AUGUSTINE

CITY OF GOD

VII

LCL 417

AUGUSTINE

THE CITY OF GOD
AGAINST THE PAGANS

BOOKS XXI–XXII
GENERAL INDEX

WITH AN ENGLISH TRANSLATION BY

WILLIAM M. GREEN

HARVARD UNIVERSITY PRESS
CAMBRIDGE, MASSACHUSETTS
LONDON, ENGLAND

ISBN 978-0-674-99459-1

*Printed on acid-free paper and bound by
Edwards Brothers, Ann Arbor, Michigan*

CONTENTS

129641

CONTENTS

INTRODUCTION

AT the end of Book XX the reader of Augustine's
last work on the *City of God* is told what he may expect to find in the two remaining books:

> There remain two books, pertaining to this task,
> to complete, with the Lord's help, what I have
> promised. One of them will be about the punish-
> ment of the wicked, the other about the happiness
> of the righteous. In them, so far as God may
> grant, I shall in particular refute those human
> arguments by which some wretched men, wise in
> their own eyes, think that they weaken the divine
> prophecies and promises, and hold in contempt, as
> false and ridiculous, the nutriment of our salutary
> faith. But those who are wise according to God
> hold that the strongest argument in favour of all
> things that seem incredible to men yet are found
> in the holy Scriptures, whose truth has already
> been upheld in many ways, is the omnipotence of
> God; they are sure that he could in no way have
> lied in the Scriptures, and that he can do what to
> the unbeliever is impossible.[1]

In other words, Augustine first gives us his portrayal
of hell (Book XXI), then of heaven (Book XXII),
solidly based on Bible texts. At the same time he

---

[1] *City of God*, 20.30, in Volume VI, pp. 451 f.

seeks to make Christian teaching on these topics seem credible, or even plausible, by citing analogies from common experience. And if anything still remains incredible it is no more so than the marvels of this world whose existence is well attested. The discussion of hell is taken up first, we are told, since " it seems harder to believe that bodies last on in eternal torment than that they continue to exist in eternal happiness without any pain." If the harder task is first disposed of, Augustine expects more easily to win general assent to his description of the corporeal immortality of the saints.[1]

I

Modern critics of Augustine have frequently noticed his diffuse style, his unnecessary repetitions, and his love of expanding a topic beyond the requirements of the case. At times, like a garrulous talker, he wanders aside into themes which have no real bearing on the main topic. Deferrari and Keeler once published a study of the *City of God* by chapters and pages, to discover what proportion of the writing could be described as " digression " from the announced plan. Admitting that their judgement was necessarily somewhat subjective, they report that of 1220 Teubner pages about 247, or one-fifth of the whole, has no immediate or essential connection with the subject.[2] Marrou speaks of

[1] 21.1, pp. 3 f. below.
[2] R. J. Deferrari and M. J. Keeler, " St. Augustine's City of God: its Plan and Development," in *American Journal of Philology*, 50 (1929), 109–137, especially p. 127.

INTRODUCTION

Augustine's visible liking for a style that is ample, well-rounded, and massive, a style most notably illustrated in the *City of God*. There he finds Augustine often "carried away by the flood of his fluency, despite all his efforts incapable of mastering himself and setting a proper limit." [1] C. I. Balmus has a chapter of thirty pages on Augustine's search for the ample style. It was achieved by the accumulation of synonyms, figures of speech, and varied forms of pleonasm taught in the schools of rhetoric. [2] Particularly tedious to the modern reader is the tautology by which a given word and its cognates are repeated frequently throughout a long passage. [3]

Augustine's prolixity is well illustrated in Books XXI and XXII. The former opens with the question whether bodies can survive in fire, and the affirmative is demonstrated by citing the case of the salamander, an animal supposed to live and thrive in fire. Volcanoes also are mentioned as burning without being consumed. The next illustration is not so apt: peacock flesh is proved immune to decay by the fact that Augustine had kept some in his house for a year. Then he goes on with a list of marvels (*mirabilia*) which may be both amazing and entertaining, but have nothing to do with the credibility of hell. [4] In

[1] H. I. Marrou, *St. Augustin et la Fin de la Culture Antique* (1938), 70, n. 5.
[2] C. I. Balmus, *Étude sur le Style de Saint Augustin dans les Confessions et la Cité de Dieu* (1930), 204–234.
[3] See, for example, 22.5, pp. 188–194 below. Forms of the word *credo* and its cognates occur eighteen times in the first seventeen lines, and then recur frequently throughout the chapter.
[4] 21.4–8 ,pp. 17–59 below.

INTRODUCTION

Book XXII the case for the resurrection and eternal life of the saints is based on the power and the promises of God. The trustworthiness of his promises is demonstrated by the fulfilment of prophecy, especially by the resurrection of Christ, along with the miracles of Christ and the apostles. When the unbeliever retorts with the question why such miracles no longer occur, Augustine declares that they are still being performed, especially in connection with the relics of the saints. Many had occurred in Hippo, some in the very presence of Augustine, and he was zealous to see that proper records were made and preserved, for the future edification of saints and conversion of sinners. Twenty-five of these miracles are related in the *City of God*,[1] some with great detail, so that the continuation of the main topic of heaven is delayed for sixteen Teubner pages.

One highly respected scholar, G. Bardy, remarks that Augustine was seventy-two years old in 426, when he was finishing this work, and suggests that Augustine's age may explain the frequent repetitions and surprising prolixity which can be noticed more in these last books than elsewhere. He refers especially to the list of marvels in Book XXI and the miracles of healing in Book XXII.[2]

II

If the opening chapters of Book XXI seem to digress widely from the central topic, the matter is

---

[1] 22.8, pp. 211–251 below.

[2] *Bibliothèque Augustinienne*, 37 (1960), 10.

taken up with sufficient directness in chapter nine. For the remainder of the book the case is well summarized by Bourke: "The sole purpose of Book XXI is to prove that hell is an awful reality."[1] Scripture texts are taken up one by one, and each is pressed to the full extent of its literal meaning. There were those who would make the "fire" and "worm" of hell (Mark 9 : 48) refer to punishment of the mind and not of the body. Augustine replies that "it is certainly absurd to say that pain either of body or of mind will be lacking there."[2] Moreover, the punishment is eternal, and it is unreasonable to object to everlasting punishment for temporary guilt.[3]

Towards the close of Book XXI Augustine takes up the controversy with tender-hearted Christians (*cum misericordibus nostris*) who sought by one argument or another to temper the sternness of the Bible teaching on hell. Six chapters are taken to set forth the six views of the "tender-hearted": (1) that hell is not eternal, and that each one will be freed after a proper period of time; (2) that men will be freed by the intercession of the saints; (3) that only those washed in baptism, who have also partaken of the eucharist will be saved; (4) or only those who have

---

[1] V. J. Bourke, *Augustine's Quest of Wisdom* (1944), 278.

[2] 21.9, p. 61 below.

[3] 21.11, pp. 69 f. Bourke (*op. cit.*, 279, n. 54) on this point quotes from Welldon, the Anglican editor of the *City of God*, who says: "The everlastingness of the punishment inflicted upon guilty souls is a belief which, if it were logically realized, would drive believers into a madhouse." Bourke then adds his comment: "Hell is indeed a terrible prospect, but modern Catholics are as certain as was Augustine that it entails punishment in real and everlasting fire."

received the sacraments in the Catholic church; (5) or only those who persevere in the Catholic faith, and that only after their wickedness has been punished in fire; (6) that all those who have shown mercy in acts of charity and forgiveness will escape.[1] The remaining five chapters of the book are devoted to a refutation of these views. Only in the case of the fifth view does Augustine relent enough to say that perhaps it is true.[2]

The only one named by Augustine as a representative of the tender-hearted is Origen. Origen had gone so far as to include the devil and his angels among those who would eventually complete the punishment due, and be delivered from the tortures of hell (*gehenna*).[3] Origen's " hell " is thus really a purgatory in which all sinners, whether men or angels, will finally be cleansed from their guilt and restored to peace with God. Nor does Origen take the fire of which the Bible speaks to be a literal, external fire. Rather, he declares, " every sinner kindles for himself the flame of his own fire," his sins providing the " wood and hay and stubble " for the fire of which the Apostle speaks. It is thus a matter of memory and conscience, as Paul intimates in another passage: " Their thoughts mutually accusing or excusing them in the day when God will judge the secrets of men."[4] This view, along with other views of Origen, had already been condemned by the church as heretical,

---

[1] 21.17–22, pp. 93–109 below.
[2] 21.26, p. 147 below.
[3] 21.17, p. 93 below.
[4] Origen, *De Principiis*, 2.10.4, translated in *Ante-Nicene Fathers* IV, 295, citing 1 Cor. 3.12 and Rom. 2.15–16.

INTRODUCTION

as Augustine points out.[1] But in the meantime
Origen's doctrine had enjoyed much popularity,
especially in the eastern churches. Their renowned
teacher Basil himself believed in eternal punishment,
but states that most ordinary Christians believed
there would be a time limit. Among these, apparently, must be included his brother Gregory of
Nyssa and his close friend Gregory of Nazianzus.[2]
Ambrose of Milan was a diligent student of the works
of Origen, and though he did not adopt the notion
of universal salvation, he does in one passage inter-
pret hell metaphorically. "There is no gnashing of
bodily teeth, nor any perpetual fire of material
flames, nor a material worm," he writes—these are
merely vivid figures of the torments of a conscience
which has awakened too late.[3]

It is impossible for us to determine who were the
contemporary proponents of the "tender-hearted"
views stated and refuted at such length by Augustine.
He speaks of meeting and conversing with men who
relied on the mercy of God and the prayers of the
saints to spare those who would otherwise be destined
to hell.[4] The theologians who had once shared
Origen's more liberal views were no longer on the

[1] 21.17, p. 93 below. Pope Anastasius had condemned the
books of Origen in the year 400. His letter to Simplicianus
of Milan is preserved as No. 95 among the letters of Jerome,
translated in N.P.N.F., sec.ser., VI, 186.

[2] J. N. D. Kelly, *Early Christian Doctrines* (1960), 483; see
also Harnack, *History of Dogma*, III, 186, where it is added
that Origen's doctrine was more and more regarded as heretical
from the end of the fourth century.

[3] *Exposition of the Gospel of Luke*, 7.205 f., cited by F. H.
Dudden, *Life and Times of St. Ambrose* (1935), II, 658 f.

[4] 21.18, pp. 95 f. below.

scene. Jovinian has been mentioned as a representative of " notorious laxity " capable of defending such non-orthodox ideas.[1] However, he was dead twenty years or more before the time of Augustine's writing, and in Jerome's long attack on his views no mention is made of unorthodox teaching on the subject of hell. Liberal views on that subject might linger on in the minds of individual Christians and become the topic of private conversations, but no representative churchman could be found to contest the established orthodoxy. Harnack describes the rejection of Origen's doctrine as " the first decisive victory of traditionalism over spiritualizing speculation." [2]

III

If the chief purpose of Book XXI is to prove to Christians by citing Bible texts that hell is an awful reality, it would seem that the chief aim of Book XXII is rather by rational argument to refute the pagans and reassure the Christians in their hope of the resurrection and of eternal life. The historical argument is presented: God's past performance of his own promises is a guarantee of future performance (chapter 3). God predicted both the resurrection of Christ and the faith of the world in that resurrection, though both these predictions must have seemed equally incredible. The world's faith is now an obvious fact, and can only be explained by the truth of the resurrection. The apostles who bore witness

[1] See note of A. Gaudel in *Bibliothèque Augustinienne*, 9 (1947), 390.
[2] *Loc. cit.*, note 18.

to the fact also performed miracles in confirmation
of their divine mission, and only hardness of heart
causes a few still to reject what all the world accepts
(chapter 5). The age of the apostles was an enlightened age, and the faith then publicly verified is
sufficiently verified for all time (chapter 7). But
God has deigned to grant our age also a demonstra-
tion of his truth by miracles, especially miracles connected with the relics of his saints (chapter 8). If
the pagans should reply that their gods also worked
miracles, Augustine challenges them to compare the
character of their gods (who were rather unholy
demons) with that of the saints and martyrs of
Christ (chapter 10).

There are also philosophical objections to the
Christian doctrine of the resurrection. Cicero had
declared that earthly bodies could dwell nowhere
except on earth (chapter 4), and the Platonists argue
from the natural weight of the elements that an
earthly body cannot be in heaven (chapter 11). Unbelievers can produce many captious objections.
Will abortive foetuses rise again? Or those with
monstrous deformities? If there is no marriage,
will there still be difference of sex? What of bodies
dispersed in fire and water, or devoured by beasts, or
even eaten as food by men under pressure of famine?
Ten chapters are filled with these riddles and their
solution (chapters 12–21). Three chapters (22–24)
discuss the evils and blessings of this life. The last
of these is especially diffuse, and is derived largely
from the Stoic exposition of the providence of God in
Cicero's dialogue *On the Nature of the Gods*.[1] Then

---

[1] 22.24, pp. 320–329; see note p. 321 below.

INTRODUCTION

Augustine returns to his controversy with the Platonists about the future life (chapters 25–28). The views of Porphyry, Plato, Labeo, and Varro are such that they could correct each other and arrive at what the Christians believe, that is, that holy souls will return to bodies, in fact their own bodies, and not return to any evils.

BIBLIOGRAPHY

Augustinus Magister: Communications. Congrès International Augustinien. Paris, 1954.

Courcelle, Pierre. *Recherches sur les Confessions de Saint Augustin.* Paris, 1950.

James, M. R. *The Apocryphal New Testament.* Oxford, 1953.

Marrou, H.-I. *Saint Augustin et la Fin de la Culture Antique.* Paris, 1938.

McClintock, John and Strong, James. *Cyclopaedia of Biblical, Theological, and Ecclesiastical Literature.* 12 Volumes. New York, 1895.

Meer, F. van der. *Augustine the Bishop.* London, 1961.

Quasten, Johannes. *Patrology.* Volumes I–III. Utrecht, 1950–1960.

TABLE OF ABBREVIATIONS

BA   *Bibliothèque Augustinienne: Oeuvres de Saint Augustin.* Bruges, Paris, 1949–.

DCA   *A Dictionary of Christian Antiquities* by William Smith and Samuel Cheetham. 2 Volumes. London, 1875–1880.

DACL   *Dictionnaire d'Archeologie Chretienne et de Liturgie*. Paris.

NPNF   Nicene and Post-Nicene Fathers. First Series, 1886–1890; Second Series 1890–1898. Buffalo.

SAINT AUGUSTINE

THE CITY OF GOD AGAINST THE PAGANS

S. AURELII AUGUSTINI

DE CIVITATE DEI CONTRA PAGANOS

LIBER XXI

I

De ordine disputationis, qua prius disserendum est de
perpetuo supplicio damnatorum cum diabolo quam
de aeterna felicitate sanctorum.

Cum per Iesum Christum Dominum nostrum, iudicem vivorum atque mortuorum, ad debitos fines
ambae pervenerint civitates, quarum est una Dei,
altera diaboli, cuius modi supplicium sit futurum
diaboli et omnium ad eum pertinentium, in hoc libro
nobis, quantum ope divina valebimus, diligentius
disputandum est. Ideo autem hunc tenere ordinem
malui ut postea disseram de felicitate sanctorum,
quoniam utrumque cum corporibus erit et incredibilius videtur esse in aeternis corpora durare cruciatibus quam sine dolore ullo in aeterna beatitudine
permanere; ac per hoc cum illam poenam non debere
esse incredibilem demonstravero, adiuvabit me plurimum, ut multo facilius omni carens molestia inmor-

SAINT AURELIUS AUGUSTINE

THE CITY OF GOD AGAINST THE PAGANS

BOOK XXI

I

On the order of my argument, which requires me to discuss the perpetual punishment of those condemned with the devil before the eternal happiness of the saints.

In this book, with the help of God, we must discuss more carefully the kind of punishment that the devil will suffer with all who belong to him, after the two cities—the one of God, the other of the devil—by command of Christ our Lord, the Judge of the living and the dead, have come to their destined ends. My reason for this arrangement, that is, leaving till later what I have to say about the happiness of the saints, is this. Since in both cases there will be bodies, and it seems harder to believe that bodies last on in eternal torment than that they continue to exist in eternal happiness without any pain, it follows that, once I have proved that such punishment is not incredible, my task will be much lightened in that the future corporeal immortality of the saints, in a life

3

talitas corporis in sanctis futura credatur. Nec a
divinis ordo iste abhorret eloquiis ubi aliquando
quidem bonorum beatitudo prius ponitur, ut est illud:
*Qui bona fecerunt in resurrectionem vitae, qui autem mala
egerunt in resurrectionem iudicii.* Sed aliquando et
posterius, ut est: *Mittet filius hominis angelos suos,
et colligent de regno eius omnia scandala et mittent in
caminum ignis ardentem; illic erit fletus et stridor den-
tium. Tunc iusti fulgebunt sicut sol in regno Patris sui,*
et illud: *Sic ibunt isti in supplicium aeternum, iusti
autem in vitam aeternam;* et in prophetis, quod commemorare longum est, nunc ille, nunc iste ordo, si
quis inspiciat invenitur. Sed ego istum qua causa
elegerim, dixi.

II

An possint corpora in ustione ignis esse perpetua.

QUID igitur ostendam unde convincantur increduli
posse humana corpora animata atque viventia non
solum numquam morte dissolvi, sed in aeternorum
quoque ignium durare tormentis? Nolunt enim hoc

---

[1] John 5.29.
[2] Matthew 13.41–43.
[3] Matthew 25.46.
[4] Augustine frequently refers to animals which were supposed to live and thrive in fire, especially the salamander.
See 12.4 (vol. IV, 21) and 21.4, p. 15 below. Aristotle
declares such life to be impossible (*Meteorologica* 4.4, 282ᵃ7;
Generation of Animals 2.3, 757ᵃ; compare Ovid, *Fasti* 6.292:
nataque de flamma corpora nulla vides.) Elsewhere (*History of
Animals* 5.19, 552ᵇ) Aristotle repeats, with reservations, the
story of the salamander. Compare Pliny, *Natural History*

free from every vexation, will much more easily win assent. Nor is this order at variance with the Scriptures. For there the blessed state of the good is sometimes placed first, as in the passage, " Those who have done good, to the resurrection of life, and those who have done evil, to the resurrection of judgement." [1] But there are also passages where it is placed second, as in this one: " The Son of man will send his angels and they will gather out of his kingdom all things that offend, and will cast them into the burning furnace of fire, where there will be weeping and gnashing of teeth. Then the just shall shine as the sun in the kingdom of their Father." [2] And again: " So these shall go into eternal punishment, but the just into eternal life." [3] In the prophets, too, first one order, then the other is found. This would be tedious to set forth, but if you look it up, you will find it to be so. As for me, I have given my reason for choosing the second order, and will say no more.

II

Whether bodies can survive in a burning fire. [4]

What proof then can I offer to convince unbelievers that it is possible for human bodies, endowed with soul and life, not merely never to be decomposed by death, but also to outlast the torments of eternal flames? They refuse to accept from us an appeal to

11.42.119; 29.33.74–76. The so-called "fire-salamander" of Mediterranean lands is a lizard-shaped black and yellow creature which lives only in moist places in woods, under logs, or in basements of houses.

ad Omnipotentis nos referre potentiam, sed aliquo
exemplo persuaderi sibi flagitant. Quibus si re-
spondebimus esse animalia profecto corruptibilia,
quia mortalia, quae tamen in mediis ignibus vivant,
nonnullum etiam genus vermium in aquarum cali-
darum scaturrigine reperiri quarum fervorem nemo
inpune contrectat, illos autem non solum sine ulla
sui laesione ibi esse, sed extra esse non posse, aut
nolunt credere, si ostendere non valemus, aut si
valuerimus sive oculis demonstrare res ipsas sive
per testes idoneos edocere, non satis esse hoc ad
exemplum rei de qua quaestio est eadem infidelitate
contendent, quia haec animalia nec semper vivunt
et in illis fervoribus sine doloribus vivunt; suae
quippe naturae convenientibus vegetantur illis, non
cruciantur elementis; quasi non incredibilius sit
vegetari quam cruciari talibus rebus. Mirabile est
enim dolere in ignibus et tamen vivere, sed mirabilius
vivere in ignibus nec dolere. Si autem hoc creditur,
cur non et illud?

III

An consequens sit ut corporeum dolorem sequatur
carnis interitus.

SED nullum est, inquiunt, corpus, quod dolere possit
nec possit mori. Et hoc unde scimus? Nam de
corporibus quis certus est daemonum, utrum in eis

the power of the Almighty, but press us to cite a precedent by way of argument. We can reply that there are animals, which are certainly liable to destruction, since they are mortal, but still survive in the midst of flames. Further, there is a kind of worm found in the gushing flow of hot springs, whose heat no one can touch with impunity. The worms, however, not only live there without any harm, but cannot live elsewhere. Here our adversaries either refuse assent unless we can display the evidence, or, if we have found means either to produce it before their eyes, or to document the fact by competent witnesses, they will argue with the same disbelief as before that this instance does not suffice to prove the matter in dispute. For these animals do not live for ever, and they live in such hot places without pain; in fact, such an environment suits them naturally, so that they thrive in it, and are not in agony. As if it were not still more incredible that anything should thrive in such a plight, rather than be in agony! It is a marvellous thing to suffer amid flames and still live, but more marvellous to live amid flames and not suffer. If we assent to the latter, why not also to the former?

III

Whether bodily pain leads inevitably to destruction of the flesh.

But there is no body, they say, which can suffer pain, yet cannot die. How do we know this? Who is sure that demons do not suffer in their bodies when

doleant, quando se affligi magnis cruciatibus con-
fitentur? Quod si respondetur terrenum corpus
solidum scilicet atque conspicuum nullum esse, atque,
ut uno potius nomine id explicem, nullam esse
carnem quae dolere possit morique non possit, quid
aliud dicitur nisi quod sensu corporis homines et
experientia collegerunt? Nullam namque carnem
nisi mortalem sciunt, et haec est eorum tota ratio,
ut quod experti non sunt nequaquam esse posse
arbitrentur. Nam cuius rationis est dolorem facere
mortis argumentum, cum vitae potius sit indicium?
Etsi enim quaerimus utrum semper possit vivere,
certum tamen est vivere omne quod dolet doloremque
omnem nisi in re vivente esse non posse. Necesse
est ergo ut vivat dolens, non est necesse ut occidat
dolor, quia nec corpora ista mortalia et utique
moritura omnis dolor occidit. Et ut dolor aliquis
possit occidere, illa causa est, quoniam sic est anima
conexa huic corpori ut summis doloribus cedat atque
discedat, quoniam et ipsa compago membrorum
atque vitalium sic infirma est ut eam vim quae
magnum vel summum dolorem facit, non valeat
sustinere. Tunc autem tali corpori anima et eo
conectetur modo ut illud vinculum, sicut nulla
temporis longitudine solvetur, ita nullo dolore
rumpatur. Proinde etiamsi caro nunc talis nulla est
quae sensum doloris perpeti possit mortemque non
possit, erit tamen tunc talis caro qualis nunc non est,
sicut talis erit et mors qualis nunc non est. Non
enim nulla, sed sempiterna mors erit, quando nec
vivere anima poterit Deum non habendo nec doloribus
corporis carere moriendo. Prima mors animam

they confess that they are afflicted with great tortures? Suppose they answer that there is no earthly body—solid, that is, and visible—or, to put it in a single word, no flesh that can suffer yet cannot die. Here they affirm only what men have gathered from bodily perception and experience. For they know no flesh except mortal flesh, and the whole of their reasoning amounts to thinking that what they have not experienced is impossible. What sort of reasoning is it to make pain a proof of death, when it is rather a sign of life? Even though we question the possibility of everlasting life, still it is certain that whatever suffers is alive, and that there can be no pain except in something alive. Therefore, one who suffers must necessarily be alive, but pain does not necessarily kill, for even our bodies that are liable to die and will surely die later are not killed by each and every attack of pain. The reason why some attacks of pain cause death is this: the soul is so bound to the body that it retreats before extreme pain and departs, for the very texture of limbs and vital organs is so flimsy that it cannot resist the shock of great, or extreme, pain. But at that time the soul will be knit to such a body, and with such a knot, that the bond will be no more broken by pain than it will be loosened by any lapse of time. Hence although there is now no flesh which can suffer pain and cannot die, nevertheless there will then be flesh of a sort that does not exist now, just as there will also be a death that does not exist now. For what will be is not no death, but an eternal death, in which the soul will neither live, for it will have no God, nor be free from pain, for it will suffer no death. The first death thrusts the soul

nolentem pellit e corpore, secunda mors animam
nolentem tenet in corpore; ab utraque morte com-
muniter id habetur, ut quod non vult anima de suo
corpore patiatur.

Adtendunt autem isti contradictores nullam esse
nunc carnem quae dolorem pati possit mortemque
non possit, et non adtendunt esse tamen aliquid tale
quod corpore maius sit. Ipse quippe animus, cuius
praesentia corpus vivit et regitur, et dolorem pati
potest et mori non potest. Ecce inventa res est
quae, cum sensum doloris habeat, inmortalis est.
Hoc igitur erit tunc etiam in corporibus damnatorum
quod nunc esse scimus in animis omnium.

Si autem consideremus diligentius, dolor, qui
dicitur corporis, magis ad animam pertinet. Animae
est enim dolere, non corporis, etiam quando ei dolendi
causa existit a corpore, cum in eo loco dolet ubi
laeditur corpus. Sicut ergo dicimus corpora sen-
tientia et corpora viventia, cum ab anima sit corpori
sensus et vita, ita corpora dicimus et dolentia, cum
dolor corpori nisi ab anima esse non possit. Dolet
itaque anima cum corpore in eo loco eius, ubi aliquid
contingit ut doleat. Dolet et sola, quamvis sit in
corpore, cum aliqua causa etiam invisibili tristis est
ipsa corpore incolumi; dolet etiam non in corpore
constituta, nam utique dolebat dives ille apud inferos
quando dicebat: *Crucior in hac flamma.* Corpus
autem nec exanime dolet nec animatum sine anima

---

[1] Revelation 20.14. For a discussion of the first and second
death see 13.2 (Vol. IV, 136, with note) and 21.11, p. 73 below.
[2] Luke 18.24.

from the body against its will, the second death [1]
holds it fast in its body against its will. What is
shared by both kinds of death is this, that the soul
must have dealt to it by its body what it does not
choose to suffer.

Moreover, while these gainsayers observe that
there is now no flesh which can suffer pain and not
suffer death, at the same time they fail to observe
that there is something greater than the body.
Surely the soul itself, by whose presence the body lives
and is governed, can both suffer pain and be unable to
die. There it is! A thing has been found which is
immortal, though it has a sense of pain. There will
be the same faculty, therefore, in the bodies of the
damned that we know exists now in the souls of all.

But if we were to examine the matter more closely,
what is said to be the body's pain belongs rather to the
soul. For pain belongs to the soul, not to the body,
even when the cause of its pain is derived from the
body, when the soul's pain is felt in a place where the
body is hurt. Just as we speak of sentient bodies and
living bodies, though the body has sensation and life
only through the presence of the soul, so also we speak
of bodies in pain though the body can have pain only
from the soul. Thus the soul feels pain with the
body in the place where there happens to be a cause
of pain. It also suffers alone, though it be dwelling
in the body, when it is sad from some cause that may
even be invisible, while the body is unharmed. It
also suffers when it is not situated in the body, for
certainly the rich man was suffering in hell when he
said, " I am tormented in this flame." [2] However,
a lifeless body does not suffer, nor does a living body

dolet. Si ergo a dolore argumentum recte sumeretur ad mortem, ut ideo mors possit accidere quia potuit accidere et dolor, magis ad animam pertineret mori, ad quam magis pertinet et dolere. Cum vero illa quae magis dolere potest non possit mori, quid momenti affert cur illa corpora, quoniam futura sunt in doloribus, ideo etiam moritura esse credamus?

Dixerunt quidem Platonici ex terrenis corporibus moribundisque membris esse animae et metuere et cupere et dolere atque gaudere; unde Vergilius: "Hinc," inquit—id est, ex moribundis terreni corporis membris—"metuunt cupiuntque, dolent gaudentque." Sed convicimus eos in duodecimo huius operis libro, habere animas secundum ipsos ab omni etiam corporis labe purgatas diram cupiditatem, qua rursus incipiunt in corpora velle reverti. Ubi autem potest esse cupiditas, profecto etiam dolor potest. Frustrata quippe cupiditas, sive non perveniendo quo tendebat sive amittendo quo pervenerat, vertitur in dolorem. Quapropter si anima, quae vel sola vel maxime dolet, habet tamen quandam pro suo modo inmortalitatem suam, non ideo mori poterunt illa corpora quia dolebunt. Postremo si corpora faciunt ut animae doleant, cur eis dolorem possunt mortem vero inferre non possunt, nisi quia non est consequens ut mortem faciat quod dolorem facit? Cur ergo incredibile est ita ignes illis cor-

---

[1] *Aeneid* 6.733.

[2] Not in the twelfth book, but in 14.3 (Vol. IV, 270), where Augustine quotes *Aeneid* 6.730–734 as a Platonic account of the soul. For Plato's view see *Phaedo* 66 B–E, and for the

suffer without a soul. Hence, if the reasoning from pain to death were true, that death can happen because pain can happen, it would rather be the soul's place to die, since pain belongs rather to it. But since the part to which rather pain belongs cannot die, what weight can we allow the argument that those bodies will die just because they will be in pain?

It has, indeed, been said by the Platonists that earthly bodies and mortal limbs are the source of the soul's fears, desires, sorrows and joys. Hence Virgil says: " From these"—that is, from earthly bodies and mortal limbs—" men fear and desire, men suffer and rejoice." [1] But we have answered their argument in the twelfth book of this work, [2] by citing their own statement that even souls cleansed from all contamination with body have a disastrous yearning, whereby " they begin once more to wish to return to bodies." [3] But where there can be desire, surely there can also be pain; indeed, desire frustrated, either by failure to attain its goal or by the loss of what it had attained, turns into pain. Therefore, if the soul, which is the only part of man to suffer, or the chief part, has nevertheless a certain limited immortality of its own, it does not follow that those bodies will be able to die because they will suffer. Finally, if bodies cause souls to suffer, why can they inflict pain on them, but not death? It must be because the proposition is false that what brings pain brings death. Why then is it incredible that fire can bring

Platonists known to Augustine see Plotinus, *Enneads* 4.8. See also 21.13, p. 77 below.
[3] Compare *Aeneid* 6.719–721, a passage cited in 14.5 (Vol. IV, 283).

poribus dolorem posse inferre, non mortem, sicut ipsa corpora dolere animas faciunt, quas tamen non ideo mori cogunt? Non est igitur necessarium futurae mortis argumentum dolor.

IV

De naturalibus exemplis quorum consideratio doceat posse inter cruciatus viventia corpora permanere.

QUAPROPTER si, ut scripserunt qui naturas animalium curiosius indagarunt, salamandra in ignibus vivit et quidam notissimi Siciliae montes, qui tanta temporis diuturnitate ac vetustate usque nunc ac deinceps flammis aestuant atque integri perseverant, satis idonei testes sunt non omne quod ardet absumi, et anima indicat non omne quod dolere potest posse etiam mori, quid adhuc a nobis rerum poscuntur exempla quibus doceamus non esse incredibile ut hominum corpora sempiterno supplicio punitorum et igne animam non amittant et sine detrimento ardeant et sine interitu doleant? Habebit enim tunc istam carnis substantia qualitatem ab illo inditam qui tam miras et varias tot rebus indidit quas videmus ut eas, quia multae sunt, non miremur. Quis enim nisi Deus creator omnium dedit carni pavonis mortui ne putesceret? Quod cum auditu incredibile vide-

---

[1] See note on Chapter II, p. 4 above.
[2] The reference is to Aetna, well known as an active volcano throughout antiquity.

pain, but not death, to those bodies, even as bodies themselves cause souls to suffer, but do not for all that compel them to die? We conclude that pain is not necessarily a proof that death will follow.

IV

Examples from nature which, if we reflect, teach that living bodies can survive under torture.

THOSE who have devoted themselves especially to the study of animals have written that the salamander lives in fire.[1] Certain well-known mountains of Sicily,[2] in spite of their age and their antiquity, still seethe with flames and remain intact, and thus are satisfactory witnesses that not all that burns is consumed. The case of the soul shows that not all that is subject to suffering is subject also to death. If these facts are granted, why are examples still demanded of us to make it seem credible that the bodies of men condemned to eternal punishment do not lose their soul by fire, but burn without damage and suffer without perishing? The substance of flesh will one day possess this quality, conferred by Him who has conferred such strange and varied qualities on so many things which we see that because of their number we cease to marvel at them. For who if not God, the creator of all things, has granted to the flesh of the dead peacock immunity from decay?[3] Although when I heard this it seemed in-

[3] This story of the preservation of peacock's flesh seems to be unique, Augustine's own contribution to the marvels of folklore.

retur, evenit ut apud Carthaginem nobis cocta
apponeretur haec avis, de cuius pectore pulparum
quantum visum est decerptum servari iussimus.
Quod post dierum tantum spatium quanto alia caro
quaecumque cocta putesceret prolatum atque obla-
tum nihil nostrum offendit olfactum. Itemque re-
positum post dies amplius quam triginta idem quod
erat inventum est, idemque post annum, nisi quod
aliquantum corpulentiae siccioris et contractioris fuit.

Quis paleae dedit vel tam frigidam vim ut obrutas
nives servet, vel tam fervidam ut poma inmatura
maturet?

De ipso igne mira quis explicet, quo quaeque
adusta nigrescunt, cum ipse sit lucidus, et paene
omnia quae ambit et lambit colore pulcherrimus
decolorat atque ex pruna fulgida carbonem taeter-
rimum reddit? Neque id quasi regulariter definitum
est, nam e contrario lapides igne candente percocti
et ipsi fiunt candidi, et quamvis magis ille rubeat,
illi albicent, congruit tamen luci quod album est,
sicut nigrum tenebris. Cum itaque ignis in lignis
ardeat ut lapides coquat, contrarios habet non in
contrariis rebus effectus. Etsi enim lapides et ligna
diversa sunt, contraria tamen non sunt, sicut album
et nigrum, quorum in lapidibus unum facit alterum
in lignis, clarus illos clarificans haec offuscans, cum in
illis deficeret nisi in istis viveret. Quid, in carbonibus
nonne miranda est et tanta infirmitas ut ictu levissimo
frangantur pressu facillimo conterantur, et tanta

credible, it happened that at Carthage a roast peacock was served to me. I ordered as much meat as
seemed good to be taken from its breast and kept.
After a period of days in which any other roast meat
would go bad, it was brought out and served without
having the least offensive odour. It was put back
again and after more than thirty days it was found
as before, and again after a year it was the same
except that its texture was somewhat more dry and
shrunken.

Who gave straw such cooling power that it can
preserve buried masses of snow, and such warming
power that it ripens green fruit?

Who can explain the wonders of fire itself? Everything it burns turns black, though fire itself is bright.
Though beautiful in colour it discolours nearly everything that its flame envelops or licks. It reduces
glowing coals to ugliest charcoal. Yet this is not
determined as by a rule, for on the other hand stones
thoroughly baked in white fire become white; and
even if the fire is red rather than white, while the
stones are white, still what is white matches any
light, just as black matches darkness. So when fire
blazes in the wood to bake stones, it has opposite
effects though the things are not opposite. For
though stones and wood are different, yet they are
not opposite like black and white, one of which fire
produces in the stones, a bright thing making them
bright, the other in the wood, which it darkens. Yet
the fire would go out in the stones unless it were alive
in the wood. Again, must we not marvel that there
is in charcoal such brittleness that it is broken by the
lightest blow and crumbled by the slightest pressure,

firmitas ut nullo umore corrumpantur, nulla aetate vincantur, usque adeo ut eos substernere soleant qui limites figunt ad convincendum litigatorem, quisquis post quantalibet tempora extiterit fixumque lapidem limitem non esse contenderit? Quis eos in terra umida infossos, ubi ligna putescerent, tamdiu durare incorruptibiliter posse, nisi rerum ille corruptor ignis effecit?

Intueamur etiam miraculum calcis. Excepto eo, de quo iam satis diximus, quod igne candicat quo alia taetra redduntur, etiam occultissime ab igne ignem concipit eumque iam gleba tangentibus frigida tam latenter servat ut nulli nostro sensui prorsus appareat, sed compertus experimento, etiam dum non apparet, sciatur inesse sopitus. Propter quod eam vivam calcem loquimur, velut ipse ignis latens anima sit invisibilis visibilis corporis. Iam vero quam mirum est quod cum extinguitur, tunc accenditur! Ut enim occulto igne careat aquae infunditur aquave perfunditur, et cum ante sit frigida inde fervescit unde ferventia cuncta frigescunt. Velut expirante ergo illa gleba discedens ignis qui latebat apparet, ac deinde tamquam morte sic frigida est ut adiecta unda non sit arsura, et quam calcem vocabamus vivam, vocemus extinctam. Quid est quod huic miraculo addi posse videatur? Et tamen additur. Nam si non adhibeas aquam sed oleum, quod magis fomes

yet it also has such durability that no moisture will
rot it and no period of time destroy it? Whence
those who set up boundary stones make a practice
of spreading charcoal beneath, to refute any litigant
who may appear after the longest lapse of time and
contend that the fixed stone is not the boundary.
What enables the charcoal, buried in moist earth
where wood rots, to endure so long unconsumed,
except fire, the great consumer of most things?

Let us consider also the marvel of lime. Aside
from the fact, on which we have already said enough,
that it is whitened by fire, which blackens other
things, it absorbs fire from fire in a most mysterious
way, and as a lump now cold to the touch it stores the
fire so secretly that it is wholly concealed from all our
senses. Only by experiment can the fire be discovered persisting asleep within, even while it is
invisible. Hence we call it " quicklime," that is,
" living lime," as if the hidden fire were the invisible
soul of a visible body. Again, how strange it is that
when it is quenched, then it is kindled! For in
order to release the hidden fire, the lime is poured
into water, or water is poured over it, and though it
was cold before, it is now made hot by the same agent
by which all hot things are cooled! Thus, as the
lump dies, so to speak, the departing fire which was
hidden now appears, and henceforth the lump is so
cold in death that it will no longer burn with the
addition of water, and what we used to call " living
lime " we now call " extinct," or " slaked lime."
What can we imagine to increase the strangeness of
this marvel? Yet there is something more. Mix it,
not with water, but oil, which is, rather than water,

est ignis, nulla eius perfusione vel infusione fervescit. Hoc miraculum si de aliquo Indico lapide legeremus sive audiremus et in nostrum experimentum venire non posset, profecto aut mendacium putaremus aut certe granditer miraremur. Quarum vero rerum ante nostros oculos cotidiana documenta versantur, non genere minus mirabili sed ipsa assiduitate vilescunt, ita ut ex ipsa India, quae remota est pars orbis a nobis, desierimus nonnulla mirari, quae ad nos potuerunt miranda perduci.

Adamantem lapidem multi apud nos habent et maxime aurifices insignitoresque gemmarum, qui lapis nec ferro nec igni nec alia vi ulla perhibetur praeter hircinum sanguinem vinci. Sed qui eum habent atque noverunt, numquid ita mirantur ut hi quibus primum potentia eius ostenditur? Quibus autem non ostenditur, fortasse nec credunt; aut si credunt, inexperta mirantur; et si contigerit experiri, adhuc quidem mirantur insolita, sed assiduitas experiendi paulatim subtrahit admirationis incitamentum.

Magnetem lapidem novimus mirabilem ferri esse raptorem. Quod cum primum vidi, vehementer inhorrui. Quippe cernebam a lapide ferreum anulum raptum atque suspensum, deinde tamquam ferro quod rapuerat vim dedisset suam communemque fecisset, idem anulus alteri admotus est eundemque suspendit, atque ut ille prior lapidi, sic alter anulus

---

[1] Pliny, *Natural History* 33.30.94, may be the source of the statement about the effect of water and oil on quicklime.

the fuel for fire; the lime will not grow hot with any amount of pouring into oil or pouring oil over it.[1] If we read, or heard, this marvel about some Indian stone and could not verify it by experiment, surely we should either think it false, or at least should marvel greatly. But when daily examples of these things occur before our eyes, though their character is no less marvellous, they seem common after frequent repetition. For example, even from India, a region far distant, there are some things that we have ceased to marvel at, because they could be brought all the way to us to arouse our wonder.

The diamond is a stone possessed by many among us, especially by goldsmiths and engravers of gems. This stone, it is said, cannot be destroyed by iron or fire or any other means except goats' blood.[2] But do you suppose that those who have the stone and know it well marvel like those to whom its power is shown for the first time? Those who do not see it perhaps do not believe, or, if they believe, they marvel at what is beyond their experience. And if the experience should happen to come, they still marvel at this as being unusual. But continued experience gradually removes all occasion for wonder.

We know that the loadstone picks up iron in a marvellous way. When I first saw it I was utterly aghast. For I actually saw an iron ring drawn up by a stone and held suspended; then, as if the stone had communicated its own power to the iron first caught up, this ring was brought near to another and held it up— as the first ring clung to the stone, so the second clung

[2] Pliny, 37.15.59; Solinus, *Collectanea* 52.56, p. 194, ed. Mommsen.

priori anulo cohaerebat; accessit eodem modo tertius, accessit et quartus. Iamque sibi per mutua circulis nexis non implicatorum intrinsecus, sed extrinsecus adhaerentium quasi catena pependerat anulorum. Quis istam virtutem lapidis non stuperet, quae illi non solum inerat, verum etiam per tot suspensa transibat et invisibilibus ea vinculis subligabat? Sed multo est mirabilius quod a fratre et coepiscopo meo Severo Milevitano de isto lapide comperi. Se ipsum namque vidisse narravit quem ad modum Bathanarius quondam comes Africae, cum apud eum convivaretur episcopus, eundem protulerit lapidem et tenuerit sub argento ferrumque super argentum posuerit. Deinde sicut subter movebat manum qua lapidem tenebat, ita ferrum desuper movebatur, atque argento medio nihilque patiente concitatissimo cursu ac recursu infra lapis ab homine, supra ferrum rapiebatur a lapide.

Dixi quod ipse conspexi, dixi quod ab illo audivi cui tamquam ipse viderim credidi. Quid etiam de isto magnete legerim dicam. Quando iuxta eum ponitur adamans non rapit ferrum, et si iam rapuerat, ut ei propinquaverit, mox remittit. India mittit hos lapides; sed si eos nos cognitos iam desistimus admirari, quanto magis illi a quibus veniunt, si eos facillimos habent, sic forsitan habent ut nos calcem, quam miro modo aqua fervescentem qua solet ignis

to the first. In the same way a third ring was added, then a fourth. Thus a chain, as it were, had been formed of rings, not linked each with the next, but clinging by their outer surface. Who would not be astonished at the power of this stone, a power which was not only present in the stone, but which passed through so many suspended objects and bound them with invisible chains? But what I learned about this stone from my brother and fellow-bishop Severus of Mileve is much more marvellous. For he says that while he was dining at the house of Bathanarius, formerly count of Africa, he saw the count bring out a loadstone, hold it under a silver plate, and put a piece of iron upon the silver. Then as he moved the hand in which he held the stone beneath the plate, the iron moved above. And so in rapid movement, this way and that, the stone below was drawn by the man's hand, and the iron above was drawn by the stone, while the silver between was unaffected.

I have told what I have seen myself, and what I have heard from one whom I believed as surely as if I had seen it myself. I will also tell what I have read about the loadstone. When a diamond is put near it it does not attract iron, and if it has already attracted a piece it releases it at the approach of the diamond.[1] India exports these stones; but if we are already ceasing to marvel at them since we have come to know them, how much more the Indians, from whose land they come! If they have them within reach, perhaps they regard them as we do lime. We see it grow hot by the action of water, which ordinarily quenches fire, while it does not grow

[1] Pliny, 37.15.61; Solinus, 52.57, p. 194.

extingui, et oleo non fervescentem quo solet ignis accendi, quia in promptu nobis est non miramur.

V

Quanta sint quorum ratio nequeat agnosci et tamen eadem vera esse non sit ambiguum.

VERUM tamen homines infideles, qui, cum divina vel praeterita vel futura miracula praedicamus quae illis experienda non valemus ostendere, rationem a nobis earum flagitant rerum, quam quoniam non possumus reddere—excedunt enim vires mentis humanae—existimant falsa esse quae dicimus, ipsi de tot mirabilibus rebus quas vel videre possumus vel videmus debent reddere rationem. Quod si fieri ab homine non posse perviderint, fatendum est eis non ideo aliquid non fuisse vel non futurum esse, quia ratio inde non potest reddi, quando quidem sunt ista de quibus similiter non potest.

Non itaque pergo per plurima, quae mandata sunt litteris, non gesta atque transacta sed in locis quibusque manentia, quo si quisquam ire voluerit et potuerit, utrum vera sint explorabit, sed pauca commemoro. Agrigentinum Siciliae salem perhibent, cum fuerit admotus igni, velut in aqua fluescere,

---

[1] Most of the material of this chapter seems to be taken from Solinus, as Mommsen shows in the preface of his edition, p. xxv. Solinus drew chiefly from Pliny, but included the

hot with oil, the ordinary fuel for fire; but because it is always within reach we do not marvel.

V

How many things whose reason cannot be discovered are still undoubtedly true.[1]

NEVERTHELESS, when we preach the marvellous works of God, whether past or future, and cannot show them to the unbelievers to be put to the test, they demand of us an explanation of these things, and since we cannot give it (for they are beyond the grasp of the human mind), they think that what we say is false. To be consistent, they themselves should give an explanation of the many marvellous things which we can see, or do see. If they perceive that no man can do this, they should admit that the inability to give an explanation is no proof that a thing has not been or will not be, since these admitted marvels exist, of which likewise no explanation can be given.

There are many things recorded in books, not as events of the past, but as descriptions of things which remain today, each in its place, so that anyone who is able and willing to go there will discover whether they are true. I will not go on through all of these, but will mention a few. They say that the salt of Agrigentum in Sicily melts when it is brought to a fire, as if dissolved in water, but when brought to

"apples of Sodom," not mentioned in that author. In several cases he "improves the story," and is closely followed by Augustine.

cum vero ipsi aquae, velut in igne crepitare.   Apud
Garamantas quendam fontem tam frigidum diebus
ut non bibatur, tam fervidum noctibus ut non
tangatur.   In Epiro alium fontem in quo faces, ut in
ceteris, extinguuntur accensae, sed, non ut in ceteris,
accenduntur extinctae.   Asbeston Arcadiae lapidem
propterea sic vocari quod accensus semel iam non
possit extingui.   Lignum cuiusdam ficus Aegyptiae,
non ut ligna cetera in aquis natare, sed mergi, et
quod est mirabilius, cum in imo aliquamdiu fuerit,
inde ad aquae superficiem rursus emergere, quando
madefactum debuit umoris pondere praegravari.
Poma in terra Sodomorum gigni quidem et ad
maturitatis faciem pervenire, sed morsu pressuve
temptata in fumum ac favillam corio fatiscente
vanescere.   Pyriten lapidem Persicum tenentis

---

¹ Pliny 31.41.86; Solinus 5.18, p. 51.   The passage in Pliny
is brief and not very clear.   W. H. Jones translates in the Loeb
edition (Vol. VIII, 431): " Salt of Agrigentum submits to fire
and sputters in water" (*ignium patiens ex aqua exilit*).   A note
suggests that this "salt" was lime, or else there is some early
mistake in the manuscripts.   Solinus then tried to clarify the
matter by inventing the account here given by Augustine.

² The spring among the Garamantes is mentioned by Pliny
5.5.36 and Solinus 29.1, p. 128.   The report of contrasting
temperatures by night and by day may easily be exaggerated.
The spring in Epirus is in Pliny 2.106.228 and Solinus 7.2, p.
55.   How a torch might be lit at such a spring is explained by
Augustine, p. 45 below.

³ By a curious transference of meaning the word *asbestos*,
"unquenchable" in Greek, came to signify "incombustible,"
hence was applied to minerals like our asbestos, which were
used to make fire-proof fabrics.   Pliny 37.54.146 speaks of
iron-coloured asbestos from Arcadia.   Solinus, doubtless
thinking of the first meaning of the word, says that this iron-
coloured stone, if once set on fire, could never be extinguished.

water it crackles, as if in fire.[1] They say that there is a spring among the Garamantes whose water is so cold in the daytime that it cannot be drunk, and so hot at night that it cannot be touched. In Epirus there is another spring in which lighted torches are extinguished, as in other springs, but extinguished torches are lit in the spring, a thing not found elsewhere.[2] They say that a stone of Arcadia is called *asbestos* (" unquenchable ") because when once set on fire it cannot be extinguished.[3] The wood of a certain fig tree in Egypt does not float in water like other wood, but sinks. And, what is more marvellous, when it has been at the bottom for some time it rises again to the surface of the water, although when water-soaked it ought to be heavier from the weight of liquid.[4] Apples in the land of Sodom grow and come to the appearance of maturity, but when they are bitten or squeezed the skin bursts in pieces and they vanish in smoke and ashes.[5] Pyrites, a Persian

---

[4] Pliny 13.14.57; Solinus 32.34–35.

[5] The earliest account of the "apples of Sodom" is in Josephus, *Jewish War* 4.484, where he describes the vestiges of the fiery destruction which the Lord brought on Sodom and Gomorrah: "Still one may see ashes reproduced in the fruits, which from their outward appearance would be thought edible, but on being plucked with the hand dissolve into smoke and ashes." Solinus 35.8, p. 155, gives a similar account.

Modern travellers have sometimes identified this "apple" with the *Solanum sodomeum*, a shrub with purplish blossoms and bright-yellow berries about the size of a plum. Others choose the *Calotropis procera*, called *osher* by the Arabs, and found by Edward Robinson growing near the Dead Sea. The trees were ten to fifteen feet high, with smooth yellow fruit the size of a large apple, or orange (see M'Clintock and Strong, *Cyclopedia* I (1895), 325 f., with illustrations of the fruit and flowers).

manum, si vehementius prematur, adurere, propter
quod ab igne nomen accepit.   In eadem Perside gigni
etiam lapidem seleniten, cuius interiorem candorem
cum luna crescere atque deficere.   In Cappadocia
etiam vento equas concipere, eosdemque fetus non
amplius triennio vivere.   Tylon Indiae insulam eo
praeferri ceteris terris quod omnis arbor quae in ea
gignitur numquam nudatur tegmine foliorum.

De his atque aliis innumerabilibus mirabilibus quae
historia non factorum et transactorum sed manentium
locorum tenet, mihi autem aliud agenti ea persequi
nimis longum est, reddant rationem, si possunt,
infideles isti qui nolunt divinis litteris credere; quid
aliud quam non putantes eas esse divinas, eo quod
res habeant incredibiles, sicuti hoc est unde nunc
agimus?   Non enim admittit, inquiunt, ulla ratio, ut
caro ardeat neque absumatur, doleat neque moriatur
—ratiocinatores videlicet magni, qui de omnibus
rebus quas esse mirabiles constat possint reddere
rationem.   Reddant ergo de his quae pauca posuimus,
quae procul dubio, si esse nescirent et ea futura

---

[1] Pliny 36.10.138; Solinus 37.16, p. 159. The name of
pyrites comes from Greek *pyr*, "fire," and denotes a stone that
will strike fire.   Pliny describes several varieties as "having
much fire" (*plurimum ignis habentis*). Solinus, apparently,
took this to mean that there was heat in the stone.

[2] Pliny 37.67.181; Solinus 37.21, p. 160. Selenite, or moon-
stone, was so named from the suggestion of the moon in the
gem's lustre. Both Pliny and Solinus repeat the notion that
the lustre waxes and wanes with the moon.

[3] The fable of mares impregnated by the wind is as old as
Homer (*Iliad* 20.223). Varro, *On Agriculture* 2.19, Pliny

stone, burns the hand which holds it if it is pressed too hard, and hence derives its name from the Greek word for fire (*pyr*).[1] In the same land of Persia is found the stone selenite, whose inner lustre waxes and wanes with the moon (*selēnē*).[2] In Cappadocia the mares are also impregnated by the wind, and their offspring do not live more than three years.[3] Tylos, an island of India, is preferred to all other lands because no tree which grows there is ever stripped of its covering of leaves.[4]

The account of these and countless other marvels belongs not to the history of past events, but to the description of places which remain; but as my interest is in other matters I cannot take time to continue the subject. Now let those unbelievers who refuse to accept the divine writings give an explanation of these marvels, if they can. Their only excuse for not thinking the writings divine is that they state supposedly incredible things, like this subject that we are now discussing. For no kind of reasoning, they say, will grant that flesh is burned and not consumed, or suffers and does not die. Great reasoners they must be, who can explain all things which are agreed to be marvels. Then let them explain these few things which I have mentioned. If they were ignorant of them and we

8.67.166, and Solinus 23.7, p. 104, tell of mares in Lisbon, Portugal, that conceived by the wind, then bore foals that lived no more than three years. Why Augustine mentions Cappadocia, departing from his usual source, is not clear.

[4] Pliny 12.21.38; Solinus 52.49, p. 192. Tylos, called Bahrein today, is described as a well-watered island of the Persian gulf, growing dates, olives, grapes and other fruits. None of the trees dropped their leaves.

esse diceremus, multo minus crederent quam quod nunc dicentibus nobis nolunt credere aliquando venturum. Quis enim eorum nobis crederet si, quem ad modum dicimus futura hominum viva corpora quae semper arsura atque dolitura nec tamen aliquando moritura sint, ita diceremus in futuro saeculo futurum salem quem faceret ignis velut in aqua fluescere, eundemque faceret aqua velut in igne crepitare; aut futurum fontem cuius aqua in refrigerio noctis sic ardeat ut non possit tangi, in aestibus vero diei sic algeat ut non possit bibi; aut futurum lapidem, vel eum qui suo calore manum constringentis adureret, vel eum qui undecumque accensus extingui omnino non posset, et cetera quae praetermissis aliis innumeris commemoranda interim duxi?

Haec ergo in illo saeculo quod futurum est, si diceremus futura nobisque increduli responderent: "Si vultis ut ea credamus, de singulis reddite rationem," nos non posse confiteremur, eo quod istis et similibus Dei miris operibus infirma mortalium ratiocinatio vinceretur. Fixam tamen apud nos esse rationem non sine ratione Omnipotentem facere unde animus humanus infirmus rationem non potest reddere; et in multis quidem rebus incertum nobis esse quid velit, illud tamen esse certissimum, nihil eorum illi esse inpossibile, quaecumque voluerit; eique nos credere praedicenti, quem neque inpotentem neque mentientem possumus credere. Hi

announced that they would come to pass, doubtless they would be even less inclined to believe than they are now to believe what we say will come. We say that there will be living human bodies which will always burn and suffer, yet will never die. If, instead, we should say that in the world to come there will be a kind of salt which fire would cause to melt, as our salt does in water, and which water would cause to crackle, as our salt does in fire, which of them would believe us? Or if we should say that there will be a spring whose water is so hot in the coolness of night that it cannot be touched, and in the heat of day so cold that it cannot be drunk? Or a stone which burns the hand of him who squeezes it, or one which can never be extinguished when once it has caught fire from any source? And which of them would believe the other examples which I have thought worth a passing mention, while I was omitting countless others?

Therefore, if we were to say that these things will be in that world which is to come, and they were to reply in unbelief, " If you wish us to believe these things, give us the explanation of each one," we should admit that we could not, for the reason that the feeble reasoning of men is surpassed by these marvellous works of God, and others like them. However, among us the reasonable view is firmly fixed that it is with good reason that the Almighty does those things concerning which the feeble human mind can give no reason. In many things it is unclear to us what His will is. This, however, is very certain, that none of the things which He has willed is impossible, and we believe His predictions since we cannot question either his strength or his truth.

tamen fidei reprehensores exactoresque rationis quid
ad ista respondent, de quibus ratio reddi ab homine
non potest et tamen sunt et ipsi rationi naturae
videntur esse contraria? Quae si futura esse
diceremus, similiter a nobis, sicut eorum quae futura
esse dicimus, ab infidelibus ratio posceretur. Ac per
hoc, cum in talibus operibus Dei deficiat ratio cordis
et sermonis humani, sicut ista non ideo non sunt,
sic non ideo etiam illa non erunt, quoniam ratio de
utrisque ab homine non potest reddi.

VI

Quod non omnia miracula naturalia sint, sed pleraque
humano ingenio modificata, pleraque autem
daemonum arte composita.

Hic forte respondeant: " Prorsus nec ista sunt nec
ista credimus; falsa de his dicta, falsa conscripta
sunt "; et adiciant ratiocinantes atque dicentes:
" Si talia credenda sunt, credite et vos quod in
easdem litteras est relatum, fuisse vel esse quoddam
Veneris fanum atque ibi candelabrum et in eo
lucernam sub divo sic ardentem, ut eam nulla
tempestas, nullus imber extingueret, unde sicut ille
lapis, ita ista λύχνος ἄσβεστος, id est lucerna inextinguibilis, nominata est." Quod propterea po-

---

[1] Pliny 2.96.210 says that Paphos had an altar of Venus on
which rain did not fall, but speaks of no unquenchable lamp.
However, at Athens, Athena had a lamp with a fireproof wick;
when the lamp was filled with oil it then burned for a year,
day and night, without refilling or relighting (Pausanias
1.26.7; W. H. S. Jones in the Loeb edition says that the fire-
proof wick of " Carpasian flax " is probably asbestos).

But these hostile critics of the faith who require explanations, what do they reply about those things that cannot be explained by man, but for all that do exist, and seem contrary to the very laws of nature? If we said that they were going to happen in the next world, the unbelievers would demand an explanation from us, just as they do of those things which we say are going to happen. In such works of God the power of human reasoning and discourse fail. But just as these admitted marvels are not for that reason untrue, so neither will those predictions fail for the reason that an explanation cannot be given by man in either case.

VI

That not all miracles are natural, but that many are controlled by human ingenuity, many contrived by the art of demons.

At this point perhaps they will answer: " These things are absolutely false, and we do not believe them. What has been said and what has been written about them is fiction." They may add, putting thoughts into words: " If such tales are worthy of belief, then believe what is related in the same work on natural history, that there was, or still is, a certain shrine of Venus with a lampstand and a large lamp on it burning under the open sky in such a way that no great wind or rain storm could extinguish it. Like the stone called *asbestos*, so this has the Greek name *lychnos asbestos* that is, ' the unquenchable lamp.' " [1] They may say this to pre-

33

terunt dicere, ut respondendi nobis angustias
ingerant; quia si dixerimus non esse credendum,
scripta illa miraculorum infirmabimus; si autem
credendum esse concesserimus, firmabimus numina
paganorum. Sed nos, sicut iam in libro duode-
vicensimo huius operis dixi, non habemus necesse
omnia credere quae historia continet gentium, cum
et ipsi inter se historici, sicut ait Varro, quasi data
opera et quasi ex industria per multa dissentiant.
Sed ea, si volumus, credimus, quae non adversantur
libris quibus non dubitamus oportere nos credere.
De his autem miraculorum locis nobis ad ea quae
futura persuadere incredulis volumus satis illa
sufficiant[1] quae nos quoque possumus experiri, et
eorum testes idoneos non difficile est invenire.

De isto autem fano Veneris et lucerna inextingui-
bili non solum in nullas coartamur angustias, verum
etiam latitudinis nobis campus aperitur. Addimus
enim ad istam lucernam inextinguibilem et huma-
narum et magicarum id est per homines daemoni-
carum artium, et ipsorum per se ipsos daemonum
multa miracula. Quae si negare voluerimus, eidem
ipsi cui credimus sacrarum litterarum adversabimur
veritati. Aut ergo in lucerna illa mechanicum
aliquid de lapide asbesto ars humana molita est aut
arte magica factum est quod homines illo mirarentur
in templo, aut daemon quispiam sub nomine Veneris

---

[1] *Many manuscripts read* sufficiunt.

sent us with a dilemma.   For if we say that the story
should not be accepted, we shall weaken the force of
recorded miracles, while if we grant that it should
be accepted, we shall give support to the gods of
the pagans.   But, as I have already said in the
eighteenth book of this work,[1] we do not think it
necessary to believe everything related in the history
of the heathen nations, since the historians themselves, as Varro says, disagree on many points, as if
they were taking pains to do it and working hard at
the task.   We do believe, if we like, such items as do
not contradict the books that we have no doubt we
are bound to believe.   But as examples to support
the points on which we wish to persuade unbelievers
that they will come to pass, let those passages suffice
that relate marvels which we ourselves can verify,
and of which we can easily find competent witnesses.

As for that shrine of Venus and its unquenchable
lamp, however, not only are we not squeezed in a
dilemma, but a broad field for reply is open to us.
For to this unquenchable lamp we add many miracles
wrought by human and magic arts, that is, demonic
arts performed through human agency, along with
miracles wrought by the demons themselves.   If
we seek to deny such miracles we shall our own selves
be contradicting the truth of the sacred writings in
which we believe.   So in that lamp, either human
skill contrived some mechanism to use the asbestos
stone, or it was made by magic art for men to marvel
at in that temple, or some demon in the name of

---

[1] 18.18 (Vol. V, p. 423).   The statement of Varro may be
from his work *On the Race of the Roman People* cited frequently
in Book 18, and again 21.8, p. 49 below.

tanta se efficacia praesentavit ut hoc ibi prodigium
et appareret hominibus et diutius permaneret.
Inliciuntur autem daemones ad inhabitandum per
creaturas quas non ipsi sed Deus condidit, delecta-
bilibus pro sua diversitate diversis, non ut animalia
cibis, sed ut spiritus signis, quae cuiusque delectationi
congruunt, per varia genera lapidum herbarum
lignorum animalium carminum rituum. Ut autem
inliciantur ab hominibus, prius eos ipsi astutissima
calliditate seducunt, vel inspirando eorum cordibus
virus occultum vel etiam fallacibus amicitiis ap-
parendo, eorumque paucos discipulos suos faciunt
plurimorumque doctores. Neque enim potuit, nisi
primum ipsis docentibus, disci quid quisque illorum
appetat, quid exhorreat, quo invitetur nomine, quo
cogatur—unde magicae artes earumque artifices
extiterunt. Maxime autem possident corda mortalium, qua potissimum possessione gloriantur, cum
se transfigurant in angelos lucis. Sunt ergo facta
eorum plurima quae quanto magis mirabilia confitemur, tanto cautius vitare debemus; sed ad hoc
unde nunc agimus, nobis etiam ipsa proficiunt. Si
enim haec inmundi daemones possunt, quanto
potentiores sunt sancti angeli, quanto potentior his
omnibus Deus, qui tantorum miraculorum effectores
etiam ipsos angelos fecit!

Quam ob rem si tot et tanta mirifica, quae μηχανή-
ματα appellant, Dei creatura utentibus humanis

---

[1] 2 Corinthians 11.14.

Venus manifested himself there so powerfully that this prodigy appeared to men's eyes and has long remained in that place. Now demons are drawn to dwell among objects created not by the demons, but by God, by different enticements suited to different demons. They are drawn, not as animals are, by food, but as spirits are, by emblems suited to each one's taste, that is, by varied kinds of stones, herbs, wood, animals, songs and rites. But in order to be drawn by men they first seduce the men with the shrewdest ingenuity, either instilling into their minds a hidden poison, or even putting on a false appearance of friendship. They make a few such men their disciples, and these teach the multitude. For unless the demons had first taught men, no one could have learned what each of them craves or loathes, or by what name each might be summoned or coerced; and these things were the origin of magic arts and their practitioners. They are especially successful in gaining the hearts of men—and it is their proudest boast to have gained them—when they transform themselves into angels of light.[1] Hence there are many accomplishments of theirs that we must shun the more carefully, the more marvellous we admit them to be, but for the topic that we are now discussing even these marvels are useful to us. For if unclean demons can do these things, how much more powerful are the holy angels, and how much more powerful than all these is God, who made even the angels themselves, the workers of such miracles!

Many notable marvels which they call *mēchanēmata* (mechanical devices) are accomplished by human skill making use of something that God created, so

artibus fiunt, ut ea qui nesciunt opinentur esse divina—unde factum est, ut in quodam templo lapidibus magnetibus in solo et camera proportione magnitudinis positis simulacrum ferreum aeris illius medio inter utrumque lapidem ignorantibus quid sursum esset ac deorsum, quasi numinis potestate penderet, quale aliquid etiam in illa lucerna Veneris de lapide asbesto ab artifice fieri potuisse iam diximus—si magorum opera, quos nostra scriptura veneficos et incantatores vocat, in tantum daemones extollere potuerunt ut congruere hominum sensibus sibi nobilis poeta videretur, de quadam femina quae tali arte polleret dicens:

Haec se carminibus promittit solvere mentes
Quas velit, ast aliis duras inmittere curas,
Sistere aquam fluviis et vertere sidera retro;
Nocturnosque ciet manes: mugire videbis
Sub pedibus terram et descendere montibus ornos:

quanto magis Deus potens est facere quae infidelibus sunt incredibilia, sed illius facilia potestati; quando quidem ipse lapidum aliarumque vim rerum et hominum ingenia, qui ea miris utuntur modis, angelicasque naturas omnibus terrenis potentiores animantibus condidit, universa mirabilia mirabili vincente virtute et operandi iubendi sinendique sapientia, utens omnibus tam mirabiliter quam creavit.

---

[1] Pliny 34.14.148.   [2] Virgil, *Aeneid* 4.487–491.

that those who are uninformed suppose them to be divine. For example, in a certain temple loadstones of proper size were placed in the floor and in the vault above, and an iron image was caused to hang in mid air between the two stones, and to those who did not know what was above and below it seemed to be supported by the power of the god.[1] Something like this, as we have said, may have been brought to pass in that unquenchable lamp of Venus, by a craftsman who made use of the asbestos stone. To such renown were the demons able to exalt the works of the magicians, whom our Scripture calls sorcerers and enchanters, that a noble poet seemed to express the sense of mankind when he said of a certain woman skilled in such arts: " She professes with her charms to free the hearts of those whom she chooses, and in others to implant heavy cares; to stop the water in flowing streams and turn back the stars; she rouses the ghosts of night; you will see the earth rumbling beneath your feet and ash trees coming down from the mountains."[2] How much more is God able to do things which are incredible to unbelievers, but easy for His power! It is He who created the power inherent in stones and other objects, as well as the ingenuity of the men who use that power in marvellous ways; angelic beings also He created, more powerful than all the living things of earth. All marvels are surpassed by His marvellous power and by His wisdom in working, in commanding, and permitting; his use of all things is as marvellous as was his creation of them.

VII

*Quod in rebus miris summa credendi ratio sit
omnipotentia Creatoris.*

CUR itaque facere non possit Deus ut et resurgant
corpora mortuorum et igne aeterno crucientur corpora damnatorum, qui fecit mundum in caelo in
terra, in aere in aquis innumerabilibus miraculis
plenum, cum sit omnibus quibus plenus est procul
dubio maius et excellentius etiam mundus ipse
miraculum? Sed isti cum quibus vel contra quos
agimus, qui et Deum esse credunt a quo factus est
mundus, et deos ab illo factos per quos ab illo ad-
ministratur mundus, et miraculorum effectrices sive
spontaneorum sive cultu et ritu quolibet impetra-
torum[1] sive etiam magicorum mundanas vel non
negant vel insuper et praedicant potestates, quando
eis rerum vim mirabilem proponimus aliarum, quae
nec animalia sunt rationalia nec ulla ratione praediti
spiritus, sicut sunt ea quorum pauca commemoravimus, respondere adsolent: " Vis est ista naturae,
natura eorum sic sese habet, propriarum sunt istae
efficaciae naturarum." Tota itaque ratio est cur
Agrigentinum salem flamma fluere faciat, aqua
crepitare, quia haec est natura eius. At hoc esse
potius contra naturam videtur, quae non igni sed
aquae dedit salem solvere, torrere autem igni non
aquae. Sed ista, inquiunt, salis huius naturalis est
vis ut his contraria patiatur. Haec igitur ratio

---

[1] *Some MSS. have* imperitorum, *others* imperatorum.

VII

*The final reason for believing in miracles is the
omnipotence of the Creator.*

WHY, then, cannot God cause the bodies of the
dead to rise, and the bodies of the lost to be tortured
in eternal fire—God who made a universe full of
countless marvels in heaven, in earth, in air, in sea?
For the universe itself is beyond doubt a greater and
more surpassing marvel than all the things of which
it is full. Those men with whom, or against whom,
we are arguing believe that there is a God by whom
the world was made, and that other gods were made
by him, through whom He governs the world.
They either do not deny, or may even go on to assert
that there are powers of this world that are workers
of miracles, some performed without prompting,
others procured by worship and ritual, others by
magic. But when we point out to them the marvellous power of other things, which are neither
rational animals nor spirits endowed with any
reasoning power, like those of which we mentioned a
few, they reply: " That is the power of nature—it is
their nature to be like that—those are the results of
their peculiar natural qualities." And so the whole
explanation why flame makes Agrigentine salt melt,
while water makes it crackle, is that this is its nature.
But all this rather seems contrary to nature, for nature
has given water, not fire, the power to dissolve salt,
and has given fire, not water, the power to scorch it.
But the nature of this salt, they say, is to be affected
in the opposite way. The same explanation is

redditur et de illo fonte Garamantico ubi una vena
friget diebus noctibus fervet, vi utraque molesta
tangentibus; haec et de illo alio qui cum sit contrectantibus frigidus et facem sicut alii fontes
extinguat accensam, dissimiliter tamen atque mirabiliter idem ipse accendit extinctam; haec et de
lapide asbesto, qui cum ignem nullum habeat
proprium, accepto tamen sic ardet alieno ut non
possit extingui; haec de ceteris, quae piget re-
texere, quibus licet vis insolita contra naturam inesse
videatur, alia tamen de illis non redditur ratio nisi ut
dicatur hanc eorum esse naturam.

Brevis sane ista est ratio, fateor, sufficiensque
responsio. Sed cum Deus auctor sit naturarum
omnium, cur nolunt fortiorem nos reddere rationem,
quando aliquid velut inpossibile nolunt credere
eisque redditionem rationis poscentibus respondemus
hanc esse voluntatem omnipotentis Dei? Qui certe
non ob aliud vocatur omnipotens nisi quoniam quidquid vult potest, qui potuit creare tam multa quae,
nisi ostenderentur aut a credendis hodieque dice-
rentur testibus, profecto inpossibilia putarentur, non
solum quae ignotissima apud nos, verum etiam quae
notissima posui. Illa enim quae [1] praeter eos quorum
de his libros legimus non habent testem, et ab eis
conscripta sunt qui non sunt divinitus docti atque
humanitus falli forte potuerunt, licet cuique sine
recta reprehensione non credere.

Nam nec ego volo temere credi cuncta quae posui,
quia nec a me ipso ita creduntur tamquam nulla de

---

[1] *Some MSS.* have quae apud nos.

offered also for that Garamantian spring, where a single stream of water is cold by day and hot by night, in each case painful to the touch, and also for the spring in Epirus which, like others, is cold to the touch and quenches a lighted torch, yet still, in a strange and marvellous way, itself lights the quenched torch. The same explanation is given for the asbestos stone, which has no fire of its own, but catches fire from without and burns so that it cannot be extinguished; so for the other cases, irksome to rehearse, in which an unusual power seems to be present contrary to nature, yet no other explanation is given except to say that such is their nature.

No doubt their explanation is short, and still it answers well enough. But since God is the author of all natural substances, why will they not let us give a better reason, and reply that this is the will of almighty God, when they refuse to believe what they say is incredible and demand an explanation? He is assuredly called almighty for no other reason except that he can do whatever he wishes. He was able to create many things which would surely be thought impossible unless they were manifest, or were affirmed even today by credible witnesses; these include not only things unknown among us, but also the well-known facts I have mentioned. For anyone may justifiably doubt reports which have no witnesses except the authors in whose books we read about them, if these are not men divinely taught, and may have gone wrong as men do.

Neither do I wish all the marvels that I have set down to be rashly believed, for I do not accept them

illis sit in mea cogitatione dubitatio, exceptis his quae
vel ipse sum expertus et cuivis facile est experiri—
sicut de calce quod fervet in aqua in oleo frigida est,
de magnete lapide quod nescio qua sorbitione in-
sensibili stipulam non moveat et ferrum rapiat, de
carne non putescente pavonis cum putuerit et
Platonis, de palea sic frigente ut fluescere nivem non
sinat, sic calente ut maturescere poma compellat,
de igne fulgido quod secundum suum fulgorem
lapides coquendo candificet et contra eundem suum
fulgorem urendo plurima offuscet. Tale est et quod
nigrae maculae offunduntur ex oleo splendido, similiter nigrae lineae de candido inprimuntur argento,
de carbonibus etiam, quod accendente igne sic
vertantur in contrarium ut de lignis pulcherrimis
taetri, fragiles de duris, inputribiles de putribilibus
fiant. Haec ipse quaedam cum multis, quaedam
cum omnibus novi, et alia plurima quae huic libro
inserere longum fuit. De his autem quae posui
non experta sed lecta—praeter de fonte illo ubi faces
et extinguuntur ardentes et accenduntur extinctae,
et de pomis terrae Sodomorum forinsecus quasi
maturis intrinsecus fumeis—nec testes aliquos idoneos
a quibus utrum vera essent audirem potui reperire.
Et illum quidem fontem non inveni qui in Epiro
vidisse se dicerent, sed qui in Gallia similem nossent
non longe a Gratianopoli civitate. De fructibus

---

[1] The spring in Epirus (21.5 and note 2, p. 26) was one where
a torch could be quenched, as in any other spring, but could
also be relit. Such a spring has been identified near Grenoble,
the Fontaine-Ardente, at Saint-Barthélemy du Guâ (Isère).
There are jets of escaping natural gas which support a small
flame, according to Marrou, *Saint Augustin et la Fin de la
Culture Antique*, 145, note 4.

myself in such a way as to exclude all doubts about them from my mind. I do believe the things that I have experienced myself and those that anyone else may easily put to the test. Such, for example, is the lime that boils in water and is cold in oil, the loadstone that draws iron by an invisible attraction but will not move a straw, the flesh of the peacock that does not decay—though even the flesh of Plato has decayed—the straw that is cold enough to prevent snow from melting and warm enough to force apples to ripen, the radiant fire that in keeping with its brightness whitens stones as it bakes them, but on the contrary darkens most things as it burns them. Similar also is the fact that black spots are made by spilling clear oil, and likewise black lines by rubbing with white silver. In making charcoal, too, the igniting fire changes everything to its opposite: from beautiful wood come ugly coals, the fragile from the solid, the unrotting from the rotting. These marvels and many others that it would be tedious to include in this book are known to me personally, some of them to many others besides, and some to all men. On the matters which I have set down without personal experience, but from reading—except the spring where burning torches are quenched and quenched torches kindled, and the apples of Sodom which look ripe on the outside but are full of smoke within— I have not been able to find any competent witnesses from whom I could learn whether the stories are true. As for the spring, I have not found any who could say that they had seen the one in Epirus, but I have found men who were acquainted with a similar spring in Gaul, not far from the city of Grenoble.[1]

autem arborum Sodomitarum non tantum litterae
fide dignae indicant, verum etiam tam multi se
loquuntur expertos ut hinc dubitare non possim.
Cetera vero sic habeo ut neque neganda neque ad-
firmanda decreverim, sed ideo etiam ipsa posui
quoniam apud eorum contra quos agimus historicos
legi, ut ostenderem qualia multa multique illorum
nulla reddita ratione in suorum litteratorum scripta
litteris credant, qui nobis credere, quando id quod
eorum experientiam sensumque transgreditur omnipotentem Deum dicimus esse facturum, nec reddita
ratione dignantur. Nam quae melior et validior
ratio de rebus talibus redditur quam cum Omnipotens
ea posse facere perhibetur et facturus dicitur quae
praenuntiasse ibi legitur, ubi alia multa praenuntiavit
quae fecisse monstratur? Ipse quippe faciet quia se
facturum esse praedixit quae inpossibilia putantur,
qui promisit et fecit ut ab incredulis gentibus incredibilia crederentur.

VIII

*Non esse contra naturam, cum in aliqua re, cuius
natura innotuit, aliquid ab eo quod erat notum
incipit esse diversum.*

Si autem respondent propterea se non credere
quae de humanis semper arsuris nec umquam mori-
turis corporibus dicimus quia humanorum corporum

As for the fruit of the trees of Sodom, not only are they mentioned in books that deserve credit, but so many say that they have seen them that I can have no doubt of the matter. I regard the other marvels as needing no decision either in favour or against, but I have included them also, for the reason that I have read them in the historians of the pagans against whom we are arguing. Thus I can show what sort of things, many in number, many of them believe without any explanation when they are recorded in the books of their own men of letters. But when we say that Almighty God will do that which goes beyond the experience of their senses, they do not see fit to believe us, even when an explanation is given. For when we say that the Almighty can do, and assert that he will do, the things that we read he has foretold, what better or stronger reason for believing can be given than the fact that in the same writings he foretold many other things which he has manifestly accomplished? He will surely do these things, for the one who has foretold what they think impossible is the one who promised, and has brought it to pass, that unbelievable things should be believed by unbelieving nations.

VIII

*It is not contrary to nature when an unexpected change
appears in a well-known object.*

THEY may reply, however, that they do not believe what we say about human bodies that will burn for ever and never die, because we know that the natural

47

naturam novimus longe aliter institutam, unde nec
illa ratio hinc reddi potest quae de illis naturis
mirabilibus reddebatur ut dici possit: " Vis ista
naturalis est, rei huius ista natura est," quoniam
scimus humanae carnis istam non esse naturam.
Habemus quidem quod respondeamus de litteris
sacris, hanc ipsam scilicet humanam carnem aliter
institutam fuisse ante peccatum, id est, ut posset
numquam perpeti mortem; aliter autem post peccatum, qualis in aerumna huius mortalitatis innotuit,
ut perpetem vitam tenere non possit; sic ergo aliter
quam nobis nota est instituetur in resurrectione
mortuorum. Sed quoniam istis non credunt litteris
ubi legitur qualis in paradiso vixerit homo quantum-
que fuerit a necessitate mortis alienus—quibus utique
si crederent, non cum illis de poena damnatorum
quae futura est operosius ageremus—de litteris
eorum qui doctissimi apud illos fuerunt aliquid pro-
ferendum est quo appareat posse fieri ut aliter se
habeat quaeque res quam prius in rebus innotuerat
suae determinatione naturae.

Est in Marci Varronis libris quorum inscriptio est
De gente populi Romani, quod eisdem verbis quibus
ibi legitur et hic ponam: " In caelo, inquit, mirabile
extitit portentum. Nam in [1] stella Veneris nobilis-
sima quam Plautus Vesperuginem, Homerus Hespe-
ron appellat pulcherrimam dicens, Castor scribit
tantum portentum extitisse ut mutaret colorem
magnitudinem, figuram, cursum; quod factum ita

---

[1] *The word* in *is supplied by editors, but not found in the
manuscripts.*

constitution of human bodies is far different. Hence,
they say, the explanation that was given for those
natural marvels, permitting us to state, " This force
is natural, such is the nature of this thing," cannot
be offered in this case, for we know that such is not
the nature of human flesh. For this we have indeed
an answer, based on our sacred writings. Before
the first sin this human flesh was of one kind, a kind
that could never suffer death; after the sin it was of
another kind, such as we have come to know in the
tribulation of this mortal life, a kind that cannot
retain life for ever. So also in the resurrection of the
dead it will be constituted differently from what we
have known here. But they do not believe the writings where we read what sort of life man lived in
paradise and how far he was removed from the
necessity of death, for certainly if they believed them
we should not be laboriously discussing with them the
future punishment of the damned. Hence we must
produce from the writings of the most learned men
among them an example to show that a thing can
come to be different from what had formerly been
known about its fixed nature.

There is a passage in the treatise of M. Varro en-
titled *The Race of the Roman People*,[1] which I shall
quote in his exact words: " In the sky," he says,
" appeared a marvellous portent. For in the splendid
star Venus, which Plautus calls ' Vesperugo,' and
Homer ' Hesperos ' with the epithet ' most beautiful,' [2] Castor writes that a portent occurred when the
star changed its colour, size, shape and course, a thing

---

[1] See Vol. V, p. xiv for a discussion of this work.
[2] Plautus, *Amphitryo* 275; Homer, *Iliad* 22.318.

neque antea nec postea sit. Hoc factum Ogygo
rege dicebant Adrastos Cyzicenos et Dion Neapo-
lites, mathematici nobiles." Hoc certe Varro tantus
auctor portentum non appellaret nisi esse contra
naturam videretur. Omnia quippe portenta contra
naturam dicimus esse, sed non sunt. Quo modo est
enim contra naturam quod Dei fit voluntate, cum
voluntas tanti utique conditoris conditae rei cuiusque
natura sit? Portentum ergo fit non contra naturam,
sed contra quam est nota natura. Quis autem
portentorum numerat multitudinem quae historia
gentium continetur? Sed nunc in hoc uno ad-
tendamus, quod ad rem de qua agimus pertinet.

Quid ita dispositum est ab auctore naturae caeli
et terrae quem ad modum cursus ordinatissimus
siderum? Quid tam ratis legibus fixisque firmatum?
Et tamen, quando ille voluit qui summo regit imperio
ac potestate quod condidit, stella prae ceteris magnitudine ac splendore notissima colorem, magnitudinem, figuram et (quod est mirabilius) sui cursus
ordinem legemque mutavit. Turbavit profecto tunc,
si ulli iam fuerunt, canones astrologorum quos velut
inerrabili computatione de praeteritis ac futuris
astrorum motibus conscriptos habent, quos canones
sequendo ausi sunt dicere hoc quod de Lucifero
contigit nec antea nec postea contigisse. Nos autem
in divinis libris legimus etiam solem ipsum et stetisse,
cum hoc a Domino Deo petivisset vir sanctus Iesus

---

[1] See 18.8 (Vol. V, 389).

which has never happened before or since. The well-known astronomers Adrastus of Cyzicus and Dion of Naples said that this happened in the reign of Ogygus." [1] As great a writer as Varro would surely not call this a portent unless it seemed contrary to nature. We commonly say, of course, that all portents are contrary to nature, but in fact they are not. For how can anything done by the will of God be contrary to nature, when the will of so great a creator constitutes the nature of each created thing? A portent therefore happens not contrary to nature, but contrary to what is known of nature. Now who can count the number of portents that the history of the pagans records? But now let us notice this one case, so far as it concerns the point that we are now discussing.

What is so exactly determined by the creator of heaven and earth as the perfectly ordered course of the stars? What is established upon such firm and immutable laws? Yet God rules what He created by his supreme command and power; hence when he so willed, a star conspicuous beyond all the rest for size and brightness changed its colour, size, shape and, what is even more marvellous, its regular and ordained course. Surely God then upset the tables of the astronomers, if there were any then, tables which they have drawn up from a supposedly unerring reckoning of the past and future motions of the stars. Following these tables they dared to assert that what happened then to Venus has never happened before or since. We read, moreover, in the Scriptures both that even the sun itself once stood still, when the holy man Joshua, the son of Nun, had

Nave, donec coeptum proelium victoria terminaret, et retrorsum redisse, ut regi Ezechiae quindecim anni ad vivendum additi hoc etiam prodigio promissioni Dei significarentur adiuncto. Sed ista quoque miracula quae meritis sunt concessa sanctorum, quando credunt isti facta, magicis artibus tribuunt. Unde illud est quod superius commemoravi dixisse Vergilium:

Sistere aquam fluviis et vertere sidera retro.

Nam et fluvium stetisse superius inferiusque fluxisse cum populus Dei ductore supra memorato Iesu Nave viam carperet, et Helia propheta transeunte ac postea discipulo eius Helisaeo id esse factum in sacris litteris legimus, et retro versum fuisse maximum sidus regnante Ezechia modo commemoravimus. Quod vero de Lucifero Varro scripsit, non est illic dictum alicui petenti homini id fuisse concessum.

Non ergo de notitia naturarum caliginem sibi faciant infideles, quasi non possit in aliqua re divinitus fieri aliud quam in eius natura per humanam suam experientiam cognoverunt; quamvis et ipsa quae in rerum natura omnibus nota sunt non minus mira sint, essentque stupenda considerantibus cunctis si solerent homines mirari mira nisi rara. Quis enim consulta ratione non videat in hominum innumerabili numerositate et tanta naturae similitudine valde mirabiliter sic habere singulos singulas facies ut, nisi

---

[1] Joshua 10.13.
[2] Isaiah 38.8.
[3] *Aeneid* 4.489.
[4] Joshua 3.16.
[5] 2 Kings 2.8, 14.

asked this of the Lord God, until he should crown
with victory the battle that he had begun,[1] and that
it also turned back, to indicate to King Hezekiah the
addition of fifteen years to his life, the prodigy being
added to confirm the promise of God.[2] But these
miracles too, which were granted to the saints as a
reward for their merits, when they are accepted as
facts by the pagans, are ascribed to magic arts. Of
these Virgil was speaking in the words which I
quoted above: "To stop the water in flowing
streams and turn back the heavenly bodies." [3]
For, as we read in the sacred writings, a river stopped
above and flowed away below when the people of
God, led by Joshua, were advancing.[4] This happened also, we read in the Scriptures, when Elijah
the prophet crossed, and later when his disciple
Elisha did so.[5] And we have just now mentioned
that in the reign of Hezekiah the greatest of the
heavenly bodies was turned back. But in what Varro
wrote about Venus, he does not state that the miracle
was granted as an answer to someone's prayer.

Therefore unbelievers are not to create a mental
fog for themselves out of their knowledge of natural
objects, as if in any matter God could bring nothing
to pass different from what they have come to know
in their human experience. Even everyday matters,
known to all, are equally marvellous, and would be a
great wonder to all who consider them, if men marvelled at any marvels except the uncommon. For
who, after reflecting on the matter, would not observe
that among the countless number of men naturally
so much alike, each individual, strangely enough,
has his individual appearance? If men were not

inter se similes essent, non discerneretur species
eorum ab animalibus ceteris, et rursum nisi inter
se dissimiles essent, non discernerentur singuli ab
hominibus ceteris? Quos ergo similes confitemur,
eosdem dissimiles invenimus. Sed mirabilior est
consideratio dissimilitudinis quoniam similitudinem
iustius videtur exposcere natura communis. Et
tamen quoniam quae sunt rara ipsa sunt mira, multo
amplius admiramur quando duos ita similes reperimus
ut in eis discernendis aut semper aut frequenter
erremus.

Sed quod dixi scriptum a Varrone, licet eorum sit
historicus idemque doctissimus, fortasse vere factum
esse non credunt. Aut quia non diu mansit alius
eiusdem sideris cursus, sed reditum est ad solitum,
minus isto moventur exemplo. Habent ergo aliud
quod etiam nunc possit ostendi eisque puto debere
sufficere quo commoneantur, cum aliquid adverterint
in aliqua institutione naturae eamque sibi notissimam
fecerint, non se inde Deo debere praescribere, quasi
eam non possit in longe aliud quam eis cognita est
vertere atque mutare. Terra Sodomorum non fuit
utique ut nunc est, sed iacebat simili ceteris facie
eademque vel etiam uberiore fecunditate pollebat,
nam Dei paradiso in divinis eloquiis comparata est.
Haec postea quam tacta de caelo est, sicut illorum
quoque adtestatur historia et nunc ab eis qui veniunt
ad loca illa conspicitur, prodigiosa fuligine horrori est

alike, their species would not be distinguished from other animals, and again, if they were not different, individuals would not be distinguished from each other. Hence we find that the same men that we admit are alike, are also unlike. But the consideration of their dissimilarity is more marvellous, since a common nature seems more properly to require similarity. However, since what is uncommon is also marvellous, we marvel much more when we find two men so much alike that we always, or frequently, go wrong in trying to tell them apart.

But perhaps they do not believe that the event which I have cited from Varro's writings really took place, though he is a pagan historian, as well as their most learned authority. Or perhaps they are less moved by this case because the altered course of Venus did not long continue, but the usual course was resumed. Well, then, they have another case, a marvel which can be displayed even today, and I think that it ought to be enough to teach them that although they may have observed something somewhere in the order of nature and have become very familiar with it, they should not lay down a rule for God in the matter, as if he could not change and alter it into something far different from what they have known. The land of Sodom certainly was not always as it is today, but presented the same features as other lands, and enjoyed the same or even greater fertility, for in the sacred writings it is compared to the paradise of God. This land was destroyed by fire from heaven, as pagan history also affirms, and as visitors there can observe. Since that event the land is a fearsome sight with its unnatural soot, and be-

et poma eius interiorem favillam mendaci superficie
maturitatis includunt. Ecce non erat talis, et talis
est. Ecce a conditore naturarum natura eius in hanc
foedissimam diversitatem mirabili mutatione conversa est, et quod post tam longum accidit tempus
tam longo tempore perseverat.

Sicut ergo non fuit inpossibile Deo quas voluit
instituere, sic ei non est inpossibile in quidquid
voluerit quas instituit mutare naturas. Unde illorum
quoque miraculorum multitudo silvescit, quae monstra
ostenta portenta prodigia nuncupantur. Quae recolere et commemorare si velim, huius operis quis
erit finis? Monstra sane dicta perhibent a mon-
strando quod aliquid significando demonstrent, et
ostenta ab ostendendo, et portenta a portendendo,
id est, praeostendendo, et prodigia quod porro
dicant, id est, futura praedicant. Sed viderint eorum
coniectores quo modo ex eis sive fallantur, sive
instinctu spirituum quibus cura est tali poena dignos
animos hominum noxiae curiositatis retibus implicare
etiam vera praedicant, sive multa dicendo aliquando
in aliquid veritatis incurrant. Nobis tamen ista
quae velut contra naturam fiunt et contra naturam
fieri dicuntur—quo more hominum locutus est et
apostolus dicendo contra naturam in olea insitum
oleastrum factum esse participem pinguedinis oleae—
et monstra ostenta portenta prodigia nuncupantur,
hoc monstrare debent, hoc ostendere vel praeosten-

---

[1] See Chapter V, p. 25 above, with note.
[2] This group of words is discussed by Cicero, *On Divination*
1.93.
[3] Romans 11.17–24.

neath the deceitful appearance of ripeness its apples enclose ashes within.[1] Behold, it was not thus, now thus it is. Behold, the Creator of every nature altered its nature by a miraculous change into something disgustingly different, and the change that came after so long a lapse of time maintains itself still so long after.

Therefore, just as it was possible for God to make such natural kinds as He wished, so it is possible for him to change those natural kinds into whatever he wishes. From this power comes the wild profusion of those marvels which are called omens, signs, portents, prodigies. If I should try to recall and enumerate these, where would this treatise end? The various names *monstra, ostenta, portenta, prodigia* come from the verbs *monstrare* 'show,' because they show something by a sign, *ostendere* 'display,' *portendere* 'spread in front,' that is, display beforehand, and *porro dicere* 'say aforetime,' that is, predict the future.[2] Let the interpreters of these signs observe how at times they are deceived by them, and at times they even speak the truth by the prompting of spirits who aim to involve men worthy of such punishment in the snares of harmful curiosity, and at times they merely stumble on some true prediction in the course of much random talk. These marvels are apparently contrary to nature, and men say that they happen " contrary to nature." Indeed, this manner of speaking is used by the Apostle when he says that the wild olive grafted into the olive becomes a partaker of the fatness of the olive contrary to nature.[3] To us these marvels, these *monstra, ostenta, portenta, prodigia*, should demonstrate, show, portend,

dere, hoc praedicere, quod facturus sit Deus quae
de corporibus hominum se praenuntiavit esse facturum, nulla impediente difficultate, nulla praescri-
bente lege naturae. Quo modo autem praenunti-
averit, satis in libro superiore docuisse me existimo,
decerpendo de scripturis sanctis et novis et veteribus
non quidem omnia ad hoc pertinentia, sed quae
sufficere huic operi iudicavi.

IX

De gehenna et aeternarum qualitate poenarum.

Quod igitur de sempiterno supplicio damnatorum
per suum prophetam Deus dixit fiet, omnino fiet:
*Vermis eorum non morietur et ignis eorum non ex-
tinguetur.* Ad hoc enim vehementius commen-
dandum etiam Dominus Iesus, cum membra quae
hominem scandalizant pro his hominibus poneret
quos ut sua membra dextra quis diligit, eaque
praeciperet amputari: *Bonum est tibi*, inquit, *debilem
introire in vitam quam duas manus habentem ire in
gehennam, in ignem inextinguibilem, ubi vermis eorum
non moritur et ignis non extinguitur.* Similiter de pede:
Bonum est tibi, inquit, *claudum introire in vitam aeternam
quam duos pedes habentem mitti in gehennam ignis
inextinguibilis, ubi vermis eorum non moritur et ignis non
extinguitur.* Non aliter ait et de oculo: *Bonum est
tibi luscum introire in regnum Dei quam duos oculos*

---

[1] Isaiah 66.24.

predict that God will do what he has declared he will do with the bodies of men, and that no difficulty will detain him, no law of nature circumscribe him. The way in which he has foretold this has been adequately set forth in the preceding book, where I gathered from the Old and New Testaments, not all the passages indeed which relate to the matter, but such as I judged sufficient for the present purpose.

IX

Gehenna, and the Nature of Eternal Punishment.

THEREFORE what God through his prophet said concerning the everlasting punishment of the lost will come to pass, yea, it will certainly come to pass: " Their worm shall not die, and their fire shall not be quenched." [1] For our Lord Jesus also, to press this point more strongly, used these words repeatedly. When he spoke of members that cause a man to stumble, letting ' members ' stand for such persons as anyone loves as much as his own right hand and foot, and advises that they should be cut off, the words are: " It is better for you to enter into life maimed than having two hands to go into gehenna, into unquenchable fire, where their worm does not die and their fire is not quenched." Likewise he says of the foot: " It is better for you to enter into eternal life lame than having two feet to be sent into the gehenna of unquenchable fire, where their worm does not die and their fire is not quenched." And not otherwise does he speak of the eye: " It is better for you to enter the kingdom of God with one eye

habentem mitti in gehennam ignis, ubi vermis eorum non moritur et ignis non extinguitur. Non eum piguit uno loco eadem verba ter dicere. Quem non terreat ista repetitio et illius poenae commendatio tam vehemens ore divino?

Utrumque autem horum, ignem scilicet atque vermem, qui volunt ad animi poenas non ad corporis pertinere, dicunt etiam uri dolore animi sero atque infructuose paenitentes eos qui fuerint a regno Dei separati, et ideo ignem pro isto dolore urente non incongrue poni potuisse contendunt. Unde illud apostoli est: *Quis scandalizatur, et non ego uror?* Eundem etiam vermem putant intellegendum esse. Nam scriptum est, inquiunt: *Sicut tinea vestimentum et vermis lignum, sic maeror excruciat cor viri.* Qui vero poenas et animi et corporis in illo supplicio futuras esse non dubitant, igne uri corpus, animum autem rodi quodam modo verme maeroris adfirmant. Quod etsi credibilius dicitur, quia utique absurdum est ibi dolorem aut corporis aut animi defuturum, ego tamen facilius est ut ad corpus dicam utrumque pertinere quam neutrum, et ideo tacitum in illis divinae scripturae verbis animi dolorem, quoniam consequens esse intellegitur, etiamsi non dicatur, ut corpore sic dolente animus quoque sterili paenitentia crucietur. Legitur quippe et in veteribus scripturis:

---

[1] Mark 9.47–48.   [2] 2 Corinthians 11.29.
[3] Proverbs 25.20 LXX, Vulgate.

than having two eyes to be thrown into the gehenna of fire where their worm does not die and their fire is not quenched." [1] He does not scruple in one passage to repeat the same words three times. Who would not be frightened by this repetition, and by the strong statement confirming this punishment, uttered by divine lips?

Those who would make both of these, the fire and the worm, refer to punishment of the mind and not to that of the body, say that those who have been separated from the kingdom of God, repenting too late and in vain, burn with mental anguish, and hence they argue that the word " fire " may have been used fittingly for burning pain. Hence the saying of the Apostle: " Who is caused to stumble, and I do not burn?" [2] And they think that the worm also should be understood in the same way. For, they say, it is written: " As the moth eats the garment and the worm the wood, so does grief afflict the heart of a man." [3] But those who do not doubt that there will be in that punishment suffering both of mind and body affirm that the body is burnt with fire, and the mind somehow gnawed by the worm of grief. Although this statement is somewhat more plausible, for it is certainly absurd to say that pain either of body or of mind will be lacking there, still it is easier for me to say that both worm and fire refer to the body, rather than neither. Mental pain is omitted in those words of Scripture because it is understood, though tacitly, that when the body is in pain the mind also must logically be tortured by a fruitless repentance. For in the ancient Scriptures we also read: " The punishment of the flesh of the wicked is

Vindicta carnis impii ignis et vermis. Potuit brevius dici: Vindicta impii. Cur ergo dictum est: *carnis impii*, nisi quia utrumque, id est et ignis et vermis, poena erit carnis? Aut si vindictam carnis propterea dicere voluit, quia hoc in homine vindicabitur quod secundum carnem vixerit—propter hoc enim veniet in mortem secundam, quam significavit apostolus dicens: *Si enim secundum carnem vixeritis, moriemini*— eligat quisque quod placet, aut ignem tribuere corpori animo vermem, hoc proprie illud tropice, aut utrumque proprie corpori.

Iam enim satis superius disputavi posse animalia etiam in ignibus vivere, in ustione sine consumptione, in dolore sine morte, per miraculum omnipotentissimi Creatoris. Cui hoc possibile esse qui negat, a quo sit quidquid in naturis omnibus miratur ignorat. Ipse est enim Deus, qui omnia in hoc mundo magna et parva miracula quae commemoravimus, et incomparabiliter plura quae non commemoravimus, fecit eademque ipso mundo uno atque omnium maximo miraculo inclusit. Eligat ergo unum e duobus quisque quod placet, utrum et vermem ad corpus proprie an ad animum translato a corporalibus ad incorporalia vocabulo existimet pertinere. Quid autem horum verum sit res ipsa expeditius indicabit quando erit scientia tanta sanctorum ut eis cognoscendarum illarum poenarum necessaria non sit ex-

---

[1] Ecclesiasticus 7.19 Vulgate (not LXX).
[2] Romans 8.13.

fire and worm." [1] It could have been put more briefly, " the punishment of the wicked." Why, then, was it said " of the flesh of the wicked " if not because both fire and worm will be the punishment of the flesh? Or perhaps the punishment of the flesh is mentioned here because that part of a man is punished that has lived according to the flesh—since that is what will bring him to the second death, which the Apostle had in mind when he said: " For if you live according to the flesh, you shall die." [2] Let each one choose what he prefers, either to refer fire to the body, worm to the mind, the one literally, the other figuratively, or to refer both literally to the body.

For I have already done enough in the foregoing to prove that animals can live even amid flames, in conflagration without being consumed, and in pain without dying by the marvellous power of the almighty Creator. And he who declares that this is impossible for him does not know him from whom all marvels in nature are derived. For it is God himself who made all the marvels in this world, small and great, that I have mentioned, and an incomparably greater number that I have not mentioned, and enclosed them in the universe itself, a single miracle, and greatest of all. So let each choose, as he likes, one of the two alternatives, whether he thinks the worm pertains literally to the body or figuratively to the mind, the word being translated from corporeal to incorporeal things. But which of these is true the fact itself will one day more conveniently show. Then such will be the knowledge of the saints that they will not need experience of those punish-

perientia, sed ea quae tunc erit plena atque perfecta ad hoc quoque sciendum sapientia sola sufficiat—nunc enim ex parte scimus donec veniat quod perfectum est—dum tamen nullo modo illa corpora talia futura esse credamus ut nullis ab igne afficiantur doloribus.

X

An ignis gehennae, si corporalis est, possit malignos spiritus, id est daemones incorporeos, tactu suo adurere.

Hic occurrit quaerere: Si non erit ignis incorporalis sicut est animi dolor, sed corporalis, tactu noxius ut eo possint corpora cruciari, quo modo in eo erit etiam poena spirituum malignorum? Idem quippe ignis erit supplicio scilicet hominum adtributus et daemonum, dicente Christo: *Discedite a me, maledicti, in ignem aeternum, qui paratus est diabolo et angelis eius.* Nisi quia sunt quaedam sua etiam daemonibus corpora, sicut doctis hominibus visum est, ex isto aere crasso atque umido cuius inpulsus vento flante sentitur. Quod genus elementi si nihil igne perpeti posset, non ureret fervefactus in balneis. Ut enim urat prior uritur, facitque cum patitur. Si autem quisquam nulla habere corpora daemones adseverat, non est de hac re aut laborandum operosa inquisitione aut contentiosa disputatione certandum. Cur

---

[1] I Corinthians 13.9–10.   [2] Matthew 25.41.

ments in order to be acquainted with them, but their inspired wisdom, which will then be full and complete, will by itself suffice to know this also, for now " we know in part," until " that which is perfect is come." [1] However, we must by no means believe that those bodies will be such as to suffer no pain from fire.

<h1 style="text-align:center">X</h1>

Whether the fire of gehenna, if it is material fire,
can burn by its contact the evil spirits,
that is, immaterial demons.

HERE the question intrudes: If the fire is not immaterial like mental suffering, but material and harmful by contact, so that bodies can be tortured by it, how will the punishment of evil spirits also take place in it? No doubt it will be the same fire that is assigned to the punishment of men and demons, as Christ says: " Depart from me, you cursed ones, into the everlasting fire that is prepared for the devil and his angels." [2] But perhaps the demons have a kind of body peculiar to themselves, as some learned men have thought, formed of the thick and humid sort of air whose pressure is felt when the wind is blowing. If this kind of element were not subject to the action of fire, it would not burn when heated in the baths, for in order to burn it is first burned, and it acts when acted upon. But if anyone asserts that demons have no bodies, it is not necessary to engage in tedious inquiry or contentious discussion on the point, for why can we not say that in

65

enim non dicamus quamvis miris tamen veris modis etiam spiritus incorporeos posse poena corporalis ignis affligi, si spiritus hominum etiam ipsi profecto incorporei et nunc potuerunt includi corporalibus membris et tunc poterunt corporum suorum vinculis insolubiliter alligari? Adhaerebunt ergo, si eis nulla sunt corpora, spiritus daemonum immo spiritus daemones licet incorporei, corporeis ignibus cruciandi, non ut ignes ipsi quibus adhaerebunt eorum iunctura inspirentur et animalia fiant quae constent spiritu et corpore, sed ut dixi miris et ineffabilibus modis adhaerendo, accipientes ex ignibus poenam non dantes ignibus vitam; quia et iste alius modus quo corporibus adhaerent spiritus et animalia fiunt omnino mirus est nec conprehendi ab homine potest, et hoc ipse homo est.

Dicerem quidem sic arsuros sine ullo suo corpore spiritus sicut ardebat apud inferos ille dives quando dicebat: *Crucior in hac flamma*, nisi convenienter responderi cernerem talem fuisse illam flammam quales oculi quos levavit et Lazarum vidit, qualis lingua cui umorem exiguum desideravit infundi, qualis digitus Lazari de quo id sibi fieri postulavit; ubi tamen erant sine corporibus animae. Sic ergo incorporalis et illa flamma qua exarsit et illa guttula quam poposcit, qualia sunt etiam visa dormientium sive in ecstasi cernentium res incorporales habentes tamen similitudinem corporum. Nam et ipse homo

---

[1] Luke 16.24.

some way, that is still a fact, however miraculous it may be, that immaterial spirits can also be made to suffer punishment by material fire? The spirits of men, though they too are certainly immaterial, have been capable of being enclosed in material members, and will then be capable of indissoluble attachment to their own bodies. So the spirits of the demons or rather, the spirit-demons, if they have no bodies, since though immaterial they must be tortured by material flames, will be so joined that the fires themselves will not be animated by the union to become living animals consisting of body and spirit, but, as I have said, they will be joined in a marvellous and indescribable way, whereby they will receive their punishment from the flames, yet not give life to them. For that other mode of joining also, by which spirits are joined to bodies and animals are created, is altogether marvellous, and cannot be understood by man—and yet man himself is such a being.

I might, in fact, say that spirits will burn without any body of their own, just as the rich man was burning in hell when he said, " I am tortured in this flame," [1] if I did not notice that it is a good answer to say that the flame was of the same sort as the eyes which he lifted up to see Lazarus, the tongue which he wished moistened with a little water, and the finger of Lazarus with which he asked this to be done for him—and that in a place where souls existed without bodies. Hence, both the flame in which he burned and the drop of water that he asked for were immaterial, like the things seen in sleep or by those who see immaterial things in a trance that still have the appearance of bodies. For in such visions,

cum spiritu non corpore sit in talibus visis, ita se
tamen tunc similem suo corpori videt ut discernere
omnino non possit. At vero gehenna illa, quod
etiam stagnum ignis et sulphuris dictum est, cor-
poreus ignis erit et cruciabit corpora damnatorum,
aut et hominum et daemonum solida hominum aeria
daemonum, aut tantum hominum corpora cum
spiritibus, daemones autem spiritus sine corporibus
haerentes sumendo poenam, non inpertiendo vitam
corporalibus ignibus. Unus quippe utrisque ignis
erit, sicut Veritas dixit.

XI

*An hoc ratio iustitiae habeat ut non sint extensiora
poenarum tempora quam fuerint peccatorum.*

Si autem quidam eorum contra quos defendimus
civitatem Dei iniustum putant ut pro peccatis quamlibet magnis, parvo scilicet tempore perpetratis,
poena quisque damnetur aeterna—quasi ullius id
umquam iustitia legis adtendat ut tanta mora
temporis quisque puniatur quanta mora temporis
unde puniretur admisit. Octo genera poenarum in
legibus esse scribit Tullius, damnum, vincla, verbera,
talionem, ignominiam, exilium, mortem, servitutem—
quid horum est quod in breve tempus pro cuiusque
peccati celeritate coartetur ut tanta vindicetur
morula quanta deprehenditur perpetratum, nisi forte

---

[1] Revelation 20.10.
[2] A fragment of uncertain source.

though the man himself is in spirit, not in body, still
he then sees himself in such a bodily likeness that he
can detect no difference. The gehenna of which we
speak, however, which is also called the lake of fire
and brimstone,[1] will be a material fire and will torture
bodies of the damned souls, either bodies in both
cases, the bodies of men being solid, those of demons
aeriform; or it will torture the bodies of men only,
along with their spirits, while the spirit-demons
without bodies will be joined to material flames so
far as to receive punishment but not to impart life
to the fire. For there will be one fire for both, as
Truth has said.

XI

*Whether justice requires that the time of punishment
should not be longer than the time of sinning.*

MOREOVER, some of those against whom we are
defending the city of God think it unjust that a man
should be condemned to eternal punishment for
crimes, however great, committed in a short period
of time. As if any just law would ever make it an
aim that punishment should equal in length the time
it took to become liable to punishment! Cicero
writes that there are eight kinds of penalties provided
by law: fine, imprisonment, scourging, retaliation,
loss of status, exile, death, slavery.[2] Which of these
is restricted to a period short enough to match the
swiftness of the crime so that punishment is as brief
when inflicted as the brief span in which the crime is
found to have been perpetrated—unless it be retalia-

talio? Id enim agit, ut hoc patiatur quisque quod fecit. Unde illud est legis: *Oculum pro oculo, dentem pro dente.* Fieri enim potest ut tam brevi tempore quisque amittat oculum severitate vindictae quam tulit ipse alteri inprobitate peccati. Porro autem si alienae feminae osculum infixum rationis sit verbere vindicare, nonne qui illud puncto temporis fecerit incomparabili horarum spatio verberatur et suavitas voluptatis exiguae diuturno dolore punitur? Quid, in vinculis numquid tamdiu quisque iudicandus est esse debere quamdiu fecit unde meruit alligari, cum iustissime annosas poenas servus in compedibus pendat qui verbo aut ictu celerrime transeunte vel lacessivit dominum vel plagavit? Iam vero damnum, ignominia, exilium, servitus cum plerumque sic infliguntur ut nulla venia relaxentur, nonne pro huius vitae modo similia poenis videntur aeternis? Ideo quippe aeterna esse non possunt, quia nec ipsa vita quae his plectitur porrigitur in aeternum. Et tamen peccata quae vindicantur longissimi temporis poenis brevissimo tempore perpetrantur, nec quisquam extitit qui censeret tam cito nocentium finienda esse tormenta quam cito factum est vel homicidium vel adulterium vel sacrilegium vel quodlibet aliud scelus non temporis longitudine sed iniquitatis et impietatis magnitudine metiendum. Qui vero pro aliquo grandi crimine morte multatur, numquid mora qua occiditur quae perbrevis est eius supplicium leges aestimant, et non quod eum in sempiternum auferunt

---

[1] The law of retaliation (*lex talionis*) belonged to early Roman law, as well as to the law of Moses.

[2] Exodus 21.24; Matthew 5.38.

tion?[1] For that concerns itself to make each man suffer what he inflicted. Hence the precept of the law: " An eye for an eye, and a tooth for a tooth."[2] For it may happen that harsh vengeance will cause a man to lose his eye in as short a time as his wicked crime took to inflict the loss on his neighbour. Moreover, if it is reasonable to punish with a lash a kiss given to another's wife, is not the man who does this in a moment of time scourged for a disproportionate period of hours, so that the sweetness of a moment's pleasure is avenged by long continued pain? What now? Should we suppose that a man ought to remain in chains only as long as it took to do the deed that brings him into bonds, while a slave who by word or by swift blow has offended or struck his master, justly pays the penalty of years in shackles? Now since fine, loss of status, exile and slavery are generally so imposed that they are not eased by any pardon, are they not comparable to eternal punishment, as far as the measure of this life allows? Note that the reason why they cannot be eternal is that the life of one punished by them is not eternally prolonged. However, the crimes that are avenged by penalties of longest duration are perpetrated in the shortest time, and no man living would propose that the torments of the guilty should be ended as quickly as the deed was done—murder, or adultery, or sacrilege, or any other crime that ought to be measured not by length of time, but by the enormity of its injustice and impiety. And when a man is punished by death for some great crime, do the laws reckon his punishment by the time in which he is being executed, which is very short, or by his

de societate viventium? Quod est autem de ista
civitate mortali homines supplicio primae mortis, hoc
est de illa civitate inmortali homines supplicio
secundae mortis auferre. Sicut enim non efficiunt
leges huius civitatis ut in eam quisque revocetur
occisus, sic nec illius, ut in vitam revocetur aeternam
secunda morte damnatus.

Quo modo ergo verum est, inquiunt quod ait
Christus vester: *In qua mensura mensi fueritis, in ea
remetietur vobis,* si temporale peccatum supplicio
punitur aeterno? Nec adtendunt non propter
aequale temporis spatium sed propter vicissitudinem
mali, id est ut qui mala fecerit mala patiatur, eandem
dictam fuisse mensuram. Quamvis hoc in ea re
proprie possit accipi de qua Dominus cum hoc diceret
loquebatur, id est de iudiciis et condemnationibus.
Proinde qui iudicat et condemnat iniuste, si iudicatur
et condemnatur iuste, in eadem mensura recipit,
quamvis non hoc quod dedit. Iudicio enim fecit,
iudicio patitur; quamvis fecerit damnatione quod
iniquum est, patiatur damnatione quod iustum est.

everlasting expulsion from the society of the living? But to expel men from this mortal city by the punishment of the first death is the same as to expel them from that immortal city by the punishment of the second death. For just as the laws of this city do not operate to recall one who has been put to death, so neither do the laws of that city operate to recall to eternal life one condemned to the second death.

" Then how," they ask, " is the word of your Christ true, ' The measure that you give will be the measure that you get back,' [1] if a sin in time is punished by timeless punishment?" They do not observe that the measure is said to be the same, not because of an equal space of time, but because of the matching of evil with evil; that is, one who has done evil must suffer evil. This statement may, however, be properly applied to the matter of which the Lord was speaking at the time, that is, judgements and condemnations. Accordingly, if one who judges and condemns unjustly is justly judged and condemned, he receives the same measure, though not the same thing, which he gave. For his act was in judging and he suffers in being judged; although in condemning he did what is unjust, in being condemned he suffers what is just.

[1] Luke 6.38.

XII

*De magnitudine praevaricationis primae, ob quam
aeterna poena omnibus debeatur qui extra gratiam
fuerint Salvatoris.*

SED poena aeterna ideo dura et iniusta sensibus
videtur humanis quia in hac infirmitate moribun-
dorum sensuum deest ille sensus altissimae puris-
simaeque sapientiae quo sentiri possit quantum nefas
in illa prima praevaricatione commissum sit. Quanto
enim magis homo fruebatur Deo, tanto maiore
impietate dereliquit Deum; et factus est malo
dignus aeterno qui hoc in se peremit bonum quod
esse posset aeternum. Hinc est universa generis
humani massa damnata, quoniam qui hoc primus
admisit cum ea quae in illo fuerat radicata sua stirpe
punitus est, ut nullus ab hoc iusto debitoque supplicio
nisi misericordi et indebita gratia liberetur, atque ita
dispertiatur genus humanum ut in quibusdam
demonstretur quid valeat misericors gratia, in ceteris
quid iusta vindicta. Neque enim utrumque demon-
straretur in omnibus, quia si omnes remanerent in
poenis iustae damnationis, in nullo appareret misericors gratia; rursus si omnes a tenebris transferrentur
in lucem, in nullo appareret veritas [1] ultionis. In
qua propterea multo plures quam in illa sunt, ut sic

---

[1] *The Benedictine editors have one MS. to support their reading* severitas.

XII

On the magnitude of the first transgression, for which eternal punishment is due to all who are excluded from the Saviour's grace.

BUT eternal punishment seems hard and unjust to men because in the weakness of our mortal perceptions there is lacking a perception of that high and pure wisdom by which man may perceive how great a crime was done in that first transgression. For the more intimately man then enjoyed God, the greater was his impiety in deserting God; and the one who destroyed this good in himself which might have been eternal became worthy of eternal evil. Hence the whole mass of mankind was condemned,[1] since he who first sinned was punished along with the stock that had its root in him, and from that just and merited punishment no one is freed except by merciful and unmerited grace. Thus the human race is cut in two, so that in the one portion is displayed the power of merciful grace, in the other the power of just vengeance. Both could not be shown in all men, for if all remained subject to the punishment of just damnation, merciful grace would appear in none, and again if all were brought from darkness to light, in none would appear the verity of vengeance. Far more experience the vengeance of God than his grace, in order that it may thus be shown what

---

[1] That the mass of mankind is condemned for Adam's sin is a doctrine emphasized by Augustine especially in his controversy with the Pelagians. See his *Manual (Enchiridion)* 27 and Rivière's note in *Bibliothèque Augustinienne* IX, 345 f.

ostendatur quid omnibus deberetur. Quod si omnibus redderetur iustitiam vindicantis iuste nemo reprehenderet, quia vero tam multi exinde liberantur est unde agantur maximae gratiae gratuito muneri liberantis.

XIII

Contra opinionem eorum, qui putant criminosis supplicia post mortem causa purgationis adhiberi.

PLATONICI quidem, quamvis inpunita nulla velint esse peccata, tamen omnes poenas emendationi adhiberi putant, vel humanis inflictas legibus vel divinis, sive in hac vita sive post mortem, si aut parcatur hic cuique aut ita plectatur ut hic non corrigatur. Hinc est Maronis illa sententia ubi, cum dixisset de terrenis corporibus moribundisque membris quod animae

Hinc metuunt cupiuntque, dolent gaudentque, nec auras

Suspiciunt, clausae tenebris et carcere caeco,

secutus adiunxit atque ait:

Quin et supremo cum lumine vita reliquit
(id est cum die novissimo reliquit eas ista vita),

Non tamen (inquit) omne malum miseris, nec funditus omnes
Corporeae excedunt pestes, penitusque necesse est
Multa diu concreta modis inolescere miris.
Ergo exercentur poenis veterumque malorum

was due to all. If vengeance were rendered to all, no one could rightly censure the justice of him who punishes justly; but since so many are freed from punishment, there is reason to give the greatest thanks for the free gift of him who frees them.

XIII

Against the opinion of those who think that punish-ments are inflicted on the guilty after death for the purpose of cleansing.

THE Platonists, though they choose to believe that no sins are unpunished, nevertheless think that all punishments are intended for correction, whether imposed by divine or human laws, whether in this life or after death, in case anyone either gets no punishment in this life, or receives punishment that does not effect correction here. On this view is based a well-known passage of Virgil. After speaking of earthly bodies and mortal frames, whence souls " derive their fears and desires, their griefs and joys, and fail to look up to heaven while locked in the darkness of their prison," he continues: " Nay, even when last they see the light, and life departs " (that is, when this life has left them on their last day), " still from their wretched souls not all the evil nor all the plagues of the body depart entirely, but many a taint long joined in growth must needs remain attached in wondrous wise. Hence they are dis-ciplined by punishments, and pay the penalties for

SAINT AUGUSTINE

Supplicia expendunt; aliae panduntur inanes
Suspensae ad ventos, aliis sub gurgite vasto
Infectum eluitur scelus aut exuritur igni.

Qui hoc opinantur nullas poenas nisi purgatorias
volunt esse post mortem, ut, quoniam terris superiora
sunt elementa aqua aer ignis, ex aliquo istorum
mundetur per expiatorias poenas quod terrena con-
tagione contractum est. Aer quippe accipitur in eo
quod ait: " Suspensae ad ventos "; aqua in eo quod
ait: " Sub gurgite vasto "; ignis autem suo nomine
expressus est cum dixit: " Aut exuritur igni."
   Nos vero etiam in hac quidem mortali vita esse
quasdam poenas purgatorias confitemur, non quibus
affliguntur quorum vita vel non inde fit melior vel
potius inde fit peior, sed illis sunt purgatoriae qui eis
coherciti corriguntur. Ceterae omnes poenae, sive
temporariae sive sempiternae, sicut unusquisque
divina providentia tractandus est, inferuntur vel pro
peccatis sive praeteritis sive in quibus adhuc vivit
ille qui plectitur, vel pro exercendis declarandisque
virtutibus per homines et angelos seu bonos seu
malos. Nam etsi quisque mali aliquid alterius inprobitate vel errore patiatur, peccat quidem homo
qui vel ignorantia vel iniustitia cuiquam mali aliquid
facit, sed non peccat Deus, qui iusto quamvis occulto
iudicio fieri sinit. Sed temporarias poenas alii in hac
vita tantum, alii post mortem, alii et nunc et tunc.
verum tamen ante iudicium illud severissimum
novissimumque patiuntur. Non autem omnes veniunt

---

¹ Virgil, *Aeneid* 6.733–742.

old misdeeds. Some are spread out exposed to the
bodiless winds, others have their stain of sin washed
out beneath a huge whirlpool, or burned out with
fire."[1] Those who hold this opinion think that there
are no penalties after death except those intended
for cleansing. Hence, since the elements of water,
air and fire are superior to earth, they think that in
one of these the guilt acquired from contact with
earth may be cleansed through expiatory penalties.
Air, of course, is meant when he says "exposed to
the bodiless winds," water when he says "beneath
a huge whirlpool," while fire is expressly mentioned
when he says "burned out with fire."

We indeed admit that even in this mortal life there
are cleansing penalties—not such afflictions as fail to
improve the character, or even make it worse, but
penalties cleansing for those who are restrained and
corrected by them. All other penalties, whether
temporal or eternal, according as divine providence
must deal with each man, are sometimes inflicted for
sins, whether these are past sins or sins in which the
man is still living, and sometimes are inflicted to
exercise and exhibit a man's virtues, through the
agency of men or angels, good or bad. For though a
man may suffer some evil by the wickedness or mistake of another, while that man sins who does evil
through ignorance or unrighteousness, yet God does
not sin in allowing it to be done, according to his just
judgement, however inscrutable. But temporary
penalties are suffered by some in this life only, by
others only after death, by others both now and
then, yet still before that stern and final judgement.
And not all who suffer temporary penalties after

in sempiternas poenas quae post illud iudicium sunt
futurae qui post mortem sustinent temporales.
Nam quibusdam quod in isto non remittitur remitti
in futuro saeculo, id est, ne futuri saeculi aeterno
supplicio puniantur, iam supra diximus.[1]

XIV

*De poenis temporalibus istius vitae, quibus subiecta
est humana condicio.*

RARISSIMI sunt autem qui nullas in hac vita, sed
tantum post eam poenas luunt. Fuisse tamen
aliquos, qui usque ad decrepitam senectutem ne
levissimam quidem febriculam senserint quietamque
duxerint vitam, et ipsi novimus et audivimus.
Quamquam vita ipsa mortalium tota poena sit quia
tota temptatio est, sicut sacrae litterae personant ubi
scriptum est: *Numquid non temptatio est vita humana
super terram?*[2] Non enim parva poena est ipsa
insipientia vel inperitia, quae usque adeo fugienda
merito iudicatur ut per poenas doloribus plenas pueri
cogantur quaeque artificia vel litteras discere.
Ipsumque discere, ad quod poenis adiguntur, tam
poenale est eis ut nonnumquam ipsas poenas per
quas compelluntur discere malint ferre quam discere.
Quis autem non exhorreat et mori eligat, si ei
proponatur aut mors perpetienda aut rursus infantia?
Quae quidem quod non a risu sed a fletu orditur

<hr>

[1] See 20.25 (Vol. VI, 415 f.), also Chapters XXIV and XXVI,
pp. 118, 146 below, with notes.
[2] Job 7.1 LXX.

death arrive among the eternal punishments that will follow that judgement. For, as we have already said, there are certain men whose sins, not forgiven in this world, will be forgiven in the next, so that they will not be punished in the eternal punishment of that world.[1]

XIV

Of the temporal punishments of this life, to which the lot of man is subject.

THERE are very few who suffer no punishments in this life, but are punished only after death. However, I have myself known some, and heard of some, who led a peaceful life till extreme old age without even the slightest illness. And yet the whole of mortal life is itself a punishment; for the whole is a trial, as the Scriptures declare: " Is not the life of man on the earth a trial? " [2] For folly itself, or ignorance, is no small punishment, and since men rightly judge that it must be shunned, boys are compelled by painful penalties to learn their trades, or letters. And the work of learning, to which they are driven by the penalties, is so much a punishment for them that sometimes they prefer to endure the penalties by which they are being driven to learn, rather than to learn.[3] Who would not shiver with dread and choose to die, if he were offered the choice of death or a second infancy? The fact that the babe begins his life not with laughter but with

---

[3] For Augustine's account of his miseries in school see *Confessions* 1.9.14.

hanc lucem, quid malorum ingressa sit nesciens
prophetat quodam modo. Solum quando natus est
ferunt risisse Zoroastrem, nec ei boni aliquid mon-
strosus risus ille portendit. Nam magicarum artium
fuisse perhibetur inventor, quae quidem illi nec
ad praesentis vitae vanam felicitatem contra suos
inimicos prodesse potuerunt; a Nino quippe rege
Assyriorum, cum esset ipse Bactrianorum, bello
superatus est. Prorsus quod scriptum est: *Grave
iugum super filios Adam a die exitus de ventre matris
eorum usque in diem sepulturae in matrem omnium*,
usque adeo impleri necesse est ut ipsi parvuli per
lavacrum regenerationis ab originalis peccati quo
solo tenebantur vinculo iam soluti mala multa
patientes nonnulli et incursus spirituum malignorum
aliquando patiantur. Quae quidem passio absit ut
eis obsit, si hanc vitam in illa aetate etiam ipsa
passione ingravescente et animam de corpore
excludente finierint.

XV

*Quod omne opus gratiae Dei eruentis nos de pro-
funditate veteris mali ad futuri saeculi pertineat
novitatem.*

VERUM tamen in gravi iugo quod positum est super
filios Adam a die exitus de ventre matris eorum usque
in diem sepulturae in matrem omnium, etiam hoc

---

[1] Pliny, *Natural History* 7.16.72.
[2] Pliny 30.2.3; Eusebius, *Chronicle* 20[a]; Justin, *Philippic
History* 1.1.7–10.

wailing is a kind of unconscious prophecy what a path of evils it has entered upon. Zoroaster alone is said to have laughed when he was born,[1] nor did that freakish laughter portend any good for him. For they say that he was the inventor of magic arts, yet these were of no avail against his enemies, even to gain the vain felicity of this present life, for he was defeated in war by Ninus, king of the Assyrians, while he himself was king of the Bactrians.[2] Truly, as it is written: " A heavy yoke is on the sons of Adam from the day when they come from their mother's womb till the day when they are buried in the mother of all," [3] so must these words be fulfilled even to the point where babes freed already by the washing of regeneration from original sin, by which alone they were bound, suffer many ills, and some at times even suffer the attacks of malignant spirits. But let it not be thought that this suffering harms them, even if they depart from life at that early age, as the suffering grows worse and expels the soul from the body.

XV

The entire work of God's grace, in lifting us from the depth of evil, relates to the new life of the world to come.

BUT as for the heavy yoke which is placed on the sons of Adam from the day when they come forth from their mother's womb until the day when they are buried in the mother of all, even this evil is found

---

[3] Ecclesiasticus 40.1.

malum mirabile reperitur, ut sobrii simus atque
intellegamus hanc vitam de peccato illo nimis nefario
quod in paradiso perpetratum est, factam nobis esse
poenalem totumque quod nobiscum agitur per
testamentum novum non pertinere nisi ad novi
saeculi hereditatem novam, ut hic pignore accepto
illud cuius hoc pignus est suo tempore consequamur,
nunc autem ambulemus in spe et proficientes de die
in diem spiritu facta carnis mortificemus. *Novit*
enim *Dominus qui sunt eius*, et *quotquot spiritu Dei*
aguntur, hi filii sunt Dei, sed gratia non natura.
Unicus enim natura Dei filius propter nos misericordia factus est hominis filius, ut nos, natura filii
hominis, filii Dei per illum gratia fieremus. Manens
quippe ille inmutabilis naturam nostram, in qua nos
susciperet, suscepit a nobis et tenax divinitatis suae
nostrae infirmitatis particeps factus est, ut nos in
melius commutati, quod peccatores mortalesque
sumus eius inmortalis et iusti participatione amit-
tamus et quod in natura nostra bonum fecit im-
pletum summo bono in eius naturae bonitate ser-
vemus. Sicut enim per unum hominem peccantem
in hoc tam grave malum devenimus, ita per unum
hominem eundemque Deum iustificantem ad illud
bonum tam sublime veniemus.

Nec quisquam se debet ab isto ad illum transisse
confidere, nisi cum ibi fuerit ubi temptatio nulla
erit, nisi pacem tenuerit quam belli huius, in quo

---

[1] Romans 9.23. [2] 2 Timothy 2.19.
[3] Romans 8.14. [4] Galatians 5.17.

to be a marvellous teacher.   It teaches that we should
be sober and understand that this life has been made
our punishment for that exceeding wicked sin which
was committed in Paradise, and that all that is done
for us in the new covenant relates to nothing else than
the new inheritance of the new world, in order that
after here receiving the pledge we may in due time
obtain that for which the pledge was given.   Meanwhile we must walk by faith, and advancing from day
to day, we must by the Spirit put to death the deeds
of the flesh.[1]   For " the Lord knoweth them that
are his," [2] and " as many as are led by the spirit of
God, these are the sons of God." [3]   But they are
sons by grace, not by nature, for the only one who
was son of God by nature became the son of man for
our sake through pity, in order that we who are sons
of man by nature might through him become sons
of God by grace.   Though he remained immutable,
he received from us our nature, thereby to receive
us to himself.   While retaining his own divinity he
became partaker of our weakness that we might be
changed for the better, and that by partaking of his
immortality and righteousness we might cast off
our sinful and mortal nature, and might fill with the
highest good the good that he created in our nature,
and preserve it by sharing in the goodness of his
nature.   For as through one man who sinned we
came into this great evil, so through one man who
justifies us, who is at the same time God, we shall
arrive at that sublime good.[4]

And no one should suppose that he has passed from
the one to the other until he arrives at the place
where there shall be no temptation, nor until he gains

caro concupiscit adversus spiritum et spiritus adversus carnem, multis et variis certaminibus quaerit. Hoc autem bellum numquam ullum esset si natura humana per liberum arbitrium in rectitudine in qua facta est perstitisset. Nunc vero quae pacem felix cum Deo habere noluit secum pugnat infelix, et cum sit hoc malum miserabile, melius est tamen quam priora vitae huius. Melius confligitur quippe cum vitiis quam [1] sine ulla conflictione dominantur. Melius est, inquam, bellum cum spe pacis aeternae quam sine ulla liberationis cogitatione captivitas. Cupimus quidem etiam hoc bello carere et ad capessendam ordinatissimam pacem, ubi firmissima stabilitate potioribus inferiora subdantur, igne divini amoris accendimur. Sed si (quod absit) illius tanti boni spes nulla esset, malle debuimus in huius conflictationis molestia remanere quam vitiis in nos dominationem non eis resistendo permittere.

XVI

Sub quibus gratiae legibus omnes regeneratorum habeantur aetates.

VERUM tanta est Dei misericordia in vasa misericordiae quae praeparavit in gloriam, ut etiam prima hominis aetas id est infantia quae sine ullo renisu subiacet carni, et secunda quae pueritia nuncupatur ubi nondum ratio suscepit hanc pugnam et fere sub

---

[1] *The Benedictine editors improve the construction by adding* cum.

---

[1] Romans 9.23.

the peace that he seeks amid the many and varied struggles of this war in which flesh lusts against the spirit and spirit against flesh. But there would never have been any such war if man's nature had remained steadfast in that rectitude in which it was created. But now the nature that refused to be happy and at peace with God is unhappy and at war with itself. Though it is in a pitiable state, yet this state is better than the state that preceded this way of life, for it is better to struggle with vices than to be ruled by them without a struggle. Better, I say, is war with the hope of eternal peace than captivity without any prospect of liberation. To be sure, we yearn to escape this war too, and we are inflamed by the fire of God's love to strive for that well-ordered peace where, in immovable stability, lower things are subject to the higher. But even if there were no hope (which God forbid!) of that great good, it would have been our duty to prefer to continue in this troubled conflict rather than to yield and be enslaved to our vices, by not resisting them.

XVI

*Of the laws of grace which govern all the periods
of life of the reborn.*

BUT great is the mercy of God toward the " vessels of mercy " [1] which he has prepared for glory, as we shall see. The first period of life, that is, infancy, is subject to the flesh without a struggle, and the second, which is called childhood, when reason has not yet taken up the battle, is at the mercy of almost all

omnibus vitiosis delectationibus iacet—quia licet
fari iam valeat et ideo infantiam transisse videatur
nondum in ea est praecepti capax infirmitas mentis—
si sacramenta Mediatoris acceperit, etiamsi hanc in
eis annis vitam finiat, translata scilicet a potestate
tenebrarum in regnum Christi, non solum poenis
non praeparetur aeternis, sed ne ulla quidem post
mortem purgatoria tormenta patiatur.   Sufficit enim
sola spiritalis regeneratio ne post mortem obsit quod
carnalis generatio cum morte contraxit.   Cum autem
ventum fuerit ad aetatem quae praeceptum iam
capit et subdi potest legis imperio, suscipiendum est
bellum contra vitia et gerendum acriter, ne ad damnabilia peccata perducat.   Et si quidem nondum
victoriarum consuetudine roborata sunt facilius
vincuntur et cedunt, si autem vincere atque imperare
consuerunt laboriosa difficultate superantur.

Neque id fit veraciter atque sinceriter nisi verae
delectatione iustitiae, haec est autem in fide Christi.
Nam si lex iubens adsit et spiritus iuvans desit, per
ipsam prohibitionem desiderio crescente atque vincente peccati etiam reatus praevaricationis accedit.
Nonnumquam sane apertissima vitia aliis vitiis
vincuntur occultis quae putantur esse virtutes, in

---

¹ The " sacraments of the Mediator " here mentioned are
the same as " the sacrament of baptism and of the body of
Christ " in Chapter XXV, p. 133 below.   Even in the case of
infants the communion was received immediately after baptism, a practice still observed in the Greek church.   In his
controversy with the Pelagians Augustine argued that just as
no one, child or adult, could enter the kingdom of God unless he
was " born of water and of the Spirit " (that is, baptized), so

sinful pleasures. For, though that age has the power of speech, hence seems to have passed beyond infancy, its weakness of discernment is not yet able to keep the commandment of God. Yet if the child has received the sacraments of the Mediator [1] and ends his life during these years, having been translated from the power of darkness into the kingdom of Christ, not only is he not destined to eternal punishment, but he does not even suffer any purgatorial torments after death. For the spiritual regeneration alone is enough to prevent any harm coming after death from what the flesh by birth brought along with its mortality. But when the age is reached that is able to keep the commandment and to be subject to the rule of law, a man must take up the war against the vices and wage it vigorously, lest he be led into damnable sins. And if the vices are not yet strengthened by the habit of victory they are more easily conquered, and yield, but if they are accustomed to conquer and rule they are overcome only with toil and difficulty.

Nor is the victory gained truly and sincerely except by a delight in true righteousness, and this comes by believing in Christ. For if the law is there commanding and the Spirit is not there assisting, through the very prohibition the desire of sin grows and conquers, till the guilt of transgression is added. Sometimes, to be sure, obvious vices are overcome by other vices which are secret and supposed to be virtues,

he could not have eternal life without "eating of the flesh" and "drinking the blood" of Christ (that is, without communion). See *On Forgiveness of Sins and Baptism* 1.26 and 34, also *Dictionary of Christian Antiquities* I, 835-837.

quibus regnat superbia et quaedam sibi placendi altitudo ruinosa. Tunc itaque victa vitia deputanda sunt cum Dei amore vincuntur, quem nisi Deus ipse non donat nec aliter nisi per mediatorem Dei et hominum, hominem Christum Iesum qui factus est particeps mortalitatis nostrae ut nos participes faceret divinitatis suae.

Paucissimi autem sunt tantae felicitatis, ut ab ipsa ineunte adulescentia nulla damnabilia peccata committant vel in flagitiis vel in facinoribus vel in nefariae cuiusquam impietatis errore, sed magna spiritus largitate opprimant, quidquid eis posset carnali delectatione dominari. Plurimi vero praecepto legis accepto, cum prius victi fuerint praevalentibus vitiis et praevaricatores eius effecti, tunc ad gratiam confugiunt adiuvantem, qua fiant et amarius paenitendo et vehementius pugnando prius Deo subdita atque ita carni praeposita mente victores. Quisquis igitur cupit poenas evadere sempiternas, non solum baptizetur, verum etiam iustificetur in Christo, ac sic vere transeat a diabolo ad Christum. Purgatorias autem poenas nullas futuras opinetur, nisi ante illud ultimum tremendumque iudicium. Nequaquam tamen negandum est etiam ipsum aeternum ignem pro diversitate meritorum quamvis malorum aliis leviorem, aliis futurum esse graviorem, sive ipsius vis atque ardor pro poena digna cuiusque varietur, sive

---

[1] 1 Timothy 2.5.

among which pride is chief, and a loftiness of self-complacency that leads to a great fall. Therefore, then only may we consider vices overcome when they are overcome by love for God. This love is granted only by God himself, and only through the mediator between God and men, the man Christ Jesus,[1] who was made a partaker of our mortality that he might make us partakers of his divinity.

But very few are so fortunate that from the beginning of their youth they commit no damnable sins (either in disgraceful deeds, or crimes, or in the error of some abominable impiety), but instead by the great bounty of the Spirit crush whatever vice might have enslaved them through carnal pleasure. Very many, on the other hand, when they first learn the precept of the law, are overcome by vices too strong for them, and become transgressors of the law. Then they flee to grace for help, whereby they become victors, for by repenting more bitterly and struggling more earnestly they first bring their mind into subjection to God and thus set it to rule over the flesh. So whoever desires to escape eternal punishment must not only be baptized, but also made righteous in Christ, thus truly passing from the devil to Christ. But as for cleansing penalties, let him not imagine that there will be any unless they precede that last and terrible judgement. However, it may be granted that even the eternal fire will be a lighter punishment for some and heavier for others, according as their deserts, though all are evil, are more or less. Perhaps its violence and heat will be varied according to the punishment each one

ipse aequaliter ardeat sed non aequali molestia
sentiatur.

XVII

*De his qui putant nullorum hominum poenas in
aeternum esse mansuras.*

NUNC iam cum misericordibus nostris agendum
esse video et pacifice disputandum, qui vel omnibus
illis hominibus quos iustissimus iudex dignos gehennae supplicio iudicabit, vel quibusdam eorum, nolunt
credere poenam sempiternam futuram, sed post certi
temporis metas pro cuiusque peccati quantitate
longioris sive brevioris eos inde existimant liberandos.
Qua in re misericordior profecto fuit Origenes, qui et
ipsum diabolum atque angelos eius post graviora pro
meritis et diuturniora supplicia ex illis cruciatibus
eruendos et sociandos sanctis angelis credidit. Sed
illum et propter hoc et propter alia nonnulla et
maxime propter alternantes sine cessatione beatitudines et miserias et statutis saeculorum intervallis
ab istis ad illas atque ab illis ad istas itus ac reditus
interminabiles non inmerito reprobavit ecclesia; quia
et hoc quod misericors videbatur amisit faciendo
sanctis veras miserias, quibus poenas luerent, et
falsas beatitudines in quibus verum ac securum, hoc
est sine timore certum, sempiterni boni gaudium non
haberent.

Longe autem aliter istorum misericordia humano

---

[1] Compare Augustine's previous criticism of Origen in
Volume III, Book 11.23.

deserves, or perhaps the fire will burn equally, but will not be felt with equal pain.

XVII

Of those who think that the punishments of no human beings will last for ever.

I SEE that the time has now come to deal with tender-hearted Christians, and argue with them in a friendly spirit. They either refuse to believe that punishment will be eternal for all of those men whom the righteous judge shall judge worthy of hell, or for certain particular ones. For they think that they should be freed from hell after a period of time which will be long or short according to the amount of each man's sin. In this matter Origen was actually even more merciful, believing that the devil, too, and his angels must be delivered from those tortures and associated with the holy angels, after the more severe and long continued punishment which is his due.[1] But the Church has rightly condemned him for this view, and for many others—especially for the notion of periods of happiness and wretchedness that alternate continually, and endless journeys back and forth from one state to the other, at fixed intervals, for ever. For he lost even the advantage of being thought merciful when he imagined real sufferings for the saints, to pay the penalty for their misdeeds, and a false happiness, in which they would not have the true and sure joy of eternal good, that is, a joy without fear of loss.

Quite different is the error, based on human

errat affectu qui hominum illo iudicio damnatorum
miserias temporales, omnium vero qui vel citius vel
tardius liberantur aeternam felicitatem putant.
Quae sententia si propterea bona et vera quia
misericors est, tanto erit melior et verior quanto
misericordior. Extendatur ergo ac profundatur fons
huius misericordiae usque ad damnatos angelos
saltem post multa atque prolixa quantumlibet saecula
liberandos. Cur usque universam naturam manat
humanam, et cum ad angelicam ventum fuerit mox
arescit? Non audent tamen se ulterius miserando
porrigere et ad liberationem ipsius quoque diaboli
pervenire. Verum si aliquis audeat, vincit nempe
istos. Et tamen tanto invenitur errare deformius et
contra recta Dei verba perversius quanto sibi videtur
sentire clementius.

XVIII

*De his qui novissimo iudicio propter intercessionem
sanctorum neminem hominum putant esse
damnandum.*

SUNT etiam, quales in conlocutionibus nostris ipse
sum expertus, qui, cum venerari videantur scripturas
sanctas, moribus inprobandi sunt, et agendo causam
suam multo maiorem quam isti misericordiam Deo
tribuunt erga humanum genus. Dicunt enim de
malis et infidelibus hominibus divinitus quidem verum

sympathy, of those who think that the misery of men condemned in that judgement will be temporary, and the happiness of all who are sooner or later freed will be eternal. If this opinion is true and good for the reason that it is merciful, then the more there is of mercy, the more there will be of goodness and truth. Let the spring of this mercy therefore be enlarged and deepened to include the lost angels, who will surely be freed at last, even if punished for many ages, prolonged as far as you like. Why does this fountain flow for all mankind, and a moment later run dry when it comes to the angels? Still, they do not dare to extend their pity so far as to reach the point of freeing the devil as well. But if someone could be so bold, he certainly surpasses them. And yet he is obviously erring the more odiously and perversely against the true word of God, the more he seems to himself to show kindness in his view of the matter.

XVIII

Of those who think that no one will be condemned in the last judgement, because of the intercession of the saints.

THERE are some men also, of a kind I have met myself in our conferences, who, though they seem to reverence the holy Scriptures, are of reprobate character, and in making a case for themselves ascribe to God much more mercy for mankind than do these others. For, they say, the voice of God truly declares that wicked and faithless men are worthy

praedictum esse quod digni sunt,[1] sed cum ad
iudicium ventum fuerit, misericordiam esse supera-
turam.   Donabit enim eos, inquiunt, misericors Deus
precibus et intercessionibus sanctorum suorum. Si
enim orabant pro illis quando eos patiebantur inimicos, quanto magis quando videbunt humiles supplices-
que prostratos! Neque enim credendum est, aiunt,
tunc amissuros sanctos viscera misericordiae cum
fuerint plenissimae ac perfectissimae sanctitatis ut
qui tunc orabant pro inimicis suis quando et ipsi
sine peccato non erant, tunc non orent pro supplicibus
suis quando nullum coeperint habere peccatum.
Aut vero Deus tunc eos non exaudiet tot et tales
filios suos, quando in tanta eorum sanctitate nullum
inveniet orationis impedimentum? Testimonium
vero psalmi, et illi quidem qui permittunt infideles
atque impios homines saltem longo tempore cruciari
et postea de malis omnibus erui, sed magis isti, pro
se dicunt esse ubi legitur: *Numquid obliviscetur
misereri Deus aut continebit in ira sua miserationes suas?*
Ira eius est, inquiunt, ut omnes indigni beatitudine
sempiterna ipso iudicante puniantur supplicio sempiterno. Sed si vel longum vel prorsus ullum esse
permiserit, profecto ut possit hoc fieri, continebit in
ira sua miserationes suas, quod eum psalmus dicit non
esse facturum. Non enim ait: "Numquid diu
continebit in ira sua miserationes suas?" sed quod
prorsus non continebit ostendit.

[1] *Various editors add* morte, poena, *or* eterno supplicio *to
supply the needed word for* "*punishment.*"

of punishment, yet when it comes to the judgement, mercy will prevail. For a merciful God, they say, will pardon them in answer to the prayers and intercessions of his saints. For if the saints prayed for their enemies while suffering their enmity, how much more will they pray when they see them prostrate in humble entreaty! For it is incredible, they say, that the saints are to lose their bowels of compassion [1] at the time when they have attained full and perfect sainthood. Nor will those who once prayed for their enemies when they were not without sin themselves, fail then to pray for suppliants when they themselves have begun to be without sin. Or will God then not hear his children—so many, and so excellent as they will be—when in their holy state he will find nothing to detract from their prayer? Both the former class, who at least allow the faithless and wicked to be tortured for a long period and later to be delivered from all evils, and, still more, this latter class, say that the Psalm speaks for them when it says: " Will God forget to pity, or shut up in his anger his tender mercies? " [2] It is by his anger, they say, while he sits as judge, that all those unworthy of eternal happiness are punished by eternal punishment. But if he allows the punishment to be long, or allows any punishment at all, then certainly to make this possible he will be shutting up in anger his tender mercies—which the Psalm says that he will not do. For it does not say: " Will he long shut up in his anger his tender mercies?" but clearly states that he will not shut them up at all.

[1] Colossians 3.12.
[2] Psalms 77.9.

Sic ergo isti volunt iudicii Dei comminationem non esse mendacem, quamvis sit neminem damnaturus, quem ad modum eius comminationem qua dixit eversurum se esse Nineven civitatem mendacem non possumus dicere; et tamen factum non est, inquiunt, quod sine ulla condicione praedixit. Non enim ait: " Nineve evertetur si non egerint paenitentiam seque correxerint," sed hoc non addito praenuntiavit futuram eversionem illius civitatis. Quam comminationem propterea veracem putant quia hoc praedixit Deus quod vere digni erant pati, quamvis hoc non esset ipse facturus. Nam etsi paenitentibus pepercit, inquiunt, utique illos paenitentiam non ignorabat acturos, et tamen absolute ac definite eorum eversionem futuram esse praedixit. Hoc ergo erat, inquiunt, in veritate severitatis, quia id erant digni; sed in ratione miserationis non erat, quam non continuit in ira sua, ut ab ea poena supplicibus parceret quam fuerat contumacibus comminatus. Si ergo tunc pepercit, aiunt, quando sanctum suum prophetam fuerat parcendo contristaturus, quanto magis tunc miserabilius supplicantibus parcet quando ut parcat omnes sancti eius orabunt!

Sed hoc quod ipsi suis cordibus suspicantur ideo putant scripturas tacuisse divinas ut multi se corrigant vel prolixarum vel aeternarum timore poenarum, et sint qui possint orare pro eis qui non se correxerint, nec tamen opinantur omni modo id

---

[1] Jonah 3.4.　　　　[2] Jonah 4.1.

Hence they explain that the threat of God's judgement is not a lie, though he is going to condemn no one, just as we cannot say that his threat to overthrow the city of Nineveh [1] was a lie, and yet, say they, the event did not occur that he had unconditionally predicted. For he did not say: "Nineveh shall be overthrown unless they repent and reform," but he predicted the overthrow of that city with no qualifying clause. They think that this threat is true inasmuch as God foretold what they truly deserved to suffer, although he was not actually going to do what he said. For though because of their repentance he spared them, he must surely have known, so they say, that they were going to repent, and yet he declared unconditionally and positively that their destruction would come to pass. Hence, they say, this was truly spoken in accordance with the sternness of God, for they were worthy of it, but untruly by the reckoning of his mercy, which he did not shut up in his anger, so that he spared them when suppliants the penalty that he had threatened when they were stubborn and proud. For if he spared men, they say, at the time when he was thereby bound to grieve his holy prophet,[2] how much more will he spare men pleading still more wretchedly, when all his saints will be praying him to spare them!

This thing that they have surmised in their own hearts is kept hidden, they think, in the Scriptures, in order that many may correct their lives through fear of prolonged, or eternal, punishment, and that there may be saints with power to pray for those who have not corrected their lives. Still, they do

eloquia divina tacuisse. Nam quo pertinet, inquiunt, quod scriptum est: *Quam multa multitudo*
dulcedinis tuae, Domine, quam abscondisti timentibus te,
nisi ut intellegamus propter timorem fuisse abscon-
ditam misericordiae divinae tam multam secretamque
dulcedinem? Addunt etiam propterea dixisse apostolum: *Conclusit enim Deus omnes in infidelitate ut*
omnium misereatur, quo significaret quod ab illo nemo
damnabitur. Nec isti tamen qui hoc sentiunt hanc
opinationem suam usque ad liberationem vel nullam
damnationem diaboli atque angelorum eius exten-
dunt. Humana quippe circa solos homines moventur
misericordia et causam maxime agunt suam, per
generalem in genus humanum quasi Dei misera-
tionem inpunitatem falsam suis perditis moribus
pollicentes. Ac per hoc superabunt eos in praedi-
canda Dei misericordia qui hanc inpunitatem etiam
principi daemonum et eius satellitibus pollicentur.

XIX

De his qui inpunitatem omnium peccatorum promittunt
etiam haereticis propter participationem corporis
Christi.

ITEM sunt alii ab aeterno supplicio liberationem nec
ipsis saltem omnibus hominibus promittentes, sed
tantummodo Christi baptismate ablutis, qui participes
fiunt corporis eius, quomodolibet vixerint, in quacum-

---

not think that the Scriptures are entirely silent on the point. For what is the meaning, they say, of the passage: " How great is thy sweetness, O Lord, which thou hast hidden from them that fear thee," [1] except that we should understand that for the sake of a wholesome fear the great and secret sweetness of God's mercy has been hidden? They add also that when the Apostle said: " For God has shut up all in unbelief that he might have mercy on all," [2] he meant that no one will be condemned by him. Yet those who hold this view do not extend their conjectures to include the release, or freedom from condemnation, of the devil and his angels. They are moved by human pity in respect to men alone, and above all they are pleading their own case, promising themselves a fictitious impunity for their own depraved character by ascribing to God a special pity for the human species. Hence, in proclaiming the mercy of God, they will be outdone by those who promise this impunity to the prince of demons also and to his retinue.

XIX

Of those who promise heretics as well impunity for all sins, because of their participation in the body of Christ.

LIKEWISE there are others who at least do not promise escape from eternal punishment to all men, but only to those washed in Christ's baptism, who become partakers of his body, no matter how they may have lived, or in what heresy or impiety they

que haeresi vel impietate fuerint, propter illud quod
ait Iesus: *Hic est panis qui de caelo descendit ut, si quis
ex ipso manducaverit, non moriatur. Ego sum panis
vivus qui de caelo descendi. Si quis manducaverit ex
hoc pane vivet in aeternum.* Ab aeterna ergo morte,
inquiunt, necesse est istos erui et ad vitam aeternam
quandocumque perduci.

XX

*De his qui non omnibus, sed eis tantum qui apud
catholicos sunt renati, etiamsi postea in multa
crimina erroresque proruperint, indulgentiam
pollicentur.*

ITEM sunt qui hoc nec omnibus habentibus baptismatis Christi et eius corporis sacramentum, sed solis
catholicis quamvis male viventibus pollicentur, quia
non solo sacramento, sed re ipsa manducaverunt
corpus Christi, in ipso eius corpore constituti de quo
dicit apostolus: *Unus panis, unum corpus multi sumus;*
ut, etiamsi postea in aliquam haeresim vel etiam in
gentilium idolatriam lapsi fuerint, tantum quia in
corpore Christi id est in catholica ecclesia sumpserunt
baptismum Christi et manducaverunt corpus Christi,
non moriantur in aeternum, sed vitam quandoque
consequantur aeternam; atque illa omnis impietas,
quanto maior fuerit, non eis valeat ad aeternitatem,
sed ad diuturnitatem magnitudinemque poenarum.

may have been involved. For they reason that Jesus said: "This is the bread that comes down out of heaven, so that if anyone has eaten of it, he may not die. I am the living bread that came down out of heaven. If anyone has eaten of this bread, he shall live for ever." [1] Therefore, they say, these persons must necessarily be delivered from eternal death, and one day be brought to eternal life.

XX

Of those who promise indulgence, not to all, but only to those reborn in the Catholic Church, even if later they fall into many sins and errors.

LIKEWISE there are some who promise this escape, not to all who have the sacrament of Christ's baptism and his body, but only to Catholics, however wickedly they live. For they have eaten the body of Christ, not only in a sacrament, but also in reality, and are established in his very body, of which the Apostle says: "We who are many are one bread, one body." [2] Hence, even if they have later lapsed into some heresy or even into heathen idolatry, for the mere reason that in the body of Christ (that is, in the Catholic Church) they have received Christ's baptism and eaten his body they will not die to remain for ever dead, but will at some time attain eternal life. And so all their impiety, however great, cannot lead to eternal punishment, but only to a punishment of greater duration and severity than that of others.

[1] John 6.50–51.   [2] 1 Corinthians 10.17.

SAINT AUGUSTINE

XXI

De his qui eos qui permanent in catholica fide, etiamsi
pessime vixerint et ob hoc uri meruerint, tamen
propter fidei fundamentum salvandos esse
definiunt.

SUNT autem qui propter id quod scriptum est: *Qui*
perseveraverit usque in finem, hic salvus erit, non nisi
in ecclesia catholica perseverantibus, quamvis in ea
male viventibus, hoc promittunt, per ignem videlicet
salvandis merito fundamenti de quo ait apostolus:
Fundamentum enim aliud nemo potest ponere praeter id
quod positum est, quod est Christus Iesus. Si quis
autem aedificat super fundamentum aurum, argentum,
lapides pretiosos, ligna, fenum, stipulam, uniuscuiusque
opus manifestabitur; dies enim declarabit, quoniam in
igne revelabitur, et uniuscuiusque opus quale sit ignis
probabit. Si cuius opus permanserit quod superaedi-
ficavit, mercedem accipiet. Si cuius autem opus arserit,
damnum patietur; ipse autem salvus erit, sic tamen quasi
per ignem. Dicunt ergo cuiuslibet vitae catholicum
Christianum Christum habere in fundamento, quod
fundamentum nulla haeresis habet a corporis eius
unitate praecisa, et ideo propter hoc fundamentum,
etiamsi malae vitae fuerit catholicus Christianus,
velut qui superaedificaverit ligna, fenum, stipulam,
putant eum salvum fieri per ignem, id est post poenas
ignis illius liberari quo igne in ultimo iudicio punientur
mali.

---

[1] Matthew 24.13.
[2] 1 Corinthians 3.11–15. Compare Chapter XXVI, pp.
138 f. below.

XXI

*Of those who fix the rule that those who persevere
in the Catholic faith, though they live most
wickedly and hence deserve to burn, nevertheless will be saved for keeping the
foundation of faith.*

THERE are those who because of the passage, " He
that endureth to the end shall be saved,"[1] promise
this only to those who persevere in the Catholic
Church, however wickedly they live in it. That is,
they are to be saved as through fire by the merit of
the foundation, of which the Apostle speaks: " For
other foundation can no one lay than that which is
laid, which is Christ Jesus. But if anyone build on
the foundation gold, silver, precious stones, wood,
hay, stubble, each one's work will be made manifest,
for the day will declare it, because it is revealed in fire
and the fire will prove each one's work, of what sort
it is. If anyone's work shall abide which he built
thereon, he will receive a reward. But if anyone's
work shall be burned he will suffer loss, but he himself
will be saved, yet so as through fire."[2] Hence they
say that a Catholic Christian, be his life what it may,
has Christ as his foundation, a foundation that no
heresy can have, cut off as it is from the unity of his
body. And so they think that even if his life be
evil, as was his who built with wood, hay or stubble,
the Catholic Christian will be saved through fire.
That is, he will be freed after a punishment in that
fire by which the wicked will be punished in the last
judgement.

XXII

De his qui putant ea crimina quae inter elemosynarum opera committuntur ad damnationis iudicium non vocari.

COMPERI etiam quosdam putare eos tantummodo arsuros illius aeternitate supplicii qui pro peccatis suis facere dignas elemosynas neglegunt, iuxta illud apostoli Iacobi: *Iudicium autem sine misericordia illi qui non fecit misericordiam.* Qui ergo fecit, inquiunt, quamvis mores in melius non mutaverit, sed inter ipsas suas elemosynas nefarie ac nequiter vixerit, iudicium illi cum misericordia futurum est, ut aut nulla damnatione plectatur aut post aliquod tempus sive parvum sive prolixum ab illa damnatione liberetur. Ideo iudicem ipsum vivorum atque mortuorum noluisse existimant aliud commemorare se esse dicturum sive dextris quibus est vitam daturus aeternam, sive sinistris quos aeterno supplicio damnaturus, nisi elemosynas sive factas sive non factas. Ad hoc pertinere aiunt et in oratione Dominica cotidianam postulationem: *Dimitte nobis debita nostra, sicut et nos dimittimus debitoribus nostris.* Quisquis enim illi qui in eum peccavit dimittit ignoscendo peccatum, procul dubio elemosynam facit. Quam rem Dominus ipse sic commendavit ut diceret: *Si enim dimiseritis peccata hominibus, dimittet vobis et pater vester peccata vestra; si autem non dimiseritis hominibus, neque pater vester qui in caelis est dimittet*

---

[1] The word "alms" (Greek, Latin *elcemosyna*) must here be taken in its original meaning, referring to any deed of mercy.

XXII

Of those who think that sins committed amid works of alms are not called into judgement of condemnation.

SOME men also, I have found, think that only those will burn in that eternal punishment who neglect proper alms [1] to atone for their sins. They quote the apostle James: " But judgement will be without mercy to him who has shown no mercy." [2] So he who has shown mercy, they say, though he has not reformed his ways, but has lived wickedly and worthlessly even while doing alms, will be judged with mercy, and either not condemned at all, or freed from his punishment after some period, short or long. That is the reason, they believe, why the judge of the living and the dead chose not to mention anything else that he will say to those on the right hand, to whom he will give eternal life, or on the left, whom he will condemn to eternal punishment, except the acts of charity which were either done or left undone.[3] They say that the daily petition in the Lord's prayer also refers to this point: " Forgive us our debts, as we forgive our debtors." [4] For whoever forgives a man who sins against him by pardoning his sin, beyond doubt is charitable. This the Lord himself has emphasized by saying: " For if ye forgive men their sins, your Father also will forgive your sins; but if ye do not forgive men, neither will your Father

[2] James 2.13.
[3] Matthew 25.34–46.
[4] Matthew 6.12.

vobis. Ergo et ad hoc genus elemosynarum pertinet quod ait apostolus Iacobus iudicium futurum sine misericordia ei qui non fecit misericordiam. Nec dixit Dominus, inquiunt, magna vel parva, sed: *Dimittet vobis pater vester peccata vestra, si et vos dimiseritis hominibus.* Ac per hoc putant etiam eis qui perdite vixerint, donec claudant diem vitae huius extremum, per hanc orationem qualiacumque et quantacumque fuerint omnia cotidie peccata dimitti, sicut ipsa cotidie frequentatur oratio, si hoc tantummodo custodire meminerint ut, quando ab eis veniam petunt qui eos peccato qualicumque laeserunt, ex corde dimittant. Cum ad haec omnia Deo donante respondero, liber iste claudendus est.

XXIII

Contra opinionem eorum qui dicunt nec diaboli nec hominum malorum perpetua futura supplicia.

Ac primum quaeri oportet atque cognosci cur ecclesia ferre nequiverit hominum disputationem diabolo etiam post maximas et diuturnissimas poenas purgationem vel indulgentiam pollicentem. Neque enim tot sancti et sacris veteribus ac novis litteris eruditi mundationem et regni caelorum beatitudinem post qualiacumque et quantacumque supplicia qualibuscumque et quantiscumque angelis inviderunt. Sed potius viderunt divinam vacuari vel infirmari non posse sententiam, quam se Dominus praenuntiavit in

---

[1] Matthew 6.15.

in heaven forgive you." [1] This kind of charity is also meant, therefore, when the apostle James says that judgement will be without mercy to him who has shown no mercy. And the Lord did not speak of "great sins " or "small," but said: " Your Father will forgive your sins if you also forgive men." And from this they think that even the sins of those who live wickedly until the last day of their life is closed, of whatever kind and number, are all daily forgiven as the prayer is daily repeated. They need only remember to watch this point, to forgive from the heart those who have harmed them by any misdeed whatever, when these ask forgiveness from them. When by God's help I have replied to all this, I will bring this book to a close.

XXIII

Against the opinion of those who say that future punishments will not be eternal, neither the devil's nor those of men.

Now first we must learn why the church has been unable to allow the reasoning of those who promised purgation or forgiveness to the devil after severe and long-continued punishment. For the many holy men who were skilled in the Scriptures, both Old and New Testament, did not begrudge the angels, of whatever kind and number, the cleansing thus promised, and the happiness of the kingdom of heaven, after punishments of any kind and number, but rather they saw that the divine sentence could not be reversed or weakened. For the Lord has

iudicio prolaturum atque dicturum: *Discedite a me, maledicti, in ignem aeternum qui paratus est diabolo et angelis eius.* Sic quippe ostendit aeterno igne diabolum et angelos eius arsuros. Et quod scriptum est in apocalypsi: *Diabolus qui seducebat eos missus est in stagnum ignis et sulphuris, quo et bestia et pseudo-propheta; et cruciabuntur die et nocte in saecula saeculorum.* Quod ibi dictum est *aeternum*, hic dictum est *in saecula saeculorum*, quibus verbis nihil scriptura divina significare consuevit nisi quod finem non habet temporis.

Quam ob rem prorsus nec alia causa nec iustior atque manifestior inveniri potest, cur verissima pietate teneatur fixum et inmobile nullum regressum ad iustitiam vitamque sanctorum diabolum et angelos eius habituros, nisi quia scriptura, quae neminem fallit, dicit eis Deum non pepercisse, et sic ab illo esse interim praedamnatos, ut carceribus caliginis inferi retrusi traderentur servandi atque ultimo iudicio puniendi, quando eos aeternus ignis accipiet, ubi cruciabuntur in saecula saeculorum. Quod si ita est, quo modo ab huius aeternitate poenae vel universi vel quidam homines post quantumlibet temporis subtrahentur, ac non statim enervabitur fides, qua creditur sempiternum daemonum futurum esse supplicium? Si enim quibus dicetur: *Discedite a me, maledicti, in ignem aeternum, qui paratus est diabolo et angelis eius,* vel universi vel aliqui eorum non semper

---

[1] Matthew 25.41.
[2] Revelation 20.10.
[3] 2 Peter 2.4.

declared that in the judgement he will pronounce the sentence: " Depart from me, ye cursed, into eternal fire, which is prepared for the devil and his angels." [1] Thus he certainly makes it clear that the devil and his angels will burn in eternal fire. And in the Apocalypse it is written: " The devil that deceived them was cast into the lake of fire and brimstone, where are also the beast and false prophet; and they shall be tormented night and day for ever and ever." [2] What is called " eternal " in the first passage is called " for ever and ever " in the second, and by these words the divine Scripture is accustomed to signify only something without end in time.

Therefore true religion holds the firm and unshaken belief that the devil and his angels will have no return to righteousness and the life of the saints, for which belief no other reason whatever can be found, none more just and clear, than the words of the Scripture, which never lies. The Scripture says that God did not spare them, but meanwhile condemned them in advance to be cast into hell and committed into pits of darkness to be kept and punished in the last judgement,[3] when eternal fire will receive them, where they will be tormented for ever and ever. If this is so, how can we grant that all men, or some men, after any interval you like, will be withdrawn from this eternal punishment, without weakening the faith by which we believe that the punishment of the demons will be eternal? For if those to whom the words will be spoken: " Depart from me, ye cursed, into eternal fire which is prepared for the devil and his angels," either all, or some of them, will not always be there, what reason

ibi erunt, quid causae est cur diabolus et angeli eius semper ibi futuri esse credantur? An forte Dei sententia quae in malos et angelos et homines proferetur, in angelos vera erit, in homines falsa? Ita plane hoc erit, si non quod Deus dixit, sed quod suspicantur homines plus valebit. Quod fieri quia non potest, non argumentari adversus Deum, sed divino potius, dum tempus est, debent parere praecepto, qui sempiterno cupiunt carere supplicio.

Deinde quale est aeternum supplicium pro igne diuturni temporis existimare et vitam aeternam credere sine fine, cum Christus eodem ipso loco in una eademque sententia dixerit utrumque complexus: *Sic ibunt isti in supplicium aeternum, iusti autem in vitam aeternam?* Si utrumque aeternum, profecto aut utrumque cum fine diuturnum aut utrumque sine fine perpetuum debet intellegi. Par pari enim relata sunt, hinc supplicium aeternum, inde vita aeterna. Dicere autem in hoc uno eodemque sensu: " Vita aeterna sine fine erit, supplicium aeternum finem habebit " multum absurdum est. Unde, quia vita aeterna sanctorum sine fine erit, supplicium quoque aeternum quibus erit finem procul dubio non habebit.

XXIV

Contra eorum sensum, qui in iudicio Dei omnibus reis propter sanctorum preces putant esse parcendum.

Hoc autem et adversus eos valet, qui suas agentes causas contra Dei venire verba velut misericordia

---

[1] Matthew 25.46.

is there to believe that the devil and his angels will always be there? Or will God's sentence, pronounced on wicked men and angels alike, be true for the angels, false for men? So it will certainly be, if what men surmise prevails over what God has said. Since that cannot be, those who desire to escape eternal punishment ought rather, while there is time, to obey the divine command and not debate against God.

Then what sort of reasoning is it, to take the eternal punishment of the wicked as a fire of long duration and believe that eternal life is without end? For Christ said in the very same place, including both in one and the same sentence: " So these will go into eternal punishment, but the righteous into eternal life." [1] If both are eternal, then surely both must be understood as " long," but having an end, or else as " everlasting," without an end. For they are matched with each other: in one clause eternal punishment, in the other eternal life. But to say in one and the same sentence: " Eternal life shall be without end, eternal punishment will have an end," is utterly absurd. Hence, since the eternal life of the saints will be without end, eternal punishment also will surely have no end, for those whose lot it is.

XXIV

Against the view of those who think that in God's judgement all the guilty will be spared because of the prayers of the saints.

THIS argument applies also to those who in pleading their own case try to answer God's words by the

maiore conantur, ut ideo videlicet vera sint quia ea quae dixit homines esse passuros, pati digni sunt, non quia passuri sunt.   Donabit enim eos, inquiunt, precibus sanctorum suorum etiam tunc tanto magis orantium pro inimicis suis quanto sunt utique sanctiores, eorumque efficacior est oratio et exauditione Dei dignior iam nullum habentium omnino peccatum.   Cur ergo eadem perfectissima sanctitate et cuncta impetrare valentibus mundissimis et misericordissimis precibus etiam pro angelis non orabunt, quibus paratus est ignis aeternus, ut Deus sententiam suam mitiget et reflectat in melius eosque ab illo igne faciat alienos?   An erit forsitan quisquam qui et hoc futurum esse praesumat, adfirmans etiam sanctos angelos simul cum sanctis hominibus, qui tunc aequales erunt angelis Dei, pro damnandis et angelis et hominibus oraturos ut misericordia non patiantur quod veritate merentur pati?   Quod nemo sanae fidei dixit, nemo dicturus est.   Alioquin nulla causa est cur non etiam nunc pro diabolo et angelis eius oret ecclesia, quam magister Deus pro inimicis suis iussit orare.

Haec igitur causa qua fit ut nunc ecclesia non oret pro malis angelis, quos suos esse novit inimicos, eadem ipsa causa est qua fiet ut in illo tunc iudicio etiam pro hominibus aeterno igne cruciandis, quamvis perfecta sit sanctitate, non oret.   Nunc enim propterea pro eis orat quos in genere humano habet inimicos quia tempus est paenitentiae fructuosae. Nam quid maxime pro eis orat, nisi *ut det illis Deus,*

pretext of a greater compassion. They argue that
the things which God says that men will suffer are
true in that men deserve to suffer them, not in that
they actually will suffer. God, they say, will grant
an answer to the prayers of the saints, who will then
pray the more for their enemies, inasmuch as they
will surely be more saintly. Their prayers too will
be more effective, more worthy to be heard by God,
when they are finally without sin. If this is so, why
will they not also pray God, with the same perfect
holiness, with pure and merciful prayers which can
obtain every request, for those angels for whom
eternal fire is prepared, to soften his sentence and
revise it for the better and exempt them from that
fire? Or does anyone perchance suppose that this
too will come to pass, affirming that even the holy
angels, along with holy men, who will then be equal
to angels of God, will pray for both angels and men
who are about to be damned, that in mercy they may
not suffer what in truth they deserve to suffer?
This no one of sound faith has said, and no one will
say it. Otherwise there is no reason why the Church
should not pray even now for the devil and his
angels, since God, her master, has ordered her to
pray for her enemies.

Thus the reason why the Church now does not pray
for wicked angels, whom it knows to be enemies, is
the same as the reason why, though perfected then
in holiness, she will not pray in the future judgement
for the men who are to be tortured in eternal fire.
The reason why she now prays for her enemies among
mankind is that there is still time for fruitful repentance. For what is her chief prayer for them, if

sicut dicit apostolus, *paenitentiam et resipiscant de diaboli laqueis, a quo captivi tenentur secundum ipsius voluntatem?*[1] Denique si de aliquibus ita certa esset, ut qui sint illi etiam nosset qui, licet adhuc in hac vita sint constituti, tamen praedestinati sunt in aeternum ignem ire cum diabolo, tam pro eis non oraret quam nec pro ipso. Sed quia de nullo certa est, orat pro omnibus dumtaxat hominibus inimicis suis in hoc corpore constitutis, nec tamen pro omnibus exauditur. Pro his enim solis exauditur qui, etsi adversantur ecclesiae, ita sunt tamen praedestinati ut pro eis exaudiatur ecclesia et filii efficiantur ecclesiae. Si qui autem usque ad mortem habebunt cor impaenitens nec ex inimicis convertentur in filios, numquid iam pro eis, id est pro talium defunctorum spiritibus, orat ecclesia? Quid ita nisi quia in parte iam diaboli computatur qui cum esset in corpore non est translatus ad Christum?[2]

Eadem itaque causa est cur non oretur tunc pro hominibus aeterno igne puniendis, quae causa est ut neque nunc neque tunc oretur pro angelis malis. Quae itidem causa est ut, quamvis pro hominibus, tamen iam nec nunc oretur pro infidelibus impiisque defunctis. Nam pro defunctis quibusdam vel ipsius ecclesiae vel quorumdam piorum exauditur oratio, sed pro his quorum in Christo regeneratorum nec usque adeo vita in corpore male gesta est ut tali misericordia iudicentur digni non esse, nec usque adeo bene ut talem misericordiam reperiantur necessariam non habere. Sicut etiam facta resur-

---

[1] 2 Timothy 2.25-26.
[2] Colossians 1.13.

not that God may grant them repentance, as the
Apostle says, "so that they may return to their senses
from the snares of the devil, by whom they are held
prisoners, subject to his will"?[1] Hence, if the
Church were as sure of the identity of any men who,
though still living, are predestined to go into eternal
fire with the devil, then she would no more pray for
them than for the devil himself. But since she is certain regarding none, she prays for all her merely
human enemies who are still living in our kind of body.
Yet her prayers are not answered in all cases, but only
when she prays for those who, though opposed to the
Church, are among the elect, so that her prayer for
them is heard and they become her sons. But if any
are to have impenitent hearts until death, and are
not converted from enemies to become sons, does the
Church still pray for them, that is, for the spirits of
such dead men? Why does she not pray, except
that the one who was not in his lifetime translated
into the kingdom of Christ[2] is now counted as part
of the devil's portion?

Thus the reason for not praying then for men who
are to be punished in eternal fire is the same as the
reason for not praying, either now or then, for the
wicked angels, and also for not praying now for the
unbelieving and impious dead, though these are
men. For on behalf of certain dead the prayer of
the Church, or of certain pious men, is heard, but
only on behalf of those who were born again in Christ
and whose life on earth was not so badly lived that
they are judged unworthy of such mercy, nor yet
so well lived that they are found to have no need of
such mercy. For even after the resurrection of the

rectione mortuorum non deerunt, quibus post poenas quas patiuntur spiritus mortuorum inpertiatur misericordia ut in ignem non mittantur aeternum. Neque enim de quibusdam veraciter diceretur quod non eis remittatur neque in hoc saeculo neque in futuro, nisi essent quibus etsi non in isto tamen remittitur in futuro. Sed cum dictum fuerit a iudice vivorum atque mortuorum: *Venite, benedicti patris mei, possidete paratum vobis regnum a constitutione mundi*, et aliis e contrario: *Discedite a me, maledicti, in ignem aeternum qui paratus est diabolo et angelis eius*, et ierint *isti in supplicium aeternum, iusti autem in vitam aeternam:* nimiae praesumptionis est dicere cuiquam eorum aeternum supplicium non futurum quos Deus ituros in supplicium dixit aeternum, et per huius praesumptionis persuasionem facere ut de ipsa quoque vita vel desperetur vel dubitetur aeterna.

Nemo itaque sic intellegat psalmum canentem: *Numquid obliviscetur misereri Deus, aut continebit in ira sua miserationes suas?* ut opinetur de hominibus bonis veram de malis falsam, aut de bonis hominibus et malis angelis veram de malis autem hominibus falsam

---

[1] Matthew 12.32. This text, along with 1 Corinthians 3.12–15, gave Augustine his Biblical support for belief in purgatory. There was also a long-established custom of prayer for the dead which was related to the belief. In his treatise *On Care to be had for the Dead* 3, he cites 2 Maccabees 12.39–45, a passage which relates that Judas Maccabeus, after burying those slain in battle, paid the cost for sacrifice to be made in Jerusalem for the sins of the dead; Augustine adds that in his time the whole church approved of such a custom. This evidently refers to the celebration of mass for the dead, which he mentions elsewhere in connection with his mother's burial (*Confessions* 9.12.32). A council at Carthage in 397

dead takes place there will be some to whom mercy
will be granted after they have suffered the punishment that belongs to spirits of the dead, so that
they will not be cast into eternal fire. It could not
be said truly of some that they will not be forgiven either in this world or in that which is to come,[1]
if there were not some who, though not forgiven here,
will nevertheless be forgiven in the world to come.
But once the judge of the living and the dead has
said: " Come, O blessed of my Father, take possession of the kingdom prepared for you from the
foundation of the world," and to others on the opposite side, " Depart from me, you cursed, into the
eternal fire which is prepared for the devil and his
angels," and once these have gone " into eternal
punishment, but the righteous into eternal life," [2]
then it is a matter of excessive presumption to say
that the punishment of any of these will not be
eternal, when God has said that they will go into
eternal punishment. To maintain this presumptuous
argument is to destroy hope or raise doubt concerning
eternal life also.

Let no one therefore understand the verse in the
Psalm which says: " Will God forget to pity, or in
anger shut up his tender mercies," [3] so as to suppose
that the pronouncement of God is true concerning
good men, but false concerning the wicked, or concerning good men and wicked angels true, but false

regulated the custom, providing that, if the mourners were
not fasting, the " commendation " of the dead should be completed with prayers only. See *DCA* II, 1436.

[2] Matthew 25.34–41.

[3] Psalms 77.9.

Dei esse sententiam. Hoc enim, quod ait psalmus, ad vasa misericordiae pertinet et ad filios promissionis, quorum erat unus etiam ipse propheta qui, cum dixisset: *Numquid obliviscetur misereri Deus aut continebit in ira sua miserationes suas?* continuo subiecit: *Et dixi: Nunc coepi, haec est inmutatio dexterae Excelsi.* Exposuit profecto quid dixerit: *Numquid continebit in ira sua miserationes suas?* Ira enim Dei est etiam ista vita mortalis ubi homo vanitati similis factus est, dies eius velut umbra praetereunt. In qua tamen ira non obliviscitur misereri Deus, faciendo solem suum oriri super bonos et malos et pluendo super iustos et iniustos, ac sic non continet in ira sua miserationes suas, maximeque in eo, quod expressit hic psalmus dicendo: *Nunc coepi, haec est inmutatio dexterae Excelsi,* quoniam in hac ipsa aerumnosissima vita, quae ira Dei est, vasa misericordiae mutat in melius, quamvis adhuc in huius corruptionis miseria maneat ira eius, quia nec in ipsa ira sua continet miserationes suas. Cum ergo isto modo compleatur divini illius cantici veritas non est eam necesse etiam illic intellegi ub non pertinentes ad civitatem Dei sempiterno supplicio punientur. Sed quibus placet istam sententiam usque ad illa impiorum tormenta protendere, saltem sic intellegant ut manente in eis ira Dei, quae in aeterno est praenuntiata supplicio, non contineat Deus in hac ira sua miserationes suas et faciat eos non tanta quanta digni sunt poenarum atrocitate

---

[1] Psalms 77.10.   [2] Psalms 144.4.   [3] Matthew 5.45.

concerning bad men. For the statement in the Psalm relates to the vessels of mercy and the sons of the promise, of whom the prophet himself was one. And after saying: "Will God forget to pity, or in anger shut up his tender mercies?" he immediately adds: "And I said, now have I begun, this is the change wrought by the right hand of the Most High." [1] These words surely explain the preceding, "Will he shut up in anger his tender mercies?" For the anger of God is precisely this mortal life, where man has become like an empty thing, and his days pass like a shadow.[2] But in this anger God does not forget to pity, but makes his sun to rise on the good and the evil, and rain to fall on the just and the unjust.[3] It is thus that he does not in his anger shut up his tender mercies. And he shows this most clearly in the words of the Psalm: "Now have I begun, this is the change wrought by the right hand of the Most High," for even in this troubled life, which is the wrath of God, he changes his vessels of mercy for the better, though in the misery of this corrupted state his wrath abides, since not even in that same wrath does he shut up his tender mercies. By this interpretation the truth of that divinely inspired hymn is fulfilled; it is not necessary to apply the words also to the time when those not belonging to the City of God will be punished with everlasting punishment. But let those who think that this statement extends even to the punishments of the ungodly at least understand it thus: while the wrath of God which is declared to be in eternal punishment still remains against them, God will not shut up in his anger his tender mercies, but will cause them not to be tormented with as great

cruciari; non ut eas poenas vel numquam subeant vel aliquando finiant, sed ut eas mitiores quam merita sunt eorum levioresque patiantur. Sic enim et ira Dei manebit, et in ipsa ira sua miserationes suas non continebit. Quod quidem non ideo confirmo, quoniam non resisto.

Ceterum eos qui putant minaciter potius quam veraciter dictum: *Discedite a me, maledicti, in ignem aeternum*, et: *Ibunt isti in supplicium aeternum*, et: *Cruciabuntur in saecula saeculorum*, et: *Vermis eorum non morietur et ignis non extinguetur*, et cetera huius modi, non tam ego quam ipsa scriptura divina planissime atque plenissime redarguit ac refellit. Ninevitae quippe in hac vita egerunt paenitentiam et ideo fructuosam, velut in hoc agro seminantes in quo Deus voluit cum lacrimis seminari quod postea cum laetitia meteretur. Et tamen quis negabit quod Dominus praedixit in eis fuisse completum, nisi parum advertat quem ad modum peccatores Deus non solum iratus verum etiam miseratus evertat? Evertuntur enim peccatores duobus modis, aut sicut Sodomitae ut pro peccatis suis ipsi homines puniantur, aut sicut Ninevitae ut ipsa hominum peccata paenitendo destruantur. Factum est ergo quod praedixit Deus: eversa est Nineve quae mala erat, et bona aedificata est quae non erat. Stantibus enim moenibus atque domibus eversa est civitas in perditis moribus. Ac sic, quamvis propheta fuerit contri-

---

[1] Matthew 25.41–46.   [2] Revelation 20.10.
[3] Isaiah 66.24.   [4] Jonah 3.5–10.
[5] Psalms 126.5.

severity as they deserve. That does not mean that they will escape these punishments, or ever reach their end, but that they will suffer punishments which are more gentle and easy than they deserve. For thus the anger of God will remain, and in his very anger he will not shut up his tender mercies. My not opposing this view does not, however, mean that I support it.

Some men think that God made a mere threat, and not a true declaration, when He said: " Depart from me, you cursed, into eternal fire," and " These shall go into eternal punishment," [1] and " They shall be tormented for ever and ever," [2] and " Their worm will not die and their fire will not be quenched," [3] and other sayings of the sort. Not I, but the Scripture itself, clearly and fully answers and refutes them. As for the Ninevites, they repented in this life,[4] and so their repentance was fruitful. They sowed, as it were, in this field in which God wished men to sow with tears seed that they should later reap with joy.[5] And yet who will deny that what God predicted was fulfilled in them, unless he fails to notice how God " overthrows " sinners not only when he is angry but also when he has mercy ? For sinners are overthrown in two ways, either like the Sodomites, so that men themselves are punished for their sins, or like the Ninevites, so that only the sins of men are destroyed by repentance. Therefore, what God predicted came to pass: the Nineveh that was wicked was overthrown, and a good Nineveh was built which did not exist before. For though the walls and houses were standing, the city was overthrown in its depraved morals. And thus, though the prophet

status quia non est factum quod illi homines timu-
erunt illo prophetante venturum, factum est tamen
quod fuerat Deo praesciente praedictum, quoniam
noverat qui praedixit quo modo in melius esset
implendum.

Ut autem noverint isti in perversum misericordes
quo pertineat quod scriptum est: *Quam multa multitudo dulcedinis tuae, Domine, quam abscondisti timentibus
te!* legant quod sequitur: *Perfecisti autem sperantibus
in te.* Quid est *abscondisti timentibus, perfecisti
sperantibus,* nisi quia illis qui timore poenarum suam
iustitiam volunt constituere quae in lege est non est
iustitia Dei dulcis, quia nesciunt eam? Non enim
gustaverunt eam. In se namque sperant non in
ipso, et ideo eis absconditur multitudo dulcedinis Dei;
quoniam timent quidem Deum, sed illo timore servili
qui non est in caritate, quia perfecta caritas foras
mittit timorem. Ideo sperantibus in eum perficit
dulcedinem suam inspirando eis caritatem suam, ut
timore casto, non quem caritas foras mittit sed
permanente in saeculum saeculi, cum gloriantur, in
Domino glorientur. Iustitia quippe Dei Christus est,
qui factus est nobis, sicut dicit apostolus, *sapientia a
Deo et iustitia et sanctificatio et redemptio ut, quem ad
modum scriptum est, qui gloriatur in Domino glorietur.*
Hanc Dei iustitiam quam donat gratia sine meritis

[1] Psalms 31.19.
[2] Romans 10.3–4.
[3] 1 John 4.18.
[4] 1 Corinthians 1.30–31.

was grieved because that which the Ninevites feared because of his prophecy did not come to pass, still that which had been predicted by the foreknowledge of God did come to pass. For he who made the prediction foreknew how it was to be fulfilled in a better sense.

But that those perversely merciful men may know the meaning of the passage: " How great is thy sweetness, O Lord, which thou hast hidden from them that fear thee," let them read what follows: " But thou hast perfected it for those who hope in thee." [1] What is the meaning of the words, " Thou hast hidden from those who fear," and " hast perfected for those who hope " ? Is it not that for those who from fear of punishment would establish their righteousness which is in the law,[2] the righteousness of God is not sweet, because they do not know it? For they have not tasted it, for truly their hope is in themselves, not in God, and hence the greatness of his sweetness is hidden from them. They fear God, to be sure, but with that slavish fear which is not in love, for perfect love casteth out fear.[3] Hence for those who hope in him, he perfects his sweetness by inspiring in them his love, to this end, that when they glory, they may glory in the Lord with a chaste fear, which is not the fear cast out by love, but a fear that endures for ever and ever. For the righteousness of God is Christ, " who was made for us," as the Apostle says, " wisdom from God and righteousness and sanctification and redemption, in order that, as it is written, he that glorieth may glory in the Lord." [4] This righteousness of God, which he bestows by grace without merit, is unknown to those who wish to

nesciunt illi qui suam iustitiam volunt constituere et ideo iustitiae Dei quod est Christus non sunt subiecti. In qua iustitia est multa multitudo dulcedinis Dei, propter quam dicitur in psalmo: *Gustate et videte quam dulcis est Dominus.* Et hanc quidem in hac peregrinatione gustantes, non ad satietatem sumentes, esurimus eam potius ac sitimus, ut ea postea saturemur cum videbimus eum sicuti est, et implebitur quod scriptum est: *Saturabor cum manifestabitur gloria tua.* Ita perficit Christus multam multitudinem dulcedinis suae sperantibus in eum. Porro autem si eam quam illi putant dulcedinem suam Deus abscondit timentibus eum, qua non est impios damnaturus ut hoc nescientes et damnari timentes recte vivant, ac sic possint esse qui orent pro non recte viventibus, quo modo eam perficit sperantibus in eum, quando quidem, sicut somniant, per hanc dulcedinem non damnaturus est eos qui non sperant in eum? Illa igitur eius dulcedo quaeratur quam perficit sperantibus in eum, non quam perficere putatur contemnentibus et blasphemantibus eum. Frustra itaque homo post hoc corpus inquirit quod in hoc corpore sibi comparare neglexit.

Illud quoque apostolicum: *Conclusit enim Deus omnes in infidelitate ut omnium misereatur*, non ideo dictum est quod sit neminem damnaturus, sed superius apparet unde sit dictum. Nam cum de Iudaeis postea credituris apostolus loqueretur ad gentes ad quas utique iam credentes conscribebat

---

[1] Romans 10.3.   [2] Psalms 34.8.
[3] 1 John 3.2.   [4] Psalms 17.15.

establish their own righteousness, and so are not submissive to the righteousness of God,[1] which is Christ. In this righteousness is found the great sweetness of God, of which it is said in the Psalm: "Taste and see how sweet is the Lord."[2] And while tasting this sweetness in this pilgrim journey, we are not filled. Rather, we hunger and thirst for it, that we may afterwards be filled, when we shall see him as he is.[3] Then will be fulfilled the Scripture: "I shall be fully fed when thy glory shall be manifested."[4] Thus Christ perfects the greatness of his sweetness for those who hope in him. Furthermore, if, as they think, God hides from them who fear him the sweetness by which he will pardon the wicked in order that men who do not know about it may fear condemnation and live rightly, that thus there may be some to pray for the ungodly, then how does he perfect his sweetness for those who hope in him? For, according to their dreams, it is those who do not hope in him that he will pardon. Then that sweetness of his must be the object of our search, that which he perfects for those who hope in him, not that other which he is supposed to perfect for those who scorn and blaspheme him. In vain, therefore, after this body is dead, does man seek what he has failed to provide for himself while living in the body.

Moreover the apostolic saying, "For God has shut up all in unbelief, that he might have mercy upon all," does not mean that he will condemn no one, but its meaning appears in what was said above. For the Apostle was speaking about the Jews who should afterwards believe, to the Gentiles addressed in the letter, who were certainly already believers.

epistulas: *Sicut enim vos*, inquit, *aliquando non credidistis Deo, nunc autem misericordiam consecuti estis illorum incredulitate, sic et hi nunc non crediderunt in vestram misericordiam, ut et ipsi misericordiam consequantur.* Deinde subiecit unde isti sibi errando blandiuntur, atque ait: *Conclusit enim Deus omnes in infidelitate, ut omnium misereatur.* Quos omnes, nisi de quibus loquebatur, tamquam dicens: Et vos et illos? Deus ergo et gentiles et Iudaeos quos praescivit et praedestinavit conformes imaginis filii sui, omnes in infidelitate conclusit, ut de amaritudine infidelitatis suae paenitendo confusi et ad dulcedinem misericordiae Dei credendo conversi clamarent illud in psalmo: *Quam multa multitudo dulcedinis tuae, Domine, quam abscondisti timentibus te, perfecisti autem sperantibus*, non in se, sed *in te!* Omnium itaque miseretur vasorum misericordiae. Quid est omnium? Et eorum scilicet quos ex gentibus, et eorum quos ex Iudaeis praedestinavit vocavit iustificavit glorificavit, non hominum omnium, sed istorum omnium neminem damnaturus.

He says: " For as you in time past did not believe in
God, but now have obtained mercy by their failure
to believe, so these have not believed now in the
mercy shown to you, in order that they also may
obtain mercy." Then he adds the words with which
they flatter themselves in their error: " For God has
shut up all in unbelief, that he might have mercy
upon all."[1] Who are the " all," except those of
whom he is speaking, as if he had said " both you and
they "? So God shut up all in unbelief, both Gentiles and Jews, whom He foreknew and predestined
to be conformed to the image of his Son,[2] that from
the bitterness of their unbelief they might by repenting be confounded, and by believing be converted to the sweetness of God's mercy, and cry, as it
is written in the Psalm: " How great is thy sweetness,
O Lord, which thou hast hidden from those that fear
thee, but hast perfected for those who hope," not in
themselves, but " in thee! "[3] And so he pities all
the vessels of his mercy. What is the meaning of
" all "? All those, of course, both from the Gentiles
and the Jews, whom he has predestined and called,
justified and glorified,[4] and of all these (not of all
men) he will condemn no one.

[1] Romans 11.30–32. [2] Romans 8.29.
[3] Psalms 31.19. [4] Romans 8.30.

SAINT AUGUSTINE

XXV

An hi qui inter haereticos baptizati sunt et deteriores postea
male vivendo sunt facti, vel hi qui apud catholicos
renati ad haereses aut schismata transierunt, vel
hi qui a catholicis apud quos renati sunt non
recedentes criminose vivere perstiterunt,
possint privilegio sacramentorum re-
missionem aeterni sperare supplicii.

SED iam respondeamus etiam illis qui non solum
diabolo et angelis eius, sicut nec isti, sed ne ipsis
quidem omnibus hominibus liberationem ab aeterno
igne promittunt, verum eis tantum qui Christi
baptismate abluti et corporis eius et sanguinis
participes facti sunt, quomodolibet vixerint, in
quacumque haeresi vel impietate fuerint. Sed
contradicit eis apostolus dicens: *Manifesta autem*
sunt opera carnis, quae sunt fornicatio, inmunditia,
luxuria, idolorum servitus, veneficia, inimicitiae, con-
tentiones, aemulationes, animositates, dissensiones,
haereses, invidiae, ebrietates, comisationes et his similia.
Quae praedico vobis, sicut praedixi, quoniam qui talia
agunt regnum Dei non possidebunt. Haec profecto
apostolica falsa sententia est si tales post quantalibet
tempora liberati regnum Dei possidebunt. Sed
quoniam falsa non est, profecto regnum Dei non
possidebunt. Et si in regni Dei possessione numquam erunt aeterno supplicio tenebuntur, quoniam

XXV

Whether men by right of the sacraments can hope for release from eternal punishment; either those who have been baptized among the heretics and later by a bad life have become worse, or those reborn among Catholics who pass over to heresy or schism, or those who do not leave the Catholic Church into which they were reborn but persist in living wickedly.

Now let us reply to those who deny release from eternal fire, not only, like these last, to the devil and his angels, but also to all men, except those who are washed in the baptism of Christ, and have become partakers of his body and blood. To these they promise release, whatever the life they have lived, and in whatever heresy or ungodliness they have been involved. But the Apostle refutes them, saying: " Now the works of the flesh are manifest, which are fornication, uncleanness, lasciviousness, idolatry, sorcery, enmities, strifes, jealousies, wraths, dissensions, heresies, envyings, drunkenness, revellings and the like. Of these I warn you, as I have before, that those who practise such things will not possess the kingdom of God." [1] This pronouncement of the Apostle is surely false if such men are to be freed from hell and possess the kingdom of God after a time, however long it be. But since it is not false, they surely will not possess the kingdom, and if they will never be in possession of the kingdom, they will be held in eternal punishment, for there is

[1] Galatians 5.19–21.

non est medius locus ubi non sit in supplicio qui illo non fuerit constitutus in regno.

Quam ob rem quod ait Dominus Iesus: *Hic est panis qui de caelo descendit ut, si quis ex ipso manducaverit, non moriatur. Ego sum panis vivus qui de caelo descendi; si quis manducaverit ex hoc pane, vivet in aeternum*, quo modo sit accipiendum merito quaeritur. Et ab istis quidem quibus nunc respondemus hunc intellectum auferunt illi, quibus deinde respondendum est; hi sunt autem qui hanc liberationem nec omnibus habentibus sacramentum baptismatis et corporis Christi, sed solis catholicis, quamvis male viventibus, pollicentur. Quia non solo, inquiunt, sacramento, sed re ipsa manducaverunt corpus Christi, in ipso scilicet eius corpore constituti, de quo corpore ait apostolus: *Unus panis, unum corpus multi sumus.* Qui ergo est in eius corporis unitate, id est in Christianorum compage membrorum, cuius corporis sacramentum fideles communicantes de altari sumere consuerunt, ipse vere dicendus est manducare corpus Christi et bibere sanguinem Christi. Ac per hoc haeretici et schismatici ab huius unitate corporis separati possunt idem percipere sacramentum, sed non sibi utile, immo vero etiam noxium, quo iudicentur gravius quam vel tardius liberentur. Non sunt quippe in eo vinculo pacis quod illo exprimitur sacramento.

Sed rursus etiam isti qui recte intellegunt non dicendum esse manducare corpus Christi qui in corpore non est Christi, non recte promittunt eis qui

---

[1] John 6.50–52.
[2] 1 Corinthians 10.17.

no middle ground where he shall escape punishment
who is not established in that kingdom.

Hence it is proper to inquire what means the saying
of the Lord Jesus: " This is the bread that came
down from heaven, that if anyone has eaten of this
bread, he may not die. I am the living bread that
came down from heaven; if anyone eats of this bread
he will live for ever." [1] If those to whom we are
now replying understand this passage in their favour,
this understanding is rejected by others to whom we
must next reply, namely, those who promise this
release from punishment, not to all who have the
sacrament of baptism and of the body of Christ,
but only to Catholics, regardless of any evil in their
lives. For, they say, not only in sacrament but in
reality these have eaten the body of Christ, for they
are established in that body of which the Apostle
says: " We being many are one bread, one body." [2]
Hence anyone must truly be said to eat the body and
drink the blood of Christ if he is in the unity of that
body, that is, in the frame of the members of Christ,
the body whose sacrament the faithful are wont to
take from the altar when they commune. And hence
heretics and schismatics who are separated from the
unity of this body may take the same sacrament,
but it will do them no good, and rather be harmful,
inasmuch as they will be judged the more severely,
rather than released even after long suffering, for
they are not in the bond of peace that is set forth
in that sacrament.

Again, there are some who correctly understand
that one not in the body of Christ cannot be said to
eat the body of Christ, but who wrongly promise

vel in haeresim vel etiam in gentilium superstitionem
ex illius corporis unitate labuntur liberationem
quandoque ab aeterni igne supplicii; primum, quia
debent adtendere quam sit intolerabile atque a sana
doctrina nimis devium ut multi ac paene omnes qui
haereses impias condiderunt exeuntes de catholica
ecclesia, et facti sunt haeresiarchae, meliores habeant
causas, quam hi qui numquam fuerunt catholici,
cum in eorum laqueos incidissent—si illos haere-
siarchas hoc facit liberari a supplicio sempiterno quod
in catholica ecclesia baptizati sunt et sacramentum
corporis Christi in vero Christi corpore primitus
acceperunt, cum peior sit utique desertor fidei et ex
desertore oppugnator eius effectus quam ille qui non
deseruit quod numquam tenuit; deinde quia et his
occurrit apostolus eadem verba proferens et enume-
ratis illis carnis operibus eadem veritate praedicens:
Quoniam qui talia agunt, regnum Dei nor possidebunt.

Unde nec illi in perditis et damnabilibus moribus
debent esse securi qui usque in finem quidem velut in
communione ecclesiae catholicae perseverant, intuentes quod dictum est: *Qui perseveraverit usque in
finem, hic salvus erit.* Et per vitae iniquitatem ipsam
vitae iustitiam quod eis Christus est deserunt, sive
fornicando sive alias inmunditias flagitiorum quas
nec exprimere apostolus voluit in suo corpore
perpetrando, sive turpitudine luxuriae diffluendo,
sive aliquid aliud eorum agendo, de quibus ait:
Quoniam qui talia agunt, regnum Dei non possidebunt.

---

[1] Galatians 5.21.
[2] Matthew 10.22.

eventual release from the punishment of eternal
fire to those who fall from the unity of that body into
heresy, or even into the superstition of the heathen.
They are wrong, first, because they should see how
intolerable and how far removed from sound doctrine
it is that many men, in fact nearly all who have left
the Catholic Church and founded impious heresies,
thus becoming heresiarchs, should have a better lot
than those who have never been Catholics before they
fell into their snares. And this would be the case if
their being baptized in the Catholic Church and first
receiving the sacrament of the body of Christ in the
true body of Christ ensured those heresiarchs of
release from eternal punishment. For he is surely
worse who deserts the faith and then assails it, than
the one who does not desert what he never held.
They are wrong, again, because the Apostle refutes
them in the words already quoted; after enumerating
those works of the flesh he declares with the same
certainty: " For those who practise such things shall
not possess the kingdom of God." [1]

Hence neither should those of depraved and
damnable character rest secure, though they remain
apparently in the communion of the Catholic Church
till the end, relying on the Scripture: " He that
endureth to the end shall be saved." [2] Through the
iniquity of their lives they desert the righteousness
of life, which is Christ to them, either by fornication
or by committing in their body other unclean deeds,
which the Apostle would not even name, or by ruining
themselves in the foulness of lasciviousness, or by
doing any of those things of which the Apostle says:
" They who practise such things shall not possess the

Ac per hoc quicumque agunt talia nisi in sempiterno supplicio non erunt, quia in Dei regno esse non poterunt. In his enim perseverando usque in huius vitae finem non utique dicendi sunt in Christo perseverasse usque in finem, quia in Christo perseverare est in eius fide perseverare, quae fides, ut eam definit idem apostolus, *per dilectionem operatur; dilectio* autem, sicut ipse alibi dicit, *malum non operatur.* Nec isti ergo dicendi sunt manducare corpus Christi, quoniam nec in membris computandi sunt Christi. Ut enim alia taceam, non possunt simul esse et membra Christi et membra meretricis. Denique ipse dicit: *Qui manducat carnem meam et bibit sanguinem meum in me manet et ego in eo.* Ostendit quid sit non sacramento tenus, sed re vera corpus Christi manducare et eius sanguinem bibere; hoc est enim in Christo manere, ut in illo maneat et Christus. Sic enim hoc dixit, tamquam diceret: " Qui non in me manet et in quo non maneo, non se dicat aut existimet manducare corpus meum aut bibere sanguinem meum." Non itaque manent in Christo qui non sunt membra eius. Non sunt autem membra Christi qui se faciunt membra meretricis, nisi malum illud paenitendo esse destiterint et ad hoc bonum reconciliatione redierint.

kingdom of God." Hence all those who practise such things will be nowhere else but in eternal punishment, since they cannot be in the kingdom of God. For if they persevere in these sins until the end of this life, they cannot be said to persevere in Christ till the end. For to persevere in Christ is to persevere in his faith, and this faith, as the Apostle definitely states, works through love,[1] and love, as he elsewhere says, works no evil.[2] Hence, these too should not be said to eat the body of Christ, for they cannot be counted among the members of Christ. For, not to mention the other sins, they cannot at the same time be members of Christ and members of a harlot.[3] Finally, Christ himself says: " He who eats my flesh and drinks my blood remains in me and I in him." [4] He thus shows what it is to eat the body of Christ and drink His blood, not only in the sacrament, but in reality, for to remain in Christ is to have Christ also remaining in him. For this is the same as if he said: " He who does not remain in me, and in whom I do not remain, may not say or think that he is eating my body or drinking my blood." So those who are not his members do not remain in Christ. But those who make themselves members of a harlot are not members of Christ, unless by repentance they abandon that evil thing, and by reconciliation return to this good thing.

[1] Galatians 5.6. [2] Romans 13.10.
[3] 1 Corinthians 6.15. [4] John 6.56.

SAINT AUGUSTINE

XXVI

Quid sit in fundamento habere Christum et quibus spondeatur salus quasi per ignis usturam.

SED habent, inquiunt, Christiani catholici in fundamento Christum, a cuius unitate non recesserunt, tametsi huic fundamento superaedificaverunt quamlibet pessimam vitam, velut ligna, fenum, stipulam. Recta itaque fides, per quam Christus est fundamentum, quamvis cum damno, quoniam illa quae superaedificata sunt exurentur, tamen poterit eos quandoque ab illius ignis perpetuitate salvare. Respondeat eis breviter apostolus Iacobus: *Si quis dicat se fidem habere, opera autem non habeat, numquid poterit fides salvare eum?* Et quis est, inquiunt, de quo dicit apostolus Paulus: *Ipse autem salvus erit, sic tamen quasi per ignem?* Simul quis iste sit, inquiramus. Hunc tamen non esse certissimum est, ne duorum apostolorum sententias mittamus in rixam, si unus dicit: "Etiamsi mala opera quis habuerit, salvabit eum per ignem fides"; alius autem: *Si opera non habeat, numquid poterit fides salvare eum?*

Inveniemus ergo quis possit salvari per ignem si prius invenerimus quid sit habere in fundamento Christum. Quod ut de ipsa similitudine quantocius advertamus: nihil in aedificio praeponitur fundamento; quisquis itaque sic habet in corde Christum ut ei terrena et temporaria nec ea quae licita sunt atque concessa praeponat, fundamentum habet Christum. Si autem praeponit, etsi videatur habere

---

[1] Compare 1 Corinthians 3.12–15.   [2] James 2.14.

XXVI

What it is to have Christ as a foundation, and who is promised salvation as it were through flames of fire.

But, they say, Catholic Christians have Christ as a foundation, and have not departed from his unity, no matter how they have built on this foundation the most wicked life, as it were, wood, hay, stubble. Thus the true faith, by which Christ is the foundation, will be able to save them at last from that eternal fire, although with loss, since the things that are built upon the foundation will be burned.[1] Let the apostle James reply to them briefly: " If anyone say that he has faith, but have not works, will faith be able to save him ? "[2] And who is it, they ask, of whom the apostle Paul says: " He himself shall be saved, yet so as through fire"? Let us investigate together who this is. In any case, it is certainly not the man of whom James speaks, for we must avoid starting a quarrel between the views of two apostles. For one says: " Even if a man should have evil works, faith will save him through fire," and the other: " If he have not works, will faith save him ? "

We shall find out, then, who can be saved through fire if first we find out what it is to have Christ as a foundation. We may quickly learn this from the simile itself. Nothing is put into a building before the foundation. Whoever, therefore, has Christ in his heart so that he does not give first place to earthly and temporal things, even things lawful and permitted, has Christ as his foundation. But if he puts them first, though he may seem to have faith in

fidem Christi, non est tamen in eo fundamentum
Christus cui talia praeponuntur. Quanto magis, si
salutaria praecepta contemnens committat inlicita,
non praeposuisse Christum sed postposuisse convincitur, quem posthabuit imperantem sive con-
cedentem, dum contra eius imperata sive concessa
suam per flagitia delegit explere libidinem! Si quis
itaque Christianus diligit meretricem eique adhaerens
unum corpus efficitur, iam in fundamento non habet
Christum. Si quis autem diligit uxorem suam, si
secundum Christum, quis ei dubitet in fundamento
esse Christum? Si vero secundum hoc saeculum, si
carnaliter, si in morbo concupiscentiarum, sicut et
gentes quae ignorant Deum, etiam hoc secundum
veniam concedit apostolus, immo per apostolum
Christus. Potest ergo et iste in fundamento habere
Christum. Si enim nihil ei talis affectionis voluptatis-
que praeponat, quamvis superaedificet ligna, fenum,
stipulam, Christus est fundamentum, propter hoc
salvus erit per ignem. Delicias quippe huius modi
amoresque terrenos, propter coniugalem quidem
copulam non damnabiles, tribulationis ignis exuret.
Ad quem pertinent ignem et orbitates et quaecumque
calamitates quae auferunt haec.

Ac per hoc ei, qui aedificavit, erit aedificatio ista
damnosa, quia non habebit quod superaedificavit, et
eorum amissione cruciabitur quibus fruendo utique
laetabatur. Sed per hunc ignem salvus erit merito
fundamenti quia, etsi utrum id habere mallet an
Christum a persecutore proponeretur, illud Christo

---

[1] 1 Corinthians 6.16.
[2] 1 Thessalonians 4.5.

Christ, still for him Christ is not the foundation if such temporal things are put first. How much more, if he despises the precepts of salvation and commits unlawful deeds, is he proved not to have put Christ first, but last? For he has put him last with his commands and permissions, since he chooses to fulfil his own lust in shameful deeds contrary to his commands and permissions. Therefore, if any Christian loves a harlot, and is joined to her and becomes one body,[1] he no longer has Christ as a foundation. But if, on the other hand, anyone loves his own wife and loves in the spirit of Christ, who can doubt that Christ is his foundation? But if he loves her according to this world, carnally, in the disorder of lust, even as the heathen who know not God,[2] even this indulgence the apostle grants, or rather, Christ through the apostle. Therefore he, too, may have Christ as a foundation. For if he puts none of such affections and pleasures before Him, though he build with wood, hay, stubble, Christ is the foundation, and for this reason he will be saved through fire. Surely the fire of tribulation will burn up delights of this kind and earthly loves which, to be sure, because of the conjugal bond are not to be condemned. To this fire belong also bereavements and any calamities that carry away these earthly things.

And so for the builder the building will be a loss, for he will not have what he built, and he will be tortured by the loss of what he enjoyed, since he certainly felt joy in the enjoyment of them. But through this fire he will be saved by the merit of the foundation, for even if he were offered by a persecutor the choice whether he preferred to have this

non praeponeretur. Vide in apostoli verbis hominem aedificantem super fundamentum aurum, argentum, lapides pretiosos: *Qui sine uxore est*, inquit, *cogitat quae sunt Dei, quo modo placeat Deo*. Vide alium aedificantem ligna, fenum, stipulam: *Qui autem matrimonio iunctus est*, inquit, *cogitat quae sunt mundi, quo modo placeat uxori. Uniuscuiusque opus manifestabitur, dies enim declarabit* (dies utique tribulationis), *quoniam in igne*, inquit, *revelabitur*. Eandem tribulationem ignem vocat, sicut alibi legitur: *Vasa figuli probat fornax et homines iustos temptatio tribulationis. Et uniuscuiusque opus quale sit ignis probabit. Si cuius opus permanserit* (permanet enim quod quisque cogitat quae sunt Dei, quo modo placeat Deo), *quod super-aedificavit, mercedem accipiet* (id est, unde cogitavit hoc sumet); *si cuius autem opus arserit, damnum patietur* (quoniam quod dilexerat non habebit), *ipse autem salvus erit* (quia nulla eum tribulatio ab illius fundamenti stabilitate semovit); *sic tamen quasi per ignem* (quod enim sine inliciente amore non habuit, sine urente dolore non perdit). Ecce, quantum mihi videtur, inventus est ignis qui nullum eorum damnet, sed unum ditet, alterum damnificet, ambos probet.

Si autem ignem illum loco isto voluerimus accipere de quo Dominus dicet sinistris: *Discedite a me, maledicti, in ignem aeternum* ut in eis etiam isti esse

---

[1] 1 Corinthians 7.32–33.
[2] Ecclesiasticus 27.5.
[3] 1 Corinthians 7.13–15.
[4] Matthew 25.41.

or Christ, he would not put it before Christ. Behold in the Apostle's words a man building upon the foundation gold, silver, precious stones: " He who is without a wife," he says, " considers the things which are God's, how he may please God." Behold another who builds wood, hay, stubble: " But he who is joined in marriage," he says, " considers the things of the world, how he may please his wife." [1] " Each man's work shall be made manifest, for the day shall declare it " (that is, the day of tribulation) " because it shall be revealed in the fire. (He calls the same tribulation fire, in accordance with another passage: " The vessels of the potter are proved by the oven, and just men by the trial of tribulation.") [2] And the fire will prove each one's work, of what sort it is. If anyone's work abides " (it abides when he acts considering the things which are God's, how he may please God), " which he built thereon, he shall receive a reward " (that is, he shall receive what he considered); " but if anyone's work shall be burned, he shall suffer loss " (for he will not have what he loved), " but he himself shall be saved " (for no tribulation has removed him from the firmness of that foundation); " yet so as through fire " [3] (for that which he did not hold without love's sweet allurement, he does not lose without burning grief). There the fire is found, I think, which condemns neither of them, but enriches one, brings loss to another, tries both.

But if we wish to take the " fire " of this passage as the same mentioned by the Lord when he says to those on his left: " Depart from me, ye cursed, into eternal fire," [4] believing that among these are those

143

credantur qui aedificant super fundamentum ligna,
fenum, stipulam, eosque ex illo igne post tempus pro
malis meritis impertitum liberet boni meritum
fundamenti, quid arbitrabimur dextros quibus dicetur:
Venite, benedicti patris mei, possidete paratum vobis
regnum nisi eos qui aedificaverunt super fundamentum
aurum, argentum, lapides pretiosos? Sed in illum
ignem de quo dictum est: *Sic tamen quasi per ignem,*
si hoc modo est intellegendus, utrique mittendi sunt,
et dextri scilicet et sinistri. Illo quippe igne
utrique probandi sunt de quo dictum est: *Dies enim*
declarabit, quoniam in igne revelabitur, et uniuscuiusque
opus quale sit ignis probabit. Si ergo utrumque
probabit ignis ut, si cuius opus permanserit, id est
non fuerit igne consumptum, quod superaedificavit
mercedem accipiat, si cuius autem opus arserit
damnum patiatur, profecto non est ipse aeternus ille
ignis. In illum enim soli sinistri novissima et
perpetua damnatione mittentur, iste autem dextros
probat. Sed alios eorum sic probat ut aedificium,
quod super Christum fundamentum ab eis invenerit
esse constructum, non exurat atque consumat; alios
autem aliter, id est, ut quod superaedificaverunt
ardeat damnumque inde patiantur, salvi fiant autem,
quoniam Christum in fundamento stabiliter positum
praecellenti caritate tenuerunt. Si autem salvi fient,
profecto et ad dexteram stabunt et cum ceteris
audient: *Venite, benedicti patris mei, possidete paratum*
vobis regnum, non ad sinistram, ubi illi erunt qui salvi

---

[1] Matthew 25.34.
[2] 1 Corinthians 3.13.

who build on the foundation wood, hay, stubble, and
that the merit of the good foundation will free them
from that fire after a time that is allotted according
to their evil deserts, what shall we think of those on
the right, who will hear the words: " Come, ye
blessed of my Father, possess the kingdom prepared
for you," [1] unless they are the ones who have built
upon the foundation gold, silver, precious stones ? But
into that fire of which it is said, " Yet so as by fire,"
both groups must be thrown, if this view is right, both
those on the right and those on the left. Both
groups surely must be proved in that fire of which it
is said: " For the day shall declare it, because it
shall be revealed in the fire, and the fire will prove
each man's work, of what sort it is." [2] If, therefore,
the fire will prove both (so that, if anyone's work
remain, that is, is not consumed by fire, he shall
receive as a reward what he built thereon, while if
anyone's work burns, he will suffer loss), surely this
is not that eternal fire. For into it will be sent only
those on the left hand, in a final and everlasting
damnation, while the other fire tests those on the
right. Some of them it tests in such a way as not to
burn and consume the building which is found con-
structed on Christ the foundation. But the opposite
is true of others, that is, what they have built burns
and hence they suffer loss, but they themselves will
be saved, since with surpassing love they keep Christ
firmly fixed as their foundation. But if they are to
be saved, they will also surely stand at the right hand
and hear with the others: " Come ye blessed of my
Father, possess the kingdom prepared for you," not
on the left, where those will be who are not saved,

non erunt et ideo audient: *Discedite a me, maledicti, in ignem aeternum.* Nemo quippe ab illo igne salvabitur, quia in supplicium aeternum ibunt illi omnes ubi vermis eorum non moritur et ignis non extinguitur quo cruciabuntur die ac nocte in saecula saeculorum.

Post istius sane corporis mortem, donec ad illum veniatur qui post resurrectionem corporum futurus est damnationis et remunerationis ultimus dies, si hoc temporis intervallo spiritus defunctorum eius modi ignem dicuntur perpeti, quem non sentiant illi qui non habuerunt tales mores et amores in huius corporis vita ut eorum ligna et fenum et stipula consumatur, alii vero sentiant qui eius modi secum aedificia portaverunt, sive ibi tantum sive et hic et ibi sive ideo hic ut non ibi, saecularia quamvis a damnatione venialia concremantem ignem transitoriae tribulationis inveniant, non redarguo, quia forsitan verum est. Potest quippe ad istam tribulationem pertinere etiam mors ipsa carnis quae de primi peccati perpetratione concepta est, ut secundum cuiusque aedificium tempus quod eam sequitur ab unoquoque sentiatur.

Persecutiones quoque quibus martyres coronati sunt et quas patiuntur quicumque Christiani probant utraque aedificia velut ignis et alia consumunt cum ipsis aedificatoribus si Christum in eis non inveniunt fundamentum, alia sine ipsis si inveniunt, quia licet cum damno salvi erunt ipsi, alia vero non con-

---

[1] Isaiah 66.24; Mark 9.44–46; Revelation 20.10.

[2] This is Augustine's view of purgatory—a conjecture with a '' perhaps '' attached. See p. 118 above, with note.

and so will hear the words: " Depart from me, ye cursed, into eternal fire." For no one will be saved from that fire, since all in that group will go into eternal punishment, where their worm does not die and their fire is not quenched, in which they will be tormented night and day for ever and ever.[1]

After the death of this body, and before that day comes which will be the final day of condemnation and reward after the resurrection, it may be said that in this interval of time there are spirits of the dead who endure a fire, a fire of a sort that is not experienced by those who in their earthly lives did not so live and love that their " wood and hay and stubble " must be consumed.[2] That fire may be experienced by the others who take buildings of this sort with them. They may encounter this fire of passing affliction, which consumes whatever is worldly though not worthy of damnation, either there alone, after death, or both here and there, or they may encounter it here in order to escape it there. I do not oppose this view, for perhaps it is true. In fact, even bodily death itself, which came upon man from the perpetration of the first sin, may belong to that tribulation, so that each man's experience after death will depend upon the nature of his building.

The persecutions also, those by which the martyrs were crowned, and those that all Christians suffer, prove both kinds of buildings as if by fire. Some they consume along with the builders, if they do not find Christ in them as their foundation; others they consume, but not the builders, if they find Christ there, for the men themselves will be saved, though with loss. There are still other buildings, however,

sumunt quia talia reperiunt quae maneant in aeternum. Erit etiam in fine saeculi tribulatio tempore Antichristi qualis numquam antea fuit. Quam multa erunt tunc aedificia, sive aurea sive fenea, super optimum fundamentum, quod est Christus Iesus, ut ignis ille probet utraque et de aliis gaudium de aliis inferat damnum, neutros tamen perdat, in quibus haec inveniet, propter stabile fundamentum!

Quicumque autem, non dico uxorem cuius etiam commixtione carnis ad carnalem utitur voluptatem, sed ipsa quae ab eius modi delectationibus aliena sunt nomina pietatis humano more carnaliter diligendo Christo anteponit, non eum habet in fundamento et ideo non per ignem salvus erit, sed salvus non erit, quia esse cum Salvatore non poterit, qui de hac re apertissime loquens ait: *Qui amat patrem aut matrem plus quam me non est me dignus; et qui amat filium aut filiam super me non est me dignus.* Verum qui has necessitudines sic amat carnaliter ut tamen eas Christo Domino non praeponat, malitque ipsis carere quam Christo, si ad hunc fuerit articulum temptationis adductus, per ignem erit salvus, quia ex earum amissione tantum necesse est urat dolor quantum haeserat amor. Porro qui patrem matrem filios filias secundum Christum dilexerit, ut ad eius regnum obtinendum eique cohaerendum illis consulat, vel hoc in eis diligat quod membra sunt Christi,

148

that they do not consume because they find in them such materials as to last for ever. At the end of this age there will also be a tribulation in the time of the Antichrist, such as never was before. How many buildings, then, will there be, whether of gold or of hay, built on the best foundation, which is Christ Jesus! Both of these that fire will prove, and from the gold bring joy, from the hay, loss. But still it will destroy the builders of neither kind in which it finds those things, on account of the sure foundation.

But if anyone places earthly love of the human sort before Christ—I am not speaking of a wife, whose carnal intercourse he uses for his carnal pleasure, but even the love of other relatives not associated with those delights, but joined by ties of duty—he does not have Christ as his foundation, and so he will not be saved through fire, nor saved at all, for he cannot be with the Saviour, who speaks most clearly on this point: " He who loves father or mother more than me is not worthy of me, and he who loves son or daughter above me is not worthy of me." [1] But if one loves such relatives in the flesh, not however putting them before Christ the Lord, and prefers to lose them rather than Christ, if he is brought to this critical moment of trial, he will be saved through fire, for he must burn with grief for their loss as much as he once clung to them in love. Furthermore, if a man has loved father, mother, sons or daughters in the spirit of Christ, taking thought so that they may obtain his kingdom and cleave to him, or loves in them their

[1] Matthew 10.37.

absit ut ista dilectio reperiatur in lignis, feno et stipula consumenda, sed prorsus aedificio aureo, argenteo, gemmeo deputabitur. Quo modo autem potest eos plus amare quam Christum quos amat utique propter Christum?

XXVII

Contra eorum persuasionem qui putant sibi non offutura peccata in quibus, cum elemosynas facerent, perstiterunt.

RESTAT eis respondere qui dicunt aeterno igne illos tantummodo arsuros qui pro peccatis suis facere dignas elemosynas neglegunt, propter illud quod ait apostolus Iacobus: *Iudicium autem sine misericordia illi qui non fecit misericordiam.* Qui ergo fecit, inquiunt, quamvis non correxerit perditos mores, sed nefarie ac nequiter inter ipsas suas elemosynas vixerit, cum misericordia illi futurum est iudicium ut aut non damnetur omnino aut post aliquod tempus a damnatione novissima liberetur. Nec ob aliud existimant Christum de solo dilectu atque neglectu elemosynarum discretionem inter dextros et sinistros esse facturum, quorum alios in regnum alios in supplicium mittat aeternum. Ut autem cotidiana sibi opinentur, quae facere omnino non cessant, qualiacumque et quantacumque sint, per elemosynas dimitti posse peccata, orationem quam docuit ipse Dominus et suffragatricem sibi adhibere conantur et testem.

---

[1] James 2.13.

being members of Christ, God forbid that this love be found worthy to be consumed as among wood, hay or stubble. Rather, it will be reckoned as a building of gold, silver, precious stones. And how, moreover, can he love more than Christ those whom he loves to begin with for the sake of Christ?

XXVII

Against the opinion of those who hold that the sins in which they persisted while they were doing alms will not harm them.

IT remains to reply to those who say that only those will burn in eternal fire who neglect to perform suitable acts of charity to atone for their sins, citing the words of the apostle James: "But judgement shall be without mercy to him who has not shown mercy." [1] Hence, they say, one who has shown mercy, though he has not corrected his depraved ways, but has lived wickedly and worthlessly even while doing alms, will be judged with mercy, and either not condemned at all, or freed from final damnation after a time. And for no other reason, they think, than the mere love or neglect of alms-giving will Christ make a distinction between those on the right hand and those on the left, of whom he will send the former into the kingdom, the others into eternal punishment. To maintain the view that daily sins, which they never leave off at all, sins of any kind and size, can be forgiven through almsgiving, they attempt to use the prayer which the Lord himself taught as their support and evidence. For, they

Sicut enim nullus est, inquiunt, dies quo a Christianis haec oratio non dicatur, ita nullum est cotidianum qualecumque peccatum quod per illam non dimittatur cum dicimus: *Dimitte nobis debita nostra*, si quod sequitur facere curemus: *Sicut et nos dimittimus debitoribus nostris.* Non enim ait Dominus, inquiunt: Si dimiseritis peccata hominibus, dimittet vobis pater vester cotidiana parva peccata, sed: *Dimittet*, inquit, *vobis peccata vestra.* Qualiacumque ergo vel quantacumque sint, etiamsi cotidie perpetrentur nec ab eis vita discedat in melius commutata, per elemosynam veniae non negatae remitti sibi posse praesumunt.

Sed bene, quod isti dignas pro peccatis elemosynas commonent esse faciendas, quoniam si dicerent qualescumque elemosynas pro peccatis et cotidianis et magnis et quantacumque scelerum consuetudine misericordiam posse impetrare divinam ut ea cotidiana remissio sequeretur, viderent se rem dicere absurdam atque ridiculam. Sic enim cogerentur fateri fieri posse ut opulentissimus homo decem nummulis diurnis in elemosynas inpensis homicidia et adulteria et nefaria quaeque facta redimeret. Quod si absurdissimum atque insanissimum est dicere, profecto si quaeratur quae dignae sint pro peccatis elemosynae, de quibus etiam Christi praecursor ille dicebat: *Facite ergo fructus dignos paenitentiae*, procul dubio non invenientur eas facere qui vitam suam usque ad mortem cotidianorum criminum perpetratione confodiunt; primum, quia in auferendis rebus alienis longe plura diripiunt ex quibus perexigua pauperibus largiendo Christum

---

[1] Matthew 6.12, 14.   [2] Matthew 3.8; Luke 3.8.

say, as there is no day when this prayer is not spoken by Christians, so there is no daily sin of any sort which is not forgiven thereby, when we say: " Forgive us our debts," if we are careful to do what follows: " as we also forgive our debtors." For, they say, the Lord does not say: " If ye forgive men their sins, your Father will forgive your small every-day sins," [1] but rather: " He will forgive your sins." So of whatever sort or however great they are, though the sins be committed daily, and the man never turn from them or change his life for the better, they presume that they can be forgiven through the good work of not refusing forgiveness to others.

But it is well that they warn us that suitable alms must be done to atone for sins. For if they said that any kind of alms could gain the divine pardon for both every-day sins and great ones and for any wicked practice, however serious, so that a daily forgiveness would follow, they would see that they were saying a thing absurd and ridiculous. For thus they would be forced to declare that a very rich man could spend ten pennies a day for alms and atone for murders and adulteries and all kinds of crimes. If it is utterly absurd and senseless to say this, and if we inquire what alms are worth enough to atone for sins (of which even Christ's forerunner said: " Bring forth therefore fruits worthy of repentance "),[2] undoubtedly none will be found and judged to be bringing forth such fruits of those who stab their lives even till death by the perpetration of daily crimes. For in the first place, in robbing others they take far greater sums, and they think that in feeding Christ by bestowing a scanty pittance of them on the

se ad hoc pascere existimant ut licentiam male-
factorum ab illo se emisse vel cotidie potius emere
credentes securi damnabilia tanta committant. Qui
si pro uno scelere omnia sua distribuerent indi-
gentibus membris Christi, nisi desisterent a talibus
factis habendo caritatem quae non agit perperam,
aliquid eis prodesse non posset.

Qui ergo dignas pro suis peccatis elemosynas facit,
prius eas facere incipiat a se ipso. Indignum est
enim, ut in se non faciat qui facit in proximum,
cum audiat dicentem Deum: *Diliges proximum tuum
tamquam te ipsum;* itemque audiat: *Miserere animae
tuae placens Deo.* Hanc elemosynam, id est, ut Deo
placeat, non faciens, animae suae quo modo dignas
pro peccatis suis elemosynas facere dicendus est?
Ad hoc enim et illud scriptum est: *Qui sibi malignus
est, cui bonus erit?* Orationes quippe adiuvant
elemosynae, et utique intuendum est quod legimus:
*Fili, peccasti, ne adicias iterum, et de praeteritis deprecare
ut tibi dimittantur.* Propter hoc ergo elemosynae
faciendae sunt ut, cum de praeteritis peccatis
deprecamur, exaudiamur; non ut in eis perseverantes
licentiam malefaciendi nos per elemosynas comparare credamus.

Ideo autem Dominus et dextris elemosynas ab eis
factas et sinistris non factas se inputaturum esse
praedixit ut hinc ostenderet quantum valeant elemo-

---

[1] 1 Corinthians 13.4.
[2] Leviticus 19.18; Matthew 22.39.
[3] Ecclesiasticus 30.23–24 Vulgate (not LXX).

poor they gain their object, with the result that they
believe that they have bought, or rather, are buying
every day, a licence from him for their misdeeds,
whereby they may commit such damnable deeds
without misgivings—whereas, if for a single crime
they distributed all their goods to the poor [1] members
of Christ, unless they were to desist from such deeds,
having a love which works no evil, nothing would do
them any good.

So he who does suitable alms to atone for sins
should first begin with himself. For it is improper
not to do for himself what he does for his neighbour,
while he hears God saying: " Thou shalt love thy
neighbour as thyself," [2] and also hears: " Pity thy
soul, pleasing God." [3] How should one who does
not do this good deed, that is, please God, be said to
do alms suitable to atone for his sins? For on this
point another text of Scripture applies: " He that
is evil to himself, to whom will he be good? " [4] No
doubt alms aid prayer, and we must by all means heed
the words: " Son, thou hast sinned; do so no more,
and for thy former sins pray that they may be forgiven thee." [5] So alms are to be done for this purpose, that we may be heard when praying concerning
past sins, not to support a belief that we gain a
licence for wrongdoing through almsgiving while we
continue in our sins.

Now when the Lord declared that he would re-
compense those on the right for alms they had done,
and those on the left for deeds left undone, his purpose was to show how far such acts avail to wipe out

[4] Ecclesiasticus 14.5.
[5] Ecclesiasticus 21.1.

synae ad priora delenda, non ad perpetua inpune committenda peccata. Tales autem elemosynas non dicendi sunt facere qui vitam nolunt a consuetudine scelerum in melius commutare. Quia et in hoc quod ait: *Quando uni ex minimis meis non fecistis, mihi non fecistis,* ostendit eos non facere etiam quando se facere existimant. Si enim Christiano esurienti panem tamquam Christiano darent, profecto sibi panem iustitiae quod ipse Christus est non negarent, quoniam Deus non cui detur sed quo animo detur adtendit. Qui ergo Christum diligit in Christiano, hoc animo ei porrigit elemosynam quo accedit ad Christum, non quo vult recedere inpunitus a Christo. Tanto enim magis quisque deserit Christum quanto magis diligit quod inprobat Christus. Nam quid cuiquam prodest quod baptizatur, si non iustificatur? Nonne qui dixit: *Nisi quis renatus fuerit ex aqua et Spiritu, non intrabit in regnum Dei,* ipse etiam dixit: *Nisi abundaverit iustitia vestra super scribarum et Pharisaeorum, non intrabitis in regnum caelorum?* Cur illud timendo multi currunt baptizari, et hoc non timendo non multi curant iustificari? Sicut ergo non fratri suo dicit: *Fatue,* qui cum hoc dicit non ipsi fraternitati, sed peccato eius infensus est—alioquin reus erit gehennae ignis—ita e contrario qui porrigit elemosynam Christiano, non Christiano porrigit qui non in eo diligit Christum, non autem diligit Christum

---

[1] Matthew 25.45.   [2] John 3.5.
[3] Matthew 5.20.   [4] Matthew 5.22.

the guilt of former deeds, not to permit continual sin to be repeated with impunity. Moreover, any who are unwilling to give up their accustomed sins and change for the better cannot be said to do alms at all. For in the saying: " When ye did it not to one of the least of my brethren, ye did it not unto me," [1] he shows that they were not doing it even when they thought that they were. For if they gave bread to a hungry Christian as to a Christian, surely they would not deny themselves the bread of righteousness, which is Christ himself. For God gives heed not to the recipient of the gift, but to the spirit of the giver. So he who loves Christ in his fellow Christian extends alms to him in the spirit in which one approaches Christ, not in the spirit of desiring to depart from Christ with impunity. For a man deserts Christ in proportion as he loves what Christ disapproves. For what does it benefit anyone that he is baptized, if he is not made righteous? For did not he who said: " Except a man be reborn of water and the Spirit, he shall not enter the kingdom of God," [2] also himself say: " Except your righteousness exceed the righteousness of the scribes and Pharisees, you shall not enter the kingdom of heaven? " [3] Why is it that many, fearing the first saying, run to be baptized, while few fear the second enough to take the trouble to become righteous? Hence, just as it is not to a brother that a man says, " Thou fool! " when he says it from hostility to his sin, and not with any hostility to his status as brother—otherwise he will be in danger of hell fire [4]—so, on the other hand, if a man gives alms to a Christian, it is not as to a Christian that he gives unless he loves Christ in him,

qui iustificari recusat in Christo. Et quem ad
modum si quis praeoccupatus fuerit hoc delicto ut
fratri suo dicat: *Fatue*, id est, non eius peccatum
volens auferre convicietur iniuste, parum est illi ad
hoc redimendum elemosynas facere, nisi etiam quod
ibi sequitur remedium reconciliationis adiungat.
Ibi enim sequitur: *Si ergo offeres munus tuum ad
altare et ibi recordatus fueris quia frater tuus habet
aliquid adversum te, relinque ibi munus tuum ad altare
et vade prius, reconciliare fratri tuo, et tunc veniens offeres
munus tuum.* Ita parum est elemosynas quantaslibet
facere pro quocumque scelere et in consuetudine
scelerum permanere.

Oratio vero cotidiana quam docuit ipse Iesus, unde
et dominica nominatur, delet quidem cotidiana peccata cum cotidie dicitur: *Dimitte nobis debita nostra*,
atque id quod sequitur non solum dicitur, sed etiam
fit: *Sicut et nos dimittimus debitoribus nostris.* Sed quia
fiunt peccata ideo dicitur, non ut ideo fiant quia
dicitur. Per hanc enim nobis voluit Salvator ostendere, quantumlibet iuste in huius vitae caligine
atque infirmitate vivamus, non nobis deesse peccata
pro quibus dimittendis debeamus orare, et eis qui in
nos peccant ut et nobis ignoscatur ignoscere. Non
itaque propterea Dominus ait: *Si dimiseritis peccata
hominibus dimittet vobis et pater vester peccata vestra*
ut de hac oratione confisi securi cotidiana scelera
faceremus, vel potentia qua non timeremus hominum

---

[1] Matthew 5.23–24.
[2] Matthew 6.12.
[3] Matthew 6.14.

nor does he love Christ if he refuses to be made
righteous in Christ. Likewise, if anyone is overtaken
by the fault of saying to his brother: " Thou fool! "
that is, reviles him unjustly when he has no desire to
take away his sin, doing alms is insufficient to atone
for this unless he adds the remedy of reconciliation,
to which a reference follows. For the text continues:
" If therefore you bring your gift to the altar and there
remember that your brother has anything against
you, leave your gift there before the altar and first
go and be reconciled to your brother and then you
shall come and offer your gift." [1] Just so it is not
enough to do acts of mercy, however great, for any
sin whatever, if a man persists in his accustomed
sinful course.

But the daily prayer that Jesus himself taught
(whence it is also called " The Lord's Prayer ") does
wipe out our daily sins when we daily say: " Forgive
us our debts," and then not only add the next words
but also act accordingly: " as we also forgive our
debtors." [2] But the prayer is repeated because sins
are committed, but not to the end that more may be
committed because it is repeated. For by this
petition the Saviour's purpose was to show that however righteously we may live amid the darkness and
instability of this life, we are never free from sins,
but must pray for their forgiveness and must pardon
those who sin against us, in order that we also may
be pardoned. And so the Lord said: " If you forgive men their sins, your Father also will forgive your
sins," [3] not that by relying on this prayer we might
commit sins daily with confidence, either exempt
from fear of the laws of men because of high position,

leges, vel astutia qua ipsos homines falleremus, sed
ut per illam disceremus non putare nos esse sine
peccatis, etiamsi a criminibus essemus inmunes;
sicut etiam legis veteris sacerdotes hoc ipsum Deus de
sacrificiis admonuit, quae iussit eos primum pro suis
deinde pro populi offerre peccatis.

Nam et ipsa verba tanti magistri et Domini nostri
vigilanter intuenda sunt. Non enim ait: " Si
dimiseritis peccata hominibus, et pater vester
dimittet vobis qualiacumque peccata," sed ait:
Peccata vestra. Cotidianam quippe orationem doce-
bat et iustificatis utique discipulis loquebatur. Quid
est ergo: *Peccata vestra* nisi " peccata sine quibus
nec vos eritis qui iustificati et sanctificati estis "?
Ubi ergo illi qui per hanc orationem occasionem per-
petrandorum cotidie scelerum quaerunt dicunt
Dominum significasse etiam magna peccata, quoniam
non dixit: " Dimittet vobis parva," sed *peccata
vestra,* ibi nos considerantes qualibus loquebatur et
audientes dictum *Peccata vestra* nihil aliud debemus
existimare quam parva, quoniam talium iam non
erant magna. Verum tamen nec ipsa magna, a
quibus omnino mutatis in melius moribus recedendum
est, dimittuntur orantibus nisi fiat quod ibi dicitur:
Sicut et nos dimittimus debitoribus nostris. Si enim
minima peccata sine quibus non est etiam vita
iustorum aliter non remittuntur, quanto magis multis
et magnis criminibus involuti, etiamsi ea perpetrare

---

[1] Leviticus 16.6.

or capable of cheating human eyes because of our craftiness. Rather, his intention was that by that prayer we should learn not to think that we are without sin, even if we do avoid great crimes. This is the same instruction that God gave to the priests of the old law through the sacrifices that he commanded them to offer first for their own sins, then for the sins of the people.[1]

For the very words of our great Master and Lord must be carefully observed. He does not say: " If you forgive men their sins, your Father also will forgive for you sins of any kind," but he says: " your sins." It was a daily prayer that he was teaching, and in any case he was speaking to disciples already made righteous. What then is the meaning of " your sins," if not " the sins which not even you will avoid, who are made both righteous and holy " ? So when those who through this prayer seek an opening for committing sins daily say that the Lord meant to include even great sins—since he did not say: " He will forgive your small sins," but " your sins "—at that point we consider the men to whom he was speaking, and when we hear the words " your sins " are bound to think of nothing but small sins, for the sins of such men were not great. However, neither are the great sins (from which it is altogether necessary to depart by a change of character for the better) remitted when we pray unless we do as the text says: " as we also forgive our debtors." For if the least sins, from which not even the life of the righteous is free, are not otherwise forgiven, how much more do those who are entangled in many great crimes fail to attain forgiveness (even if they cease now to com-

iam desinant, nullam indulgentiam consequuntur, si
ad remittendum aliis quod in eos quisque peccaverit
inexorabiles fuerint, cum dicat Dominus: *Si autem
non dimiseritis hominibus, neque pater vester dimittet
vobis.*

Ad hoc enim valet quod etiam Iacobus apostolus
ait iudicium futurum sine misericordia illi qui non
fecit misericordiam. Venire quippe debet in mentem
etiam servus ille cui debitori dominus eius relaxavit
decem milia talentorum, quae postea iussit ut redderet, quia ipse non misertus est conservi sui qui ei
debebat centum denarios. In his ergo qui filii sunt
promissionis et vasa misericordiae valet quod ait
idem apostolus consequenter adiungens: *Superexultat autem misericordia iudicio*, quoniam et illi iusti
qui tanta sanctitate vixerunt ut alios quoque recipiant
in tabernacula aeterna (a quibus amici facti sunt de
mammona iniquitatis ut tales essent) misericordia
liberati sunt ab eo qui iustificat impium, imputans
mercedem secundum gratiam, non secundum debitum. In eorum quippe numero est apostolus qui
dicit: *Misericordiam consecutus sum, ut fidelis essem.*

Illi autem qui recipiuntur a talibus in tabernacula
aeterna, fatendum est quod non sint his moribus
praediti ut eis liberandis sine suffragio sanctorum sua
possit vita sufficere, ac per hoc multo amplius in eis
superexultat misericordia iudicio. Nec tamen ideo
putandus est quisquam sceleratissimus, nequaquam
vita vel bona vel tolerabiliore mutatus, recipi in

---

1 Matthew 6.15. 2 James 2.13.
3 Matthew 18.23–34. 4 James 2.13.
5 Luke 16.9. 6 1 Corinthians 7.25.

mit them) if they refuse all entreaties to forgive
others any sins that anyone has committed against
them! For the Lord says: " If you do not forgive
men, neither will your Father forgive you." [1]

What the apostle James says also applies to the
point, that judgement will be without mercy to him
who has shown no mercy.[2] Here no doubt that
servant should be called to mind for whom his master
forgave the debt of ten thousand talents, but later
ordered him to pay them back because he did not
have pity on his fellow servant who owed him a
hundred shillings.[3] So in the case of those who are
sons of the promise and vessels of mercy, the words of
the same Apostle in the same context apply: " But
mercy triumphs over judgement." [4] For even those
righteous men who have lived in such holiness that
they receive others also into eternal tabernacles
(men who have gained their friendship by means of
the mammon of unrighteousness,[5] in order to be such
as they are) have been freed as an act of mercy by
him who justifies the ·unrighteous, reckoning the
reward as a matter of grace, not of debt. For in
their number is the Apostle who says: " I have
obtained mercy, so as to be faithful." [6]

But of those who are received by such men into
eternal tabernacles, it must be admitted that they
are not endowed with such character that their life
is enough to free them without the help of the saints,
and hence in their case much more does mercy triumph
over judgement. But neither must it be supposed
that any wicked man, without any change at all in
his life so that it is good, or better than before, is
received into the eternal tabernacles because he

tabernacula aeterna quoniam obsecutus est sanctis de mammona iniquitatis. Id est de pecunia vel divitiis quae male fuerant adquisitae, aut etiamsi bene, non tamen veris sed quas iniquitas putat esse divitias, quoniam nescit quae sint verae divitiae quibus illi abundabant qui et alios recipiunt in tabernacula aeterna. Est itaque quidam vitae modus nec tam malae ut his qui eam vivunt nihil prosit ad capessendum regnum caelorum largitas elemosynarum, quibus etiam iustorum sustentatur inopia, et fiunt amici qui in tabernacula aeterna suscipiant, nec tam bonae ut ad tantam beatitudinem adipiscendam eis ipsa sufficiat, nisi eorum meritis quos amicos fecerint misericordiam consequantur.

Mirari autem soleo etiam apud Vergilium reperiri istam Domini sententiam, ubi ait: *Facite vobis amicos de mammona iniquitatis, ut et ipsi recipiant vos in tabernacula aeterna;* cui est et illa simillima: *Qui recipit prophetam in nomine prophetae, mercedem prophetae accipiet; et qui recipit iustum in nomine iusti, mercedem iusti accipiet.* Nam cum Elysios campos poeta ille describeret, ubi putant habitare animas beatorum, non solum ibi posuit eos qui propriis meritis ad illas sedes pervenire potuerunt, sed adiecit atque ait:

Quique sui memores alios fecere merendo,

id est, qui promeruerunt alios eosque sui memores promerendo fecerunt—prorsus tamquam eis dicerent,

---

[1] Luke 16.9.
[2] Matthew 10.41.
[3] *Aeneid,* 6.664.

has courted the saints with the mammon of unrighteousness. This term refers to money or riches
that are wrongly acquired—or, if properly acquired,
still not true riches, but what unrighteousness sup-
poses to be riches, not knowing what are the true
riches of which those had a superfluity who receive
others with them into eternal tabernacles. And so
there is a certain manner of life which is neither so
wicked that those who live it cannot be helped to
reach the kingdom of heaven by their generous almsgiving (by which not only is the poverty of the
righteous supported, but friends are also gained to
receive the givers into eternal tabernacles), nor so
good that it is sufficient of itself to gain so great
happiness, unless they obtain mercy by the merits of
those whose friendship they gain.

I often marvel that in Virgil also is found a thought
which the Lord puts in the words: " Make for your-
selves friends with the mammon of unrighteousness,
that they in turn may receive you into eternal tabernacles." [1] Very like it is the well-known promise:
" He who receives a prophet in the name of a prophet
shall receive a prophet's reward, and he who receives
a righteous man in the name of a righteous man shall
receive a righteous man's reward." [2] For when the
great poet describes the Elysian fields, where it is
supposed that the souls of the happy live, not only
does he place there those who were able to reach that
place of residence by their own merits, but he adds:
" And those who have made others mindful of them
by service," [3] that is, those who have served others
and made them mindful of them by their service.
It is just as if they used the words in speaking to them

quod frequentatur ore Christiano, cum se cuique sanctorum humilis quisque commendat et dicit: "Memor mei esto," atque id ut esse possit pro- merendo efficit.

Sed quis iste sit modus, et quae sint ipsa peccata quae ita impediunt perventionem ad regnum Dei ut tamen sanctorum amicorum meritis inpetrent indulgentiam, difficillimum est invenire, periculo- sissimum definire. Ego certe usque ad hoc tempus cum inde satagerem ad eorum indaginem pervenire non potui. Et fortassis propterea latent ne studium proficiendi ad omnia cavenda peccata pigrescat. Quoniam si scirentur quae vel qualia sint delicta pro quibus etiam permanentibus nec provectu vitae melioris absumptis intercessio sit inquirenda et speranda iustorum, eis secura se obvolveret humana segnitia, nec evolvi talibus implicamentis ullius virtutis expeditione curaret, sed tantummodo quaere- ret aliorum meritis liberari quos amicos sibi de mammona iniquitatis elemosynarum largitate fecisset. Nunc vero dum venialis inquitatis, etiamsi per- severet, ignoratur modus, profecto et studium in meliora proficiendi orando et instando vigilantius adhibetur et faciendi de mammona inquitatis sanctos amicos cura non spernitur.

Verum ista liberatio quae fit sive suis quibusque orationibus sive intercedentibus sanctis id agit ut in ignem quisque non mittatur aeternum, non ut cum

that are often heard on Christian lips, when a humble soul commends himself to one of the saints and says: " Be mindful of me," and makes it possible for him to be mindful by some worthy act.

But it is very hard to learn and ticklish to define what is the manner of life, and what are the sins that stand in the way of reaching the kingdom of God, but still allow the sinners to win indulgence by the merits of the saints, their friends. At least, up to the present time I have not been able to arrive at the answer, though I have applied myself to the subject. And perhaps it is purposely hidden, lest zeal for progress in avoiding all sins should grow slothful. For if men knew for what sins or what kind of sins they might seek and expect the intercession of the saints even though the sins remain and are not overcome by progress toward a better life, then man's sloth would wrap itself securely in the sins, and not strive to escape from such entanglements by any energetic pursuit of virtue; they would only seek to be freed by the merits of others whom they had gained as friends by the mammon of unrighteousness generously spent in almsgiving. But as it is, as long as the amount of iniquity that can be forgiven though it be persisted in is unknown, there is certainly so much the more vigilant zeal displayed in prayer and striving for improvement in character, and the effort to make the saints one's friends by means of the mammon of unrighteousness is not despised.

But that liberation which is gained by a man's own prayers or by the intercession of the saints only brings it about that a soul is not dispatched into eternal fire; once it is so dispatched, naught avails

fuerit missus post quantumcumque inde tempus eruatur. Nam et illi qui putant sic intellegendum esse quod scriptum est, adferre terram bonam uberem fructum, aliam tricenum, aliam sexagenum, aliam centenum, ut sancti pro suorum diversitate meritorum alii tricenos homines liberent, alii sexagenos, alii centenos, hoc in die iudicii futurum suspicari solent, non post iudicium. Qua opinione quidam cum videret homines inpunitatem sibi perversissime pollicentes, eo quod omnes isto modo ad liberationem pertinere posse videantur, elegantissime respondisse perhibetur, bene potius esse vivendum, ut inter eos quisque reperiatur qui pro aliis intercessuri sunt liberandis, ne tam pauci sint ut cito ad numerum suum vel tricenum vel sexagenum vel centenum unoquoque eorum perveniente multi remaneant qui erui iam de poenis illorum intercessione non possint, et in eis inveniatur quisquis sibi spem fructus alieni temeritate vanissima pollicetur.

Haec me illis respondisse suffecerit qui sacrarum litterarum quas communes habemus auctoritatem non spernunt, sed eas male intellegendo non quod illae loquuntur, sed hoc potius putant futurum esse quod ipsi volunt. Hac itaque responsione reddita librum sicut promisimus terminamus.

to effect its deliverance thence, no matter how long a time it may have been there. For even those who hold that when Scripture says that the good ground bears a plentiful harvest, some thirty-fold, some sixty, some a hundred,[1] it should be understood to mean that the saints, according to the diversity of their merits free, some thirty men each, some sixty, some a hundred, suppose that this will happen on the day of judgement, not after the judgement. There was a certain man, they say, who saw people perversely promising themselves impunity because of this notion, whereby it seems that in this way all may come to be freed from hell. He made the apt retort, it is said, that it is better to live a good life, whereby a person may be found among those who will intercede for the liberation of others, lest the intercessors be so few that when each has speedily filled out his quota of thirty, sixty or a hundred, many others should be left unable to gain deliverance from punishment by their intercession, and lest among these be found every one who with baseless audacity promises himself the hope of profiting by another's merit.

With this I have said enough in answer to those who do not reject the authority of the sacred writings which we have in common, but by misinterpreting them expect that what they themselves wish will come to pass, rather than what the Scriptures say. So now, having completed our reply, we end the book as we promised.

[1] Matthew 13.8.

BOOK XXII

LIBER XXII

I

De conditione angelorum et hominum.

SICUT in proximo libro superiore promisimus, iste huius totius operis ultimus disputationem de civitatis Dei aeterna beatitudine continebit, quae non propter aetatis per multa saecula longitudinem tamen quandocumque finiendam aeternitatis nomen accepit, sed quem ad modum scriptum est in evangelio, *regni eius non erit finis*; nec ita ut aliis moriendo decedentibus, aliis succedentibus oriendo species in ea perpetuitatis appareat, sicut in arbore quae perenni fronde vestitur eadem videtur viriditas permanere, dum labentibus et cadentibus foliis subinde alia quae nascuntur faciem conservant opacitatis; sed omnes in ea cives inmortales erunt, adipiscentibus et hominibus quod numquam sancti angeli perdiderunt. Faciet hoc Deus omnipotentissimus eius conditor. Promisit enim nec mentiri potest, et

---

[1] The words "eternal" and "eternity," from Latin *aeternus, aeternitas,* are related to *aevum,* which means both "unending time" and "a period of time"; for the second meaning the commoner word is *aetas.* Augustine seeks to

BOOK XXII

I

The condition of angels and men.

As we promised in the preceding book, this book, the last of the whole work, will contain a discussion of the eternal happiness of the City of God. The term " eternal," as applied here, does not refer to a long period of time (*aetas*) lasting through many ages, but still at some time bound to end.[1] Rather, as it stands written in the gospel, " of his kingdom there shall be no end." [2] Nor is it eternal in the sense that there is an outward appearance of continuity in its case because, as some sink in death, so others rise to replace them. When a tree, for instance, wears its robe of leaves throughout the year, it seems to keep permanently the same greenery, for, though leaves detach themselves and fall, yet new ones burgeoning maintain the front unbroken. But in that city all the citizens are immortal, for human beings will also attain to the status that the holy angels never lost. God, its most almighty Creator, shall bring this to pass, for he has promised and cannot lie, and as an earnest of his

make it clear that the " eternal " happiness of the saints is unending happiness, that is, an unending immortality for each individual.

[2] Luke 1.33.

quibus fidem hinc quoque faceret, multa sua et non promissa et promissa iam fecit.

Ipse est enim, qui in principio condidit mundum, plenum bonis omnibus visibilibus atque intellegibilibus rebus, in quo nihil melius instituit quam spiritus quibus intellegentiam dedit, et suae contemplationis habiles capacesque sui praestitit atque una societate devinxit quam sanctam et supernam dicimus civitatem, in qua res qua sustententur beatique sint Deus ipse illis est, tamquam vita victusque communis. Qui liberum arbitrium eidem intellectuali naturae tribuit tale ut, si vellet, desereret Deum, beatitudinem scilicet suam, miseria continuo secutura. Qui, cum praesciret angelos quosdam per elationem qua ipsi sibi ad beatam vitam sufficere vellent tanti boni desertores futuros, non eis ademit hanc potestatem, potentius et melius esse iudicans etiam de malis bene facere quam mala esse non sinere.

Quae omnino nulla essent, nisi natura mutabilis, quamvis bona et a summo Deo atque incommutabili bono qui bona omnia condidit instituta, peccando ea sibi ipsa fecisset. Quo etiam peccato suo teste convincitur bonam conditam se esse naturam. Nisi enim magnum et ipsa, licet non aequale Conditori, bonum esset, profecto desertio Dei tamquam luminis sui malum eius esse non posset. Nam sicut caecitas oculi vitium est et idem ipsum indicat

good faith he has already performed many things that he promised, as well as things not promised.

For it is he who in the beginning created the world, full of all good things, visible to eye or mind, and in it he put nothing better than those spirits to whom he gave intelligence. These he created capable of contemplating and receiving himself, and bound them in one fellowship which we call the holy and heavenly city. There God himself is the substance by which they are sustained and made happy, their common food, so to speak, and source of life. To the same group who were endowed with intelligence he granted free will of a kind that permitted them, if they wished, to desert God—their true joy, be it noted, so that misery would immediately follow. Though he foreknew that certain angels would forsake their great blessedness through the pride that made them wish to be self-sufficient in a happy life, he did not take the power of choice away from them, but judged that it was more in keeping with his might and goodness to make evil a source of good rather than not to permit any evils to exist.

There would be no evil at all in existence if a nature subject to change—good though it was and created by God and his unchangeable goodness who made all things good—had not sinned and so created its own evil for itself. Even this sin is a witness against such a nature to prove that God created it good. For unless it were itself a great good (though not equal in goodness to the creator) certainly the desertion of God, its light, could not be its ruin. To illustrate, blindness is a defect of the eye, and this very fact shows that the eye was created to see the

ad lumen videndum esse oculum creatum ac per hoc etiam ipso vitio suo excellentius ostenditur ceteris membris membrum capax luminis—non enim alia causa esset vitium eius carere lumine—ita natura, quae fruebatur Deo, optimam se institutam docet etiam ipso vitio, quo ideo misera est quia non fruitur Deo. Qui casum angelorum voluntarium iustissima poena sempiternae infelicitatis obstrinxit atque in eo summo bono permanentibus ceteris, ut de sua sine fine permansione certi essent, tamquam ipsius praemium permansionis dedit.

Qui fecit hominem etiam ipsum rectum cum eodem libero arbitrio, terrenum quidem animal, sed caelo dignum si suo cohaereret auctori, miseria similiter si eum desereret secutura, qualis naturae huius modi conveniret. Quem similiter cum praevaricatione legis Dei per Dei desertionem peccaturum esse praesciret, nec illi ademit liberi arbitrii potestatem, simul praevidens quid boni de malo eius esset ipse facturus. Qui de mortali progenie merito iusteque damnata tantum populum gratia sua colligit ut inde suppleat et instauret partem quae lapsa est angelorum, ac sic illa dilecta et superna civitas non fraudetur suorum numero civium, quin etiam fortassis et uberiore laetetur.

---

[1] On Augustine's notion that the saints will replenish the population of heaven so as to replace the number of fallen

light.   Hence, by its very defect the member capable of illumination is proved to be more excellent than the other members, for there can be no other reason why its lack of light should be a defect.   Just so the nature which once enjoyed God shows that it was created most excellent by the very defect whereby it is wretched just because it does not now enjoy God.   The freely willed fall of the angels he constrained by the utterly just penalty of eternal unhappiness.   To all the rest who remained firm in him, their highest good, he granted as a reward for so remaining the certitude of remaining in him for ever.

And he made man himself also an upright creature, with the same free will, an earthbound animal, but worthy of heaven if he should cling to his creator. In like manner misery was to follow if he should desert him, a misery suited to a nature of this kind. In the man's case also, though God foreknew that he would sin by transgressing the law of God and deserting God, he did not take away the power of free will, foreseeing at the same time the good that he would create out of the evil which the man did. For from the man's mortal progeny, though deservedly and justly sentenced, God by his grace is gathering a people so numerous as to replace and renew the gap left by the fallen angels.[1]   Thus that beloved and heavenly city will not be cheated of the full number of its citizens; nay, it may perhaps rejoice in a number even more abundant than the former.

angels, see his *Manual* (*Enchiridion*), 9.29 with Rivière's note in *BA* 9, 351.

II

De aeterna Dei et incommutabili voluntate.

MULTA enim fiunt quidem a malis contra voluntatem Dei, sed tantae est ille sapientiae tantaeque virtutis ut in eos exitus sive fines quos bonos et iustos ipse praescivit tendant omnia quae voluntati eius videntur adversa. Ac per hoc cum Deus mutare dicitur voluntatem, ut quibus lenis erat verbi gratia reddatur iratus, illi potius quam ipse mutantur et eum quodam modo mutatum in his quae patiuntur inveniunt; sicut mutatur sol oculis sauciatis et asper quodam modo ex miti et ex delectabili molestus efficitur, cum ipse apud se ipsum maneat idem qui fuit. Dicitur etiam voluntas Dei, quam facit in cordibus oboedientium mandatis eius, de qua dicit apostolus: *Deus enim est, qui operatur in vobis et velle*, sicut iustitia Dei non solum qua ipse iustus est dicitur, sed illa etiam quam in homine qui ab illo iustificatur facit. Sic et lex eius vocatur, quae potius est hominum, sed ab ipso data. Nam utique homines erant quibus ait Iesus: *In lege vestra scriptum est*, cum alio loco legamus: *Lex Dei eius in corde eius*. Secundum hanc voluntatem quam Deus operatur in hominibus etiam velle dicitur, quod non ipse vult, sed suos id volentes facit; sicut dicitur cognovisse, quod ut cognosceretur fecit a quibus ignorabatur.

---

[1] Philippians 2.13.
[2] John 8.17; Psalm 37.31.

II

Of God's eternal and unchangeable will.

MANY things, to be sure, are done by the wicked against the will of God, but he is of such wisdom and power that all things which seem opposed to his will move towards those ends and outcomes which he knew beforehand to be good and right. Hence, when God is said to change his will, for example, when he becomes angry with those to whom he was gentle, it is they who change, rather than he, and they find him changed, so to speak, in the things that they suffer. Just so the sun is " changed " for inflamed eyes: it becomes harsh somehow instead of mild, painful instead of pleasant, although the sun in itself remains the same as ever. The phrase " will of God " is used of that will which God creates in the hearts of those who obey his commands, of which the Apostle says: " For it is God who worketh in you even to will." [1] It is just so that the phrase " righteousness of God " is used not only of that righteousness by which he himself is righteous, but also of that which he creates in the man who is made righteous by him. So also the law is called his, though it belongs rather to men, but was given by him. For surely those to whom Jesus said, " It is written in your law," were men, though in another place we read, " The law of his God is in his heart." [2] Thus also it is the will which God implants in men by which he is said to will, not what he himself wills, but what he causes his servants to will. Likewise he is said to know a thing, when he causes it to be known by others to whom the

Neque enim dicente apostolo: *Nunc autem cognoscentes Deum, immo cogniti a Deo,* fas est ut credamus quod eos tunc cognoverit Deus praecognitos ante constitutionem mundi; sed tunc cognovisse dictus est, quod tunc ut cognosceretur effecit. De his locutionum modis iam et in superioribus libris memini disputatum. Secundum hanc ergo voluntatem qua Deum velle dicimus quod alios efficit velle a quibus futura nesciuntur, multa vult nec facit.

Multa enim volunt fieri sancti eius ab illo inspirata sancta voluntate, nec fiunt, sicut orant pro quibusdam pie sancteque, et quod orant non facit, cum ipse in eis hanc orandi voluntatem sancto Spiritu suo fecerit. Ac per hoc, quando secundum Deum volunt et orant sancti ut quisque sit salvus, possumus illo modo locutionis dicere: "Vult Deus et non facit"—ut ipsum dicamus velle, qui ut velint isti facit. Secundum illam vero voluntatem suam quae cum eius praescientia sempiterna est, profecto in caelo et in terra omnia quaecumque voluit non solum praeterita vel praesentia, sed etiam futura iam fecit. Verum antequam veniat tempus quo voluit ut fieret, quod ante tempora universa praescivit atque disposuit, dicimus: "Fiet quando Deus voluerit." Si autem non solum tempus quo futurum est verum etiam utrum futurum sit ignoramus, dicimus: "Fiet, si Deus voluerit," non quia Deus novam voluntatem

---

[1] Galatians 4.9.
[2] 1 Peter 1.20; Ephesians 1.4.

matter was previously unknown. For when the
Apostle says, " But now knowing God, or rather
being known by God," [1] it is an error to suppose that
God then first knew men who were really foreknown
before the foundation of the world; [2] rather he is said
then to " know " what he then caused to be known.
I recall having discussed these forms of expression
also in former books.[3] So by this " will " which we
call " God's will," when he causes others to whom the
future is unknown to will it, he " wills " many things
which he does not do.

For his saints wish many things to be done, with a
holy will inspired by him, and yet they are not done.
They pray for certain men in piety and holiness, and
God does not do what they ask, though he himself
by his Holy Spirit created in them this desire to pray.
And hence, when the saints according to God's will
will and pray that all should be saved, we can say,
by this mode of speech, " God wills it and does not
do it," meaning that he wills in causing them to will.
But on the other hand, according to that will of God
which is eternal like his foreknowledge, he has
already surely accomplished everything which he
has willed in heaven and on earth, not only things
past and present, but also things to come. But until
the time comes for the occurrence (a time which he
foreknew and fixed before all times), we say, " It will
happen when God wills." And if we not only have
no knowledge when it will happen but even have
none whether it will happen at all, we say, " It will
happen if God wills." This does not mean that God

[3] Compare 11.8 and 21 (Vol. III); 16.5 and 32 (Vol. V, pp.
31, 155).

quam non habuit tunc habebit, sed quia id quod ex
aeternitate in eius inmutabili praeparatum est
voluntate tunc erit.

III

De promissione aeternae beatitudinis sanctorum et
perpetuis suppliciis impiorum.

QUAPROPTER, ut cetera tam multa praeteream,
sicut nunc in Christo videmus impleri quod promisit
Abrahae dicens: *In semine tuo benedicentur omnes*
gentes, ita quod eidem semini eius promisit implebitur,
ubi ait per prophetam: *Resurgent qui erant in monu-*
mentis, et quod ait: *Erit caelum novum et terra nova, et*
non erunt memores priorum nec ascendet in cor ipsorum,
sed laetitiam et exultationem invenient in ea. Ecce ego
faciam Hierusalem exultationem et populum meum
laetitiam, et exultabo in Hierusalem et laetabor in populo
meo, et ultra non audietur in illa vox fletus. Et per
alium prophetam quod praenuntiavit dicens eidem
prophetae: *In tempore illo salvabitur populus tuus*
omnis qui inventus fuerit scriptus in libro. Et multi
dormientium in terrae pulvere (sive, ut quidam interpretati sunt, *aggere*) *exurgent, hi in vitam aeternam et*
hi in opprobrium et in confusionem aeternam. Et alio
loco per eundem prophetam: *Accipient regnum sancti*
Altissimi et obtinebunt illud usque in saeculum et usque
in saeculum saeculorum. Et paulo post: *Regnum,*

---

[1] The paradoxical relation of God's will, man's will and the
course of events is further discussed in *Manual* 26.102.

[2] Genesis 22.18.   [3] Isaiah 26.19 LXX.

[4] Isaiah 65.17–19 LXX.   [5] Daniel 12.1–2.

will then have a new will which he did not have
before, but rather that the event which was from
eternity made ready in his unchanging will is then to
take place.[1]

III

The promise of eternal happiness for the saints,
and endless punishment for the wicked.

To pass over so many other matters, we now see
fulfilled in Christ what God promised to Abraham:
" In thy seed shall all nations be blessed." [2] So
also his promise to that same seed of Abraham will
be fulfilled, where he says through the prophet:
" Those who were in the tombs shall arise." [3] And
again: " There shall be a new heaven and a new
earth, and the former things shall not be remembered
or come into mind, but they shall find gladness and
rejoicing there. Behold, I will make Jerusalem a
rejoicing and my people gladness, and I will rejoice in
Jerusalem and be glad in my people, and the voice
of weeping shall no longer be heard in her." [4] And
through another prophet, saying what he had foretold to the same prophet: " In that time shall all
thy people be saved who are found written in the
book. And many of those who sleep in the dust of
the earth (or " mound," as some translate) shall
awake, some to eternal life, and some to shame and
eternal confusion." [5] And elsewhere in the same
prophet we read: " The saints of the Most High
shall receive the kingdom and possess it for ever,
even for ever and ever." And a little later: " His

inquit, *eius regnum sempiternum.* Et alia quae ad hoc
pertinentia in libro vicensimo posui, sive quae non
posui et tamen in eisdem litteris scripta sunt—
venient et haec sicut ista venerunt quae increduli
non putabant esse ventura. Idem quippe Deus
utraque promisit, utraque ventura esse praedixit,
quem perhorrescunt numina paganorum, etiam teste
Porphyrio, nobilissimo philosopho paganorum.

IV

*Contra sapientes mundi, qui putant terrena hominum
corpora ad caeleste habitaculum non posse
transferri.*

SED videlicet homines docti atque sapientes, contra
vim tantae auctoritatis quae omnia genera hominum,
sicut tanto ante praedixit, in hoc credendum speran-
dumque convertit, acute sibi argumentari videntur
adversus corporum resurrectionem et dicere quod in
tertio de re publica libro a Cicerone commemoratum
est. Nam cum Herculem et Romulum ex hominibus
deos esse factos asseveraret: " Quorum non corpora,"
inquit, " sunt in caelum elata, neque enim natura
pateretur ut id quod esset e terra nisi in terra
maneret." Haec est magna ratio sapientium,
quorum *Dominus novit cogitationes quoniam vanae sunt.*

---

[1] Daniel 7.18, 27.
[2] 20.21 (Vol. VI, 381).
[3] The statement is from Porphyry's work on *Oracular*

kingdom is an everlasting kingdom."[1] Other prophecies which relate to this I have set down in my
twentieth book;[2] some I have not set down, yet
they are written in the same Scriptures. All these
things will come to pass, like the other things which
unbelievers did not think would come, for the same
God promised both and declared that both would
come to pass. Before him the gods of the pagans
tremble, according to the testimony even of Porphyry,
the most renowned philosopher among the pagans.[3]

IV

*Against the wise men of the world who think that
men's earthly bodies cannot be transferred to a
heavenly home.*

In spite of the weight of an authority which, as
it long ago foretold, has converted all kinds of men
to this belief and hope, there are, however, we
must note, wise and learned men who think they are
using a shrewd argument against the resurrection of
the body when they repeat the words of Cicero in the
third book of his *Republic*.[4] When asserting that
Hercules and Romulus were changed from men to
gods, he says: " It was not their bodies that were
carried to heaven, for nature would not allow what
is formed of earth to dwell anywhere except on
earth." This is the great argument of the wise,
whose thoughts " the Lord knoweth, that they are

Philosophy, previously discussed at some length 19.23 (Vol.
VI, 214–231); it is also mentioned 20.24 (VI, 403 f.).
[4] Cicero, *Republic* 3.28.40.

Si enim animae tantummodo essemus, id est sine ullo corpore spiritus, et in caelo habitantes terrena animalia nesciremus nobisque futurum esse diceretur ut terrenis corporibus animandis quodam vinculo mirabili necteremur, nonne multo fortius argumentaremur id credere recusantes et diceremus naturam non pati ut res incorporea ligamento corporeo vinciretur? Et tamen plena est terra vegetantibus animis haec membra terrena, miro sibi modo connexa et implicita.

Cur ergo eodem volente Deo qui fecit hoc animal, non poterit terrenum corpus in caeleste corpus attolli, si animus omni ac per hoc etiam caelesti corpore praestabilior terreno corpori potuit inligari? An terrena particula tam exigua potuit aliquid caelesti corpore melius apud se tenere ut sensum haberet et vitam, et eam sentientem atque viventem dedignabitur caelum suscipere aut susceptam non poterit sustinere, cum de re sentiat et vivat ista meliore quam est corpus omne caeleste? Sed ideo nunc non fit quia nondum est tempus quo id fieri voluit qui hoc quod videndo iam viluit multo mirabilius quam illud quod ab istis non creditur fecit. Cur enim non vehementius admiramur incorporeos animos caelesti corpore potiores terrenis inligari corporibus quam corpora licet terrena sedibus quamvis caelestibus tamen corporeis sublimari, nisi quia hoc videre

---

[1] Psalm 94.11. Augustine's defence of the Christian doctrine of the resurrection extends through Chapter XX. For a summary of the argument see Thonnard's note in *BA* 37, 820–822.

vain." [1]   Suppose that we were mere souls, that is, spirits without a body, and while dwelling in heaven knew nothing of earthly animals.   If we were told that we should be joined to earthly bodies by a marvellous bond in order to give them life, should we not argue much more strongly, refusing to believe this, saying that nature does not allow an incorporeal thing to be bound by a corporeal tie?   And yet the earth is filled with souls which give life to these earthly limbs, marvellously bound up and entangled with them.

Then why cannot an earthly body be raised to be a heavenly body, if God, who gave it life, so wills? For the soul is more excellent than any body, hence even than a celestial body.   Yet it has been possible for it to be tied to an earthly body.   And while so slight a lump of earth can hold enclosed something that is better than even a heavenly body, in order to have life and sensation, will heaven disdain to receive that lump, now that it is living and sentient? Or will heaven not be able to retain it after receiving it, although its sensation and life come from a thing that is better than any heavenly body?   This does not happen now for the reason that it is not yet the time at which God willed it to happen.   Yet a thing which has long seemed common from daily observation is a work of God far more marvellous than that which our opponents refuse to believe.   For why are we not more amazed that incorporeal spirits, which are better than even heavenly bodies, are bound to earthly bodies, than that earthly bodies will be lifted up to a home which, though heavenly, is nevertheless corporeal?   Is it not because we are wont to see the

consuevimus et hoc sumus, illud vero nondum sumus nec aliquando adhuc vidimus? Nam profecto sobria ratione consulta mirabilioris esse divini operis reperitur incorporalibus corporalia quodam modo attexere quam licet diversa, quia illa caelestia ista terrestria, tamen corpora et corpora copulare.

V

De resurrectione carnis, quam quidam mundo credente non credunt.

SED hoc incredibile fuerit aliquando: ecce iam credidit mundus sublatum terrenum Christi corpus in caelum. Resurrectionem carnis et ascensionem in supernas sedes, paucissimis remanentibus atque stupentibus vel doctis vel indoctis, iam crediderunt et docti et indocti. Si rem credibilem crediderunt, videant quam sint stolidi qui non credunt; si autem res incredibilis credita est, etiam hoc utique incredibile est, sic creditum esse quod incredibile est. Haec igitur duo incredibilia, resurrectionem scilicet nostri corporis in aeternum et rem tam incredibilem mundum esse crediturum, idem Deus, antequam vel unum eorum fieret, ambo futura esse praedixit. Unum duorum incredibilium iam factum videmus, ut quod erat incredibile crederet mundus. Cur id quod reliquum est desperatur, ut etiam hoc veniat quod incredibile credidit mundus, sicut iam venit

one marvel daily, and in fact are that marvel ourselves, but are not yet that other thing, nor have we
ever hitherto seen it? For surely if we consult our
sober thoughts, it appears a more marvellous work
of God to join corporeal things in some way to incorporeal than to unite things which, though different,
since one is celestial, the other terrestrial, yet are
nevertheless both of them corporeal.

V

*On the resurrection of the flesh, which some do not
believe, though the world does believe.*

THIS may have seemed incredible once, but lo,
today the world has come to believe that the earthly
body of Christ was raised up to heaven. Both learned
and unlearned have come to believe in the resurrection of the flesh and its ascension to a heavenly home,
while only a few, whether of learned or unlearned,
continue in unbelief and amazement. If it is a
credible thing which they have believed, let unbelievers observe how stupid they are! But if it is
incredible, it is also certainly incredible that an
incredible thing has thus been believed. So these
two incredible things, that is, the resurrection of our
body for eternity, and the world's belief in so incredible a thing, were both predicted by the same God
before either one of them took place. One of the
two we see now accomplished, that is, that the world
should believe what was incredible. Why is it hope-
less that the other thing should come to pass that the
world thought incredible? For this has already

SAINT AUGUSTINE

quod similiter incredibile fuit, ut rem tam incredibilem crederet mundus? Quando quidem hoc
utrumque incredibile, quorum videmus unum alterum
credimus, in eisdem litteris praedictum sit per quas
credidit mundus?

Et ipse modus quo mundus credidit, si consideretur,
incredibilior invenitur. Ineruditos liberalibus disci-
plinis et omnino quantum ad istorum doctrinas
adtinet inpolitos, non peritos grammatica, non
armatos dialectica, non rhetorica inflatos, piscatores
Christus cum retibus fidei ad mare huius saeculi
paucissimos misit. Atque ita et ex omni genere tam
multos pisces, et tanto mirabiliores quanto rariores
etiam ipsos philosophos cepit. Duobus illis incredibilibus, si placet, immo quia placere debet,
addamus hoc tertium. Iam ergo tria sunt incredibilia, quae tamen facta sunt. Incredibile est
Christum resurrexisse in carne et in caelum ascendisse
cum carne. Incredibile est mundum rem tam incredibilem credidisse. Incredibile est homines ignobiles, infimos, paucissimos, inperitos rem tam incredibilem tam efficaciter mundo et in illo etiam doctis
persuadere potuisse. Horum trium incredibilium
primum nolunt isti cum quibus agimus credere,
secundum coguntur et cernere, quod non inveniunt
unde sit factum si non credunt tertium.

---

[1] Grammar, dialectic and rhetoric were the first three of
the seven "liberal arts," known as the trivium in the middle
ages. Dialectic was roughly equivalent to the division of
philosophy known as logic; more precisely it was the art of

come to pass which was likewise incredible, that is, that the world should believe a thing so incredible. For both incredible things, one of which we see, the other believe, were predicted in the same writings, the writings through which the world has come to believe.

And the very manner by which the world has come to believe, when duly considered, seems even more incredible. For it was only a very few fishermen whom Christ sent with the nets of faith out on the sea of the world, men untrained in the liberal arts and altogether untaught in the learning of the pagans, not skilled in grammar, not armed with dialectic, not puffed up with rhetoric.[1] And thus he has taken many " fish " of every kind, including even philosophers—the scarcer they are, the greater the miracle. To these two incredible things, if you please (or rather, because it ought to please), let us add this third; there are then three incredible things which have come to pass. First, it is incredible that Christ has risen in the flesh and ascended to heaven with his flesh. Second, it is incredible that the world should have believed a thing so incredible. Third, it is incredible that a very few unknown, lowly, unskilled men should have been able so effectively to persuade the world and even learned men in it. Of these three the men with whom we are arguing refuse to believe the first, but are compelled actually to see the second, while they cannot find out how it has happened unless they believe the third.

disputation by questioning. About the time of his conversion Augustine had undertaken to prepare a series of textbooks on the liberal arts. See Marrou, *Saint Augustin*, 187–193.

Resurrectio certe Christi et in caelum cum carne in
qua resurrexit ascensio toto iam mundo praedicatur
et creditur.   Si credibilis non est, unde toto terrarum
orbe iam credita est ?   Si multi nobiles sublimes docti
eam se vidisse dixerunt, et quod viderunt diffamare
curarunt, eis mundum credidisse non mirum est, sed
istos adhuc credere nolle perdurum est.   Si autem,
ut verum est, paucis obscuris minimis indoctis eam se
vidisse dicentibus et scribentibus credidit mundus,
cur pauci obstinatissimi qui remanserunt ipsi mundo
iam credenti adhuc usque non credunt ?   Qui
propterea numero exiguo ignobilium infimorum
inperitorum hominum credidit, quia in tam con-
temptibilibus testibus multo mirabilius divinitas se
ipsa persuasit. Eloquia namque persuadentium
quae dicebant, mira fuerunt facta non verba.   Qui
enim Christum in carne resurrexisse et cum illa in
caelum ascendisse non viderant, id se vidisse nar-
rantibus, non loquentibus tantum sed etiam mirifica
facientibus signa credebant.

Homines quippe, quos unius vel ut multum duarum
linguarum fuisse noverant, repente linguis omnium
gentium loquentes mirabiliter audiebant.   Claudum
ab uberibus matris ad eorum verbum in Christi
nomine post quadraginta annos incolumem consti-
tisse, sudaria de corporibus eorum ablata sanandis
profuisse languentibus, in via qua fuerant transituri

In any case, the resurrection of Christ and his ascension to heaven with the flesh in which he rose is now being preached and believed throughout the world. If it is not credible, why is it now believed in every land? If many noble, eminent, learned men had said that they saw it, and had taken pains to spread the news of what they saw, it would not be strange for the world to believe them, and it would be very hard for our opponents still to refuse to believe. But if the world has believed the testimony of a few men who were obscure, unimportant and unlearned when they said and wrote that they saw it (and this is the fact of the matter), why do the few stubborn men who are left still refuse to believe the testimony of the world which now believes? And the world has believed a small number of ignoble, lowly, untaught men for the reason that Divinity itself has made itself much more marvellously convincing in such contemptible witnesses. For the eloquence of those who convinced when they spoke was the miracle of deeds, not words. For those who had not seen Christ risen and ascending to heaven in the flesh believed those who declared that they had seen it, because these men not only spoke, but confirmed their words by marvellous signs.

They knew that these men spoke but one language, or at most two, yet miraculously they suddenly heard them speaking with the tongues of all the nations. They beheld a man lame from his mother's breasts stand up whole after forty years when the apostles spoke to him in the name of Christ. They saw that napkins brought from their bodies were useful to heal the sick. They saw countless men suffering from

positos in ordine innumerabiles morbis variis labo-
rantes ut ambulantium super eos umbra transiret
continuo salutem solere recipere, et alia multa
stupenda in Christi nomine per eos facta, postremo
etiam mortuos resurrexisse cernebant. Quae si ut
leguntur gesta esse concedunt, ecce tot incredibilia
tribus illis incredibilibus addimus, et ut credatur
unum incredibile, quod de carnis resurrectione atque
in caelum ascensione dicitur, multorum incredibilium
testimonia tanta congerimus. Et nondum ad credendum horrenda duritia incredulos flectimus. Si vero
per apostolos Christi, ut eis crederetur resurrectionem atque ascensionem praedicantibus Christi,
etiam ista miracula facta esse non credunt, hoc nobis
unum grande miraculum sufficit, quod eam terrarum
orbis sine ullis miraculis credidit.

VI

*Quod Roma conditorem suum Romulum diligendo deum
fecerit, ecclesia autem Christum Deum credendo
dilexerit.*

RECOLAMUS etiam hoc loco illud quod de Romuli
credita divinitate Tullius admiratur. Verba eius ut
scripta sunt inseram. " Magis est, inquit, in Romulo
admirandum quod ceteri qui dii ex hominibus facti
esse dicuntur minus eruditis hominum saeculis

---

[1] Augustine here mentions well-known miracles of Acts
2.5–11; 3.2–8; 4.22; 19.12; 5.15; 9.36–41; 20.9–12.

various diseases placed in a row in the street in which
the apostles were going to pass, in order that their
shadow might pass over them as they walked, and
they commonly saw the sick immediately recover
their health. Many other amazing things also they
saw done by them in the name of Christ, and finally
they saw the dead raised.[1] If they grant the truth
of this record, then we may add these many miracles
to the three we have named, and to convince them
of one incredible thing, the doctrine of the resurrection of the flesh and its ascent to heaven, we heap up
the abundant evidence of many incredible things.
And still we do not bring the unbelievers to believe,
because of their ghastly hardness of heart. But if
they do not believe that these miracles either were
wrought by the apostles of Christ to confirm their
word as they preached the resurrection and ascension
of Christ, then this one great miracle is enough for
us, that the world has believed it without any
miracles.

VI

*That Rome made a god of her founder Romulus
in her love for him, while the church came to
love Christ as God by believing in him.*

At this point let us also consider a fact that Cicero
finds remarkable in connection with the belief in the
apotheosis of Romulus. I will include his words as he
wrote them: " The case of Romulus is more remarkable in that the other men who are said to have been
transformed into gods lived in ages when men were

fuerunt, ut fingendi proclivis esset ratio, cum imperiti facile ad credendum impellerentur. Romuli autem aetatem minus his sescentis annis iam inveteratis litteris atque doctrinis omnique illo antiquo ex inculta hominum vita errore sublato fuisse cernimus." Et paulo post de eodem Romulo ita loquitur, quod ad hunc pertinet sensum: "Ex quo intellegi potest," inquit, "permultis annis ante Homerum fuisse quam Romulum, ut iam doctis hominibus ac temporibus ipsis eruditis ad fingendum vix quicquam esset loci. Antiquitas enim recepit fabulas, fictas etiam nonnumquam incondite; haec aetas autem iam exculta praesertim eludens omne quod fieri non potest respuit." Unus e numero doctissimorum hominum idemque eloquentissimus omnium Marcus Tullius Cicero propterea dicit divinitatem Romuli mirabiliter creditam quod erudita iam tempora fuerunt, quae falsitatem non reciperent fabularum. Quis autem Romulum deum nisi Roma credidit, atque id parva et incipiens? Tum deinde posteris servare fuerat necesse quod acceperant a maioribus, ut cum ista superstitione in lacte quodam modo matris ebibita cresceret civitas atque ad tam magnum perveniret imperium ut ex eius fastigio velut ex altiore quodam loco alias quoque gentes, quibus dominaretur, hac sua opinione perfunderet, ut non quidem crederent, sed tamen dicerent deum Romulum, ne civitatem cui

---

[1] Cicero, *Republic* 2.10.18–19. The dramatic date of the dialogue is 129 B.C. According to Cicero's reckoning Romulus

more ignorant and more inclined to the invention of tales, and untaught men were easily led to believe them. But we are aware that Romulus lived less than six hundred years ago, when writing and education were long familiar and all the primitive ignorance of uncivilized life had been superseded." And a little farther on he speaks of the same Romulus in words to this effect: "Hence it can be understood that Homer lived many years before Romulus, so that, as men were now learned and times enlightened, there was scarcely any room for the invention of fables. Antiquity accepted myths which were often uncouth inventions, but this age was already notably cultured, so as to mock and reject everything that was impossible." [1] Marcus Tullius Cicero was one of a number of very learned men, and was himself the most eloquent of all men. He declared that it was a miracle for men to believe in the deification of Romulus because the times were now too enlightened to accept lying fables. But who besides Rome, and a small and infant Rome at that, ever believed Romulus a god? After that it was necessary for posterity to maintain what their ancestors had received, so that the city, along with the superstition which it imbibed with its mother's milk, so to speak, might grow and come to rule a great empire. Hence, from its eminence, as from some point of vantage, it could flood other nations also, over which it ruled, with its way of thinking, so that they said that Romulus was a god, though they might not believe it, for they feared to offend a city to which they were in

reigned from 751 to 714 B.C., so that less than 600 years had elapsed since his death.

serviebant de conditore eius offenderent, aliter eum nominando quam Roma, quae id non amore quidem huius erroris, sed tamen amoris errore crediderat.

Christus autem quamquam sit caelestis et sempiternae conditor civitatis, non tamen eum quoniam ab illo condita est Deum credidit, sed ideo potius est condenda quia credit. Roma conditorem suum iam constructa et dedicata tamquam deum coluit in templo; haec autem Hierusalem conditorem suum Deum Christum, ut construi posset et dedicari, posuit in fidei fundamento. Illa illum amando esse deum credidit, ista istum Deum esse credendo amavit. Sicut ergo praecessit unde amaret illa et de amato iam libenter etiam falsum bonum crederet, ita praecessit unde ista crederet, ut recta fide non temere quod falsum, sed quod verum erat amaret. Exceptis enim tot et tantis miraculis quae persuaserunt Deum esse Christum, prophetiae quoque divinae fide dignissimae praecesserunt, quae in illo non sicut a patribus adhuc creduntur implendae, sed iam demonstrantur impletae. De Romulo autem, quia condidit Romam in eaque regnavit, auditur legiturve quod factum est, non quod antequam fieret prophetatum. Sed quod sit receptus in deos, creditum tenent litterae, non factum docent.

Nullis quippe rerum mirabilium signis id ei vere provenisse monstratur. Lupa quippe illa nutrix,

servitude by calling its founder something else than what Rome calls him. Rome had once put faith in this story, not from any love of this error, but still by an error of love.

Although Christ is the founder of a heavenly and eternal city, his city did not believe in him as God because it was founded by him, but rather it is to be founded because it believes. Rome worshipped her founder as a god in a temple when she was already built and dedicated, while our Jerusalem placed its Founder and its God, Christ, in its foundation of faith to the end that it might be built and dedicated. The one city, loving its founder, put faith in him as a god; the other believing its founder to be God, gave her love to him. In the same way as Rome's reason for loving came first, and after it her willingness to believe even a false tale to the credit of her beloved, so Jerusalem's reason for believing came first to preserve her by right faith from a rash love of the false and ensure her love of the true. For, besides the many great miracles which convinced men that Christ is God, there were also divine prophecies, most worthy of belief, which anticipated the event. We no longer believe, as our fathers did, that these are to be fulfilled in him, but rather that they have their fulfilment already demonstrated. Concerning Romulus, however, we hear and read the fact that he founded Rome and reigned there, not that the fact was prophesied before it happened. As for his being received among the gods, history records the belief, but does not teach it as historical fact.

Certainly it is not shown by any miraculous signs that this truly happened to him. To be sure, the

quod videtur quasi magnum extitisse portentum,
quale aut quantum est ad demonstrandum deum?
Certe enim etsi non meretrix fuit lupa illa, sed bestia,
cum commune fuerit ambobus, frater tamen eius non
habetur deus. Quis autem prohibitus est aut
Romulum aut Herculem aut alios tales homines deos
dicere, et mori maluit quam non dicere? Aut vero
aliqua gentium coleret inter deos suos Romulum,
nisi Romani nominis metus cogeret? Quis porro
numeret quam multi quantalibet saevitia crudelitatis
occidi quam Christum Deum negare maluerunt?
Proinde metus quamlibet levis indignationis, quae ab
animis Romanorum si non fieret posse putabatur
existere, compellebat aliquas civitates positas sub
iure Romano tamquam deum colere Romulum. A
Christo autem Deo non solum colendo verum etiam
confitendo tantam per orbis terrae populos martyrum
multitudinem metus revocare non potuit non levis
offensionis animorum, sed inmensarum variarumque
poenarum et ipsius mortis, quae plus ceteris formi-
datur. Neque tunc civitas Christi, quamvis adhuc
peregrinaretur in terris et haberet tamen magnorum
agmina populorum, adversus impios persecutores
suos pro temporali salute pugnavit; sed potius, ut
obtineret aeternam, non repugnavit. Ligabantur,
includebantur, caedebantur, torquebantur, ure-

---

[1] The word *lupa*, "she-wolf," was sometimes used of a harlot. Livy 1.4.7 suggests that Larentia, the foster-mother of

she-wolf who nursed him is supposed to be a great
omen, but what sort of proof, how strange a proof of
his deity is that? For in any case, even if that
" bitch " of a wolf was not a harlot, but a wild animal,[1]
though she was the nurse of both twins alike, his
brother is not for all that regarded as a god. And
who, when forbidden to say that Romulus or Hercules
or other such men were gods, chose to die rather than
not to say it? Or would any of the nations really
worship Romulus among their gods unless fear of the
Roman name compelled them? But who could
count the number who have chosen to die by the
most cruel torture rather than deny that Christ is
God? Likewise fear of displeasure, however slight,
which it was supposed might arise in the minds of the
Romans, if the cult were neglected, compelled some
states under Roman rule to worship Romulus as a
god. But fear could not prevent a great multitude
of martyrs among all the peoples of earth from
worshipping Christ as God, and, what is more, from
openly confessing their faith. And that was not the
fear of a slight displeasure, but of unlimited torture
of every kind, and of death itself, which is feared
more than all else. And the City of Christ, though
still living as a stranger in the world, yet mustering
in her train great companies of nations, did not do
battle then with impious persecutors to gain temporal
safety, but rather, in order to gain eternal safety,
refused to do battle in return. They were bound,
imprisoned, stabbed, tortured, burned, hewn limb

the twins, acquired that reputation and name, thus giving rise
to the wolf-legend. The matter is mentioned also 18.21 (Vol.
V, 437).

bantur, laniabantur, trucidabantur—et multiplicabantur. Non erat eis pro salute pugnare nisi salutem pro Salvatore contemnere.

Scio in libro Ciceronis tertio, nisi fallor, de re publica disputari nullum bellum suscipi a civitate optima, nisi aut pro fide aut pro salute. Quid autem dicat pro salute vel intellegi quam salutem velit, alio loco demonstrans: " Sed his poenis, inquit, quas etiam stultissimi sentiunt—egestate, exilio, vinculis, verberibus—elabuntur saepe privati oblata mortis celeritate. Civitatibus autem mors ipsa poena est, quae videtur a poena singulos vindicare. Debet enim constituta sic esse civitas, ut aeterna sit. Itaque nullus interitus est rei publicae naturalis, ut hominis, in quo mors non modo necessaria est verum etiam optanda persaepe. Civitas autem cum tollitur, deletur, extinguitur. Simile est quodam modo, ut parva magnis conferamus, ac si omnis hic mundus intereat et concidat." Hoc ideo dixit Cicero quia mundum non interiturum cum Platonicis sentit. Constat ergo eum pro ea salute voluisse bellum suscipi a civitate, qua fit ut maneat hic civitas, sicut dicit, aeterna, quamvis morientibus et nascentibus singulis, sicut perennis est opacitas oleae vel lauri atque huius modi ceterarum arborum singulorum lapsu ortuque foliorum. Mors quippe, ut dicit, non hominum singulorum, sed universae poena est civitatis, quae a poena plerumque singulos vindicat.

Unde merito quaeritur utrum recte fecerint

---

[1] Cicero, *Republic* 3.23.34.

from limb, massacred—and yet they multiplied. They fought to save themselves only by disdaining safety for their Saviour's sake.

In the third book, if I am not mistaken, of Cicero's work on the *Republic*, it is maintained that no war should be undertaken by the best kind of state except to keep faith or secure safety. But what he means by saying " safety," or what kind of safety he refers to, appears in another passage where he says: " But from those penalties which even the dullest feel— poverty, exile, bonds, blows—individuals often escape when the chance of a speedy death presents itself. But while death seems to release individuals from punishment, it is in itself a penalty for states. For a state should be so established that it will live for ever. Hence it is not natural for a state to perish in any way, as it is for a man. For in man death is not only inevitable, but often desirable. But when a state is removed, it is wiped away, it is stamped out. It is, on a small scale, as if this whole universe should collapse and perish." [1] Cicero said this because he agrees with the Platonists in thinking that the world will never perish. And so it is clear that the safety for which he was willing to have a state go to war is the safety that ensures its going on here, as he says, for ever, though men one by one die and are born. This is illustrated by the perennial shade of the olive and laurel and other evergreen trees, whose leaves fall one by one and bud anew. Thus death, he says, is a punishment not for individuals, but for the state as a whole, for it commonly frees individuals from punishment.

Hence, it is a proper question whether the

Saguntini, quando universam civitatem suam in-
terire maluerunt quam fidem frangere qua cum ipsa
Romana re publica tenebantur. In quo suo facto
laudantur ab omnibus [1] terrenae rei publicae civibus.
Sed quo modo huic disputationi possent oboedire,
non video, ubi dicitur nullum suscipiendum esse
bellum nisi aut pro fide aut pro salute, nec dicitur,
si in unum simul periculum ita duo ista concurrerint
ut teneri alterum sine alterius amissione non possit,
quid sit potius eligendum. Profecto enim Saguntini
si salutem eligerent, fides eis fuerat deserenda; si
fides tenenda, amittenda utique salus, sicut factum
est. Salus autem civitatis Dei talis est, ut cum fide
ac per fidem teneri vel potius adquiri possit, fide
autem perdita ad eam quisque venire non possit.
Quae cogitatio firmissimi ac patientissimi cordis tot
ac tantos martyres fecit qualem ne unum quidem
habuit vel habere potuit quando est deus creditus
Romulus.

VII

*Quod ut mundus in Christum crederet, virtutis fuerit
divinae, non persuasionis humanae.*

SED valde ridiculum est de Romuli falsa divinitate
cum de Christo loquimur facere mentionem. Verum

---

[1] *The Benedictine edition, along with some MSS., has* hominibus.

---

[1] The story of the Saguntines, destroyed for their loyalty to
Rome, has been told 3.20 (Vol. I, 357).

Saguntines did right when they preferred destruction
for their whole state rather than to break faith with
the Romans. For this deed they are praised by all
citizens of the earthly state. But I do not see how
they could have been following the principle laid
down here that no war should be undertaken except
to keep faith or to secure safety, when there is no
rule that dictates which should be chosen if in a single
moment of peril these two clash, so that one cannot
be maintained without the loss of the other. For
certainly if the Saguntines had chosen safety, they
would have had to desert good faith; and if it was
their duty to keep faith, they had to let safety go,
as they actually did.[1] But the safety [2] of the City
of God is such that it can be kept, or rather gained,
along with good faith, and by means of good faith,
while if faith is lost no one can reach that City.
This way of thinking produced all these many noble
martyrs who were so strong and steadfast in their
courage. But Romulus had not a single such martyr,
nor could he have had, at the time when his divinity
first gained credence.

VII

*The conversion of the world to Christ was accom-
plished by divine power, not by human
persuasion*

It is really absurd to mention Romulus' false claim
of divinity when our subject is Christ. However,

[2] Or "salvation"; in Christian Latin *salus* has acquired
this second meaning.

tamen cum sescentis ferme annis ante Ciceronem
Romulus fuerit atque illa aetas iam fuisse doctrinis
dicatur exculta, ut quod fieri non potest omne
respueret, quanto magis post sescentos annos ipsius
tempore Ciceronis maximeque postea sub Augusto
atque Tiberio, eruditioribus utique temporibus,
resurrectionem carnis Christi atque in caelum ascensionem, tamquam id quod fieri non potest, mens
humana ferre non posset eludensque ab auribus
cordibusque respueret, nisi eam fieri potuisse atque
factam esse divinitas ipsius veritatis vel divinitatis
veritas et contestantia miraculorum signa mon-
strarent; ut terrentibus et contradicentibus tam
multis tamque magnis persecutionibus praecedens in
Christo deinde in ceteris ad novum saeculum secutura
resurrectio atque inmortalitas carnis et fidelissime
crederetur et praedicaretur intrepide et per orbem
terrae pullulatura fecundius cum martyrum sanguine
sereretur. Legebantur enim praeconia praecedentia
prophetarum, concurrebant ostenta virtutum, et per-
suadebatur veritas nova consuetudini, non contraria
rationi, donec orbis terrae, qui persequebatur furore,
sequeretur fide.

since Romulus lived about six hundred years before Cicero, and that age is said to have been already so enlightened by education that it rejected the impossible, how much more would this be true in the time of Cicero himself, six hundred years later? And most emphatically would it be true still later, in the reigns of Augustus and Tiberius, when times were still more advanced. Then the human mind could not have believed in the resurrection of Christ in the flesh and his ascension to heaven, but would have mocked at the story, closed their ears, and rejected it from their hearts as impossible, if the possibility and the fact had not been demonstrated by the divinity of Truth itself, and by the truth of Divinity, as well as by the miraculous signs that confirmed the fact. Thus it happened that, in spite of the fearful obstacle of many great persecutions, men confidently believed and boldly proclaimed the resurrection and bodily immortality of Christ, which came first in time, and that of all others, which will follow in the new age. The seed of faith that was destined to bear fruit throughout the world was being sown, and made more fruitful by the blood of the martyrs. For the preceding proclamations of the prophets were read, the display of mighty works added its support, and men were convinced of the truth, new to their experience but not contrary to reason, until all the world, which once madly persecuted the truth, now followed it in faith.

VIII

*De miraculis quae ut mundus in Christum crederet
facta sunt et fieri mundo credente non desinunt.*

Cur, inquiunt, nunc illa miracula quae praedicatis
facta esse non fiunt? Possem quidem dicere necessaria fuisse, priusquam crederet mundus, ad hoc ut
crederet mundus. Quisquis adhuc prodigia ut credat
inquirit, magnum est ipse prodigium qui mundo
credente non credit. Verum hoc ideo dicunt ut nec
tunc illa miracula facta fuisse credantur. Unde ergo
tanta fide Christus usquequaque cantatur in caelum
cum carne sublatus? Unde temporibus eruditis et
omne quod fieri non potest respuentibus sine ullis
miraculis nimium mirabiliter incredibilia credidit
mundus? An forte credibilia fuisse et ideo credita
esse dicturi sunt? Cur ergo ipsi non credunt?
Brevis est igitur nostra complexio: Aut incredibilis
rei quae non videbatur, alia incredibilia quae tamen
fiebant et videbantur, fecerunt fidem; aut certe res
ita credibilis ut nullis quibus persuaderetur miraculis
indigeret, istorum nimiam redarguit infidelitatem.
Hoc ad refellendos vanissimos dixerim. Nam facta
esse multa miracula quae adtestarentur illi uni
grandi salubrique miraculo quo Christus in caelum
cum carne in qua resurrexit ascendit, negare non
possumus. In eisdem quippe veracissimis libris

---

[1] Only in his later years did Augustine become a believer in
contemporary miracles. His gradual change of viewpoint is
discussed by P. Courcelle, *Recherches sur les Confessions*, 139–
153; G. Bardy in *BA* 37, 825–831; F. van der Meer, *Augustine
the Bishop*, 539–557.

VIII

Miracles which were performed that the world might believe, and are still performed in a believing world. [1]

WHY, our opponents ask, are not those miracles which you say were once performed being performed today? I could, of course, reply that before the world believed, they were necessary to establish faith, and that whoever still asks for wonders in order to be convinced is himself a great wonder, for refusing to believe though all the world believes. But they say this in order that people may not believe in those former miracles either. Then why is it that men everywhere repeat with such assurance that Christ was taken up to heaven in bodily form? Why is it that in enlightened times, when every incredible story was rejected, the world without any miracles so miraculously credited a thing incredible? Or will they say, perchance, that the deeds were credible, and hence were credited? Then why do they not themselves believe? Our argument can be briefly stated: Either the belief in an incredible event which no one saw was established by other incredible events which really took place and were seen, or else the event was so credible that it needed no miracles to confirm it, and so their unreasonable incredulity is refuted. This I might say to put down idle talkers. For we cannot deny that many miracles were performed to confirm the one great, life-giving miracle by which Christ ascended to heaven with the flesh in which he rose from the dead. For it is all written

cuncta conscripta sunt, et quae facta sunt, et propter
quod credendum facta sunt. Haec ut fidem facerent
innotuerunt, haec per fidem quam fecerunt multo
clarius innotescunt. Leguntur quippe in populis ut
credantur, nec in populis tamen nisi credita lege-
rentur.

Nam etiam nunc fiunt miracula in eius nomine, sive
per sacramenta eius sive per orationes vel memorias
sanctorum eius. Sed non eadem claritate in-
lustrantur ut tanta quanta illa gloria diffamentur.
Canon quippe sacrarum litterarum, quem definitum
esse oportebat, illa facit ubique recitari et memoriae
cunctorum inhaerere populorum; haec autem ubicumque fiunt, ibi sciuntur vix a tota ipsa civitate
vel quocumque commanentium loco. Nam plerumque etiam ibi paucissimi sciunt ignorantibus ceteris,
maxime si magna sit civitas. Et quando alibi aliisque
narrantur, non tanta ea commendat auctoritas ut
sine difficultate vel dubitatione credantur, quamvis
Christianis fidelibus a fidelibus indicentur.

Miraculum, quod Mediolani factum est cum illic
essemus, quando inluminatus est caecus, ad multorum
notitiam potuit pervenire, quia et grandis est civitas
et ibi erat tunc imperator et inmenso populo teste res
gesta est concurrente ad corpora martyrum Protasii

---

[1] The *memoria* of a martyr might be either a relic, or a
memorial shrine. The relic might consist of his body, or a
portion of it, or something connected with it. Most miracles
of Augustine's time were associated with relics, but some also
with baptismal water, some with prayer alone.

down in the same trustworthy books, both the deeds which were done, and the faith which was to be confirmed by them. The deeds were published to establish the faith, and through the faith thus established the deeds are becoming still more widely known. For books are being read among all peoples, in order that they may be believed, yet they would not be read among all peoples if they were not believed.

For miracles are still being performed in his name, both through his sacraments, through prayers, and through the relics of his saints.[1] But these miracles do not have the same light of publicity, so as to be known with the same renown as the former. For the canon of sacred Scripture, which it was obligatory to close, explains why those miracles are rehearsed everywhere and fixed in the memory of all peoples, while these later miracles are known only where they are performed and there scarcely by all the people of the city or other local group. For commonly even there very few know the facts, while the rest are unaware of them, especially if the city is large. And when the events are related elsewhere to other people, the weight of testimony is not such that they are easily or promptly believed, even though they are proclaimed to Christian believers by other believers.

To be sure, the miracle which took place at Milan when I was there, when a blind man regained his sight, was not prevented from coming to the knowledge of many. The city is large, the emperor was then in the city, and the deed was witnessed by an immense throng of those who flocked to the spot where the bodies of the martyrs Protasius and

et Gervasii. Quae cum laterent et penitus nescirentur, episcopo Ambrosio per somnium revelata reperta sunt; ubi caecus ille depulsis veteribus tenebris diem vidit.

Apud Carthaginem autem quis novit praeter admodum paucissimos salutem quae facta est Innocentio, ex advocato vicariae praefecturae, ubi nos interfuimus et oculis aspeximus nostris? Venientes enim de transmarinis me et fratrem meum Alypium, nondum quidem clericos sed iam Deo servientes, ut erat cum tota domo sua religiosissimus, ipse susceperat, et apud eum tunc habitabamus. Curabatur a medicis fistulas quas numerosas atque perplexas habuit in posteriore atque ima corporis parte. Iam secuerant eum et artis suae cetera medicamentis agebant. Passus autem fuerat in sectione illa et diuturnos et acerbos dolores. Sed unus inter multos sinus fefellerat medicos atque ita latuerat ut eum non tangerent, quem ferro aperire debuerant.

---

[1] The miraculous discovery of the two bodies in Milan is reported by Augustine in his *Confessions* 9.7.16 and elsewhere, also by Ambrose in several accounts which have survived. The Milanese martyrs had a shrine in Hippo (see p. 227 below). For a critical discussion see Courcelle, cited in note 1, p. 208.

[2] On this interesting medical case I have consulted Dr. Walter Birnbaum, of the staff of the University of California Medical School in San Francisco. I quote extracts from his letter to me:

" A fistula, as we now define it, is an abnormal tube-like passage connecting one hollow viscus organ with another, or a hollow viscus with the outside of the body. . . . From the context it can reasonably be assumed that this was a case of

Gervasius could be seen. Though these bodies were hidden and completely unknown, they were revealed in a dream to the bishop, Ambrose, and so discovered. It was then that the blind man threw off the ancient darkness from his eyes and saw the light of day.[1]

And at Carthage, who except a very few learned of the healing of Innocentius, an ex-advocate of the deputy prefecture? I was present at the time and saw it with my own eyes. When my brother Alypius and I came from overseas, when we were not yet priests but were already serving God, Innocentius had received us as guests, for he with his whole household was very devout, and we were living with him for a time. The doctors were treating him for fistulas which were numerous and complicated in the lowest part of his body behind.[2] They had already operated, and were continuing treatment with remedies known to their profession. In the operation he had suffered sharp and long-continued pain. But the doctors had overlooked one of the many ulcerous recesses, one so deeply hidden that they did not touch it, though it should have been lanced with the others. Finally, all the ulcers which

rectal abscess. Characteristically, a rectal abscess forms in this region as a result of an infection from within the rectum and then is either surgically drained to the outside or ruptures spontaneously, leaving behind a fistulous tract. If treatment is inadequate or too long postponed, other abscesses and fistulas are formed by extension of the original process. . . .

"It is most important in the surgical repair of fistula to remove the entire tract or tracts, particularly the internal opening. Interestingly enough, the case history that you cite could well serve as an example of an overlooked tract or an incomplete operation in our teaching of today."

Denique sanatis omnibus quae aperta curabant, iste remanserat solus cui frustra inpendebatur labor. Quas moras ille suspectas habens multumque formidans ne iterum secaretur (quod ei praedixerat alius medicus domesticus eius, quem non admiserant illi ut saltem videret, cum primum sectus est, quo modo id facerent, iratusque illum domo abiecerat vixque receperat), erupit atque ait: Iterum me secturi estis? Ad illius quem noluistis esse praesentem verba venturus sum? Inridere illi medicum imperitum metumque hominis bonis verbis promissionibusque lenire. Praeterierunt alii dies plurimi nihilque proficiebat omne quod fiebat. Medici tamen in sua pollicitatione sistebant,[1] non se illum sinum ferro sed medicamentis esse clausuros. Adhibuerunt et alium grandaevum iam medicum satisque in illa arte laudatum (adhuc enim vivebat), Ammonium, qui loco inspecto idem quod illi ex eorum diligentia peritiaque promisit. Cuius ille factus auctoritate securus, domestico suo medico qui futuram praedixerat aliam sectionem faceta hilaritate velut iam salvus inlusit.

Quid plura? Tot dies postea inaniter consumpti transierunt ut fessi atque confusi faterentur eum nisi ferro nullo modo posse sanari. Expavit, expalluit nimio turbatus timore, atque ubi se collegit farique

---

[1] Some MSS. and some editors have the word persistebant.

they had opened and cared for were cured, and only this one remained, and on it all their efforts were in vain. He was suspicious of this delay, and very fearful lest they operate on him again. His household physician, who had not even been allowed to look on when the first operation was performed and observe the procedure, had predicted the need of a second. Innocentius had driven him out of the house in anger, and only with difficulty was persuaded to take him back. So now he broke out with the question: "Are you going to cut into me again? Am I going to find that the man whose presence you did not allow was right after all?" They only laughed at the mention of the unskilled doctor, and tried to soothe the man's fear by kind words and promises. Many more days passed, and all that was done proved useless. The doctors, however, continued to promise that they would cure the ulcer with drugs, and not with the knife. They brought in also another doctor, renowned for his skill, the aged Ammonius, who was then still living. He examined the place and made the same promise as the others had made on the basis of their careful study and skill. Reassured by his authority, Innocentius, as if already cured, in merry humour taunted his own doctor for having predicted another operation.

Why prolong the story? After that so many days went by without any improvement that the doctors grew weary and bewildered, and admitted that he could be cured only by the knife. The patient was terrified, and turned white with fear. When he regained composure and could speak, he ordered

potuit, abire illos iussit et ad se amplius non accedere, nec aliud occurrit fatigato lacrimis et illa iam necessitate constricto, nisi ut adhiberet Alexandrinum quendam, qui tunc chirurgus mirabilis habebatur, ut ipse faceret quod ab illis fieri nolebat iratus. Sed postea quam venit ille laboremque illorum in cicatricibus sicut artifex vidit, boni viri functus officio persuasit homini ut illi potius, qui in eo tantum laboraverant quantum ipse inspiciens mirabatur, suae curationis fine fruerentur, adiciens quod re vera nisi sectus esset salvus esse non posset; valde abhorrere a suis moribus ut hominibus, quorum artificiosissimam operam industriam diligentiam mirans in cicatricibus eius videret, propter exiguum quod remansit palmam tanti laboris auferret. Redditi sunt animo eius, et placuit ut eodem Alexandrino adsistente ipsi sinum illum ferro, qui iam consensu omnium aliter insanabilis putabatur, aperirent. Quae res dilata est in consequentem diem.

Sed cum abissent illi, ex maerore nimio domini tantus est in domo illa exortus dolor ut tamquam funeris planctus vix conprimeretur a nobis. Visitabant eum cotidie sancti viri, episcopus tunc Uzalensis, beatae memoriae Saturninus, et presbyter Gulosus

---

[1] Dr. Birnbaum continues: "The reaction of the Alexandrian surgeon could well have occurred today. The manner in which he lauds the previous physicians, minimizes their failure to effect a cure and declines further care of the patient himself is a paragon of medical ethics. Perhaps it is cynical to believe, however, that his inspection revealed

them to go away and not come near him again. Weary with weeping, and finally compelled by necessity, he could think of no alternative except to summon a certain surgeon of Alexandria who then had a marvellous reputation, and let him do what the angry patient would not allow the others to do. But after he came and with his professional eye saw by the scars what the other surgeons had done, he acted as an honest man should and persuaded Innocentius that the doctors who had done so much for him, as he observed with admiration, should rather have the privilege of completing their treatment.[1] He added that the patient really could not be saved without an operation, and that it was entirely contrary to his character to take the case from men whose skilful work and painstaking care he could see and admire in the scars, and so, for doing the little which remained, claim the credit for such a great piece of work. The doctors were thus restored to his favour, and it was decided that the Alexandrian surgeon should stand by while they opened with the knife the abscess which all now agreed was otherwise incurable. The business was put off till the next day.

But when the doctors left, on account of the excessive distress of the master there arose in the house so great a lamentation that it was like the wailing at a funeral, and I could hardly quiet it. Every day holy men would visit him, including Saturninus of blessed memory, then bishop of Uzala, the priest

spontaneous healing of the lesion, and that no further therapy was required in any event." For another fistula which healed spontaneously, see p. 233 below.

ac diaconi Carthaginensis ecclesiae. In quibus erat et ex quibus solus est nunc in rebus humanis iam episcopus cum honore a nobis debito nominandus Aurelius, cum quo recordantes mirabilia operum Dei de hac re saepe conlocuti sumus eumque valde meminisse quod commemoramus invenimus. Qui cum eum sicut solebant vespere visitarent, rogavit eos miserabilibus lacrimis ut mane dignarentur esse praesentes suo funeri, potius quam dolori. Tantus enim eum metus ex prioribus invaserat poenis ut se inter medicorum manus non dubitaret esse moriturum. Consolati sunt eum illi et hortati ut in Deo fideret eiusque voluntatem viriliter ferret.

Inde ad orationem ingressi sumus, ubi nobis ex more genua figentibus atque incumbentibus terrae ille se ita proiecit, tamquam fuisset aliquo graviter inpellente prostratus, et coepit orare. Quibus modis, quo affectu, quo motu animi, quo fluvio lacrimarum, quibus gemitibus atque singultibus succutientibus omnia membra eius et paene intercludentibus spiritum, quis ullis explicet verbis? Utrum orarent alii nec in haec eorum averteretur intentio, nesciebam. Ego tamen prorsus orare non poteram; hoc tantummodo breviter in corde meo dixi: " Domine, quas tuorum preces exaudis, si has non exaudis? " Nihil enim mihi videbatur addi iam posse nisi ut expiraret orando. Surreximus et accepta ab episcopo benedictione discessimus, rogante illo ut mane adessent, illis ut aequo animo esset hortantibus. Inluxit dies qui metuebatur, aderant servi Dei, sicut se adfuturos esse promiserant, ingressi sunt medici,

Gulosus and deacons of the church in Carthage. Among these, and the only one now surviving, was the present bishop Aurelius, whom I must mention with due honour. I have often spoken with him about this event as we recalled the marvellous works of God, and I found that he well remembered what I am relating. When these men were visiting him in the evening according to their custom, he asked them with pitiful weeping to come next morning to witness his funeral rather than his suffering. For he was filled with such fear, after his former sufferings, that he did not doubt that he would die in the hands of the doctors. They consoled him and urged him to trust in God, and submit to his will like a man.

Then we began to pray, and as we knelt and bowed according to custom, he fell down to the earth as if someone had struck him down, and began to pray. Who will ever find words to relate how he prayed— with what feeling, with what emotion, with what a flood of tears, with what groans and sobs that shook all his limbs and almost cut off his breath? Whether the rest continued to pray, or had their attention diverted by all this, I do not know. For my part I was quite unable to pray, but said in my heart only these few words: " Lord, what prayers of thy people dost thou hear, if thou dost not hear these? " For it seemed to me that he could go no farther except to breathe his last while praying. We rose, received the bishop's blessing, and departed. Innocentius asked us to come on the morrow, and the others urged him to keep up his courage. The fearful morning came, the servants of God were there as they had promised, the doctors came in, and all the prepara-

parantur omnia quae hora illa poscebat, tremenda
ferramenta proferuntur adtonitis suspensisque omnibus. Eis autem, quorum erat maior auctoritas,
defectum animi eius consolando erigentibus ad manus
secturi membra in lectulo componuntur, solvuntur
nodi ligamentorum, nudatur locus, inspicit medicus et
secandum illum sinum armatus atque intentus inquirit. Scrutatur oculis digitisque contrectat, tempt-
tat denique modis omnibus—invenit firmissimam
cicatricem. Iam laetitia illa et laus atque gratiarum
actio misericordi et omnipotenti Deo, quae fusa est
ore omnium lacrimantibus gaudiis, non est committenda meis verbis; cogitetur potius quam dicatur.

In eadem Carthagine Innocentia, religiosissima
femina, de primariis ipsius civitatis, in mamilla
cancrum habebat, rem, sicut medici dicunt, nullis
medicamentis sanabilem. Aut ergo praecidi solet et
a corpore separari membrum ubi nascitur aut, ut
aliquanto diutius homo vivat, tamen inde morte
quamlibet tardius adfutura, secundum Hippocratis ut
ferunt sententiam omnis est omittenda curatio. Hoc
illa a perito medico et suae domui familiarissimo
acceperat et ad solum Deum se orando converterat.
Admonetur in somnis propinquante Pascha, ut in
parte feminarum observanti ad baptisterium, quaecumque illi baptizata primitus occurrisset, signaret ei
locum signo Christi. Fecit, confestim sanitas con-

---

[1] Large numbers of people were regularly baptized at Easter.
However, excavations at Hippo show that the baptistry was
small, about six feet by nine, with room only for the bishop, one
person to be baptized, and one deacon or deaconess (Meer, 21).
The sign of the cross was evidently thought more effective when
made by one coming up cleansed by the water of baptism.

tions required for the occasion were made. The
gruesome knives were brought out and all were in
stunned suspense. While those whose encouragement had most weight sustained his failing courage
with consoling words, his limbs were placed on the
couch ready for the hands of the surgeon. The
knots of the bandage were loosed, the place was laid
bare, the doctor examined it, and with knife in hand
looked intently for the abscess which was to be
opened. He searched the place with his eyes, felt
it with his fingers, and examined it in every way,
but found a solid scar. I will not try to express
in words of mine the joy that now arose, the praise
and thanksgiving which was poured out from the lips
of all to the merciful and almighty God, along with
their tears of joy. Let it be imagined rather than
described.

In the same city of Carthage lived Innocentia, a
very devout woman who was descended from the best
families of the city. She had a cancer of the breast,
a thing which doctors say cannot be cured by any
kind of treatment. Hence, the practice is either to
operate and remove the affected part from the body,
or to omit all treatment, as Hippocrates is said to
advise. Thus the patient will live somewhat longer,
but death, though delayed, is sure to come of it. She
had been told this by a skilled doctor well known to
her household, and had turned to God alone in
prayer. As Easter approached she was told in a
dream to watch at the baptistery on the women's
side, and see that the first woman who came towards
her newly baptized made the sign of the cross over the
place.[1] She did so, and healing immediately fol-

secuta est. Medicus sane, qui ei dixerat ut nihil curationis adhiberet si paulo diutius vellet vivere, cum inspexisset eam postea et sanissimam comperisset quam prius habere illud malum tali inspectione cognoverat, quaesivit ab ea vehementer quid adhibuisset curationis,[1] cupiens, quantum intellegi datur, nosse medicamentum quo Hippocratis definitio vinceretur. Cumque ab ea quid factum esset audisset, voce velut contemnentis et vultu, ita ut illa metueret ne aliquod contumeliosum verbum proferret in Christum, religiosa urbanitate respondisse fertur: "Putabam," inquit, "magnum aliquid te mihi fuisse dicturam." Atque illa iam exhorrescente, mox addidit: "Quid grande fecit Christus sanare cancrum, qui quadriduanum mortuum suscitavit?"

Hoc ego cum audissem et vehementer stomacharer in illa civitate atque in illa persona non utique obscura factum tam ingens miraculum sic latere, hinc eam et admonendam et paene obiurgandam putavi. Quae cum mihi respondisset non se inde tacuisse, quaesivi ab eis quas forte tunc matronas amicissimas secum habebat, utrum hoc antea scissent. Responderunt se omnino nescisse. Ecce, inquam, quo modo non taces, ut nec istae audiant quae tibi tanta familiaritate iunguntur. Et quia breviter ab ea quaesiveram, feci ut illis audientibus multumque mirantibus et glorificantibus Deum totum ex ordine, quem ad modum gestum fuerit, indicaret.

[1] *The word* curationis, *"remedy" is omitted by many MSS. and by the Benedictine editors.*

lowed. The doctor who had told her to attempt no treatment, if she wished to prolong her life, examined her afterwards and found her entirely cured. It was by a similar examination that he had learned that she had the disease. So he eagerly asked her what remedy she had used, desiring, as far as can be discovered, to know a treatment by which the precept of Hippocrates might be overthrown. When she told him what had happened he answered with a tone and look that seemed scornful, so that she was afraid he might utter some blasphemous word against Christ. But with scrupulous politeness he is reported to have said: " I supposed that you were going to tell me some great thing." She was already horrified at what he said, but he went on: " How is it a mighty work for Christ to heal a cancer, when he once brought to life a man who was dead four days ? "

When I heard this story I was full of wrath that in that city, when that woman, certainly no obscure person, was concerned, so great a miracle was so unknown. Indeed, I thought she should be admonished, if not rebuked. When she answered that she had not failed to tell about it, I asked the women who happened to be with her then, and were very close friends, whether they had known the story before. They answered that they had never heard of it. " Well," I said, " that's the way you tell about it— so that not even these women who are your best friends hear about it ! " And since I had questioned her only briefly, I made her relate the whole story from beginning to end just as it took place, while the women listened and marvelled greatly and glorified God.

Medicum quendam podagrum in eadem urbe, qui cum dedisset nomen ad baptismum et pridie quam baptizaretur in somnis a pueris nigris cirratis quos intellegebat daemones baptizari eodem anno prohibitus fuisset, eisque non obtemperans etiam conculcantibus pedes eius in dolorem acerrimum qualem numquam expertus est isset magisque eos vincens lavacro regenerationis, ut voverat, ablui non distulisset, in baptismate ipso non solum dolore, quo ultra solitum cruciabatur, verum etiam podagra caruisse nec amplius, cum diu postea vixisset, pedes doluisse quis novit? Nos tamen novimus et paucissimi fratres ad quos id potuit pervenire.

Ex mimo quidam Curubitanus non solum a paralysi, verum etiam ab informi pondere genitalium cum baptizaretur salvus effectus est, et liberatus utraque molestia tamquam mali nihil habuisset in corpore de fonte regenerationis ascendit. Quis hoc praeter Curubim novit et praeter rarissimos aliquos qui hoc ubicumque audire potuerunt? Nos autem cum hoc comperissemus, iubente sancto episcopo Aurelio etiam ut veniret Carthaginem fecimus, quamvis a talibus prius audierimus de quorum fide dubitare non possemus.

Vir tribunicius Hesperius apud nos est. Habet in territorio Fussalensi fundum, Zubedi appellatur. Ubi cum adflictione animalium et servorum suorum domum suam spirituum malignorum vim noxiam perpeti comperisset, rogavit nostros me absente presbyteros ut aliquis eorum illo pergeret, cuius

There was a gouty doctor in the same city who had given in his name for baptism, but on the day before he was to be baptized black, fuzzy-haired boys, whom he took to be demons, appeared in his sleep and forbade him to be baptized that year. He went on without giving in to them, even though they caused excruciating pain by trampling on his feet beyond all that he had ever before experienced. Rather he carried the day, and did not postpone his cleansing in the water of regeneration, to which he was pledged. In the very act of baptism he was freed not only from the pain by which he was being tortured more than usual, but also from the gout itself, and never afterwards, though he lived a long time, did his feet give him pain. Yet who knows this story? I know it at least, and a very few brothers whose ears it could reach,

A former actor of Curubis was cured of paralysis when he was baptized, and also of an abnormal enlargement of his genital organs. Freed of both evils he came up from the font of regeneration as if he had had nothing wrong with his body. Who knows of this, except the people of Curubis, and a very few who have had opportunity to hear the story elsewhere? When I heard of it I arranged that the man should come to Carthage by order of the holy bishop Aurelius, although we had earlier heard the facts from men of whose honesty we could not doubt.

There lives near us an ex-tribune, Hesperius, who has an estate called Zubedi in the region of Fussala. Through the afflictions of his animals and slaves he learned that his household was suffering from damage inflicted by evil spirits. In my absence he asked my priests that one of them should go there to drive off

orationibus cederent. Perrexit unus, obtulit ibi
sacrificium corporis Christi, orans quantum potuit ut
cessaret illa vexatio, Deo protinus miserante cessavit.
Acceperat autem ab amico suo terram sanctam
de Hierosolymis adlatam, ubi sepultus Christus die
tertio resurrexit, eamque suspenderat in cubiculo suo
ne quid mali etiam ipse pateretur. Ast ubi domus
eius ab illa infestatione purgata est, quid de illa
terra fieret cogitabat, quam diutius in cubiculo suo
reverentiae causa habere nolebat. Forte accidit ut
ego et collega tunc meus, episcopus Sinitensis
ecclesiae Maximinus, in proximo essemus. Ut
veniremus rogavit, et venimus. Cumque nobis omnia
rettulisset, etiam hoc petivit, ut infoderetur alicubi
atque ibi orationum locus fieret ubi etiam Christiani
possent ad celebranda quae Dei sunt congregari.
Non restitimus, factum est. Erat ibi iuvenis para-
lyticus rusticanus. Hoc audito petivit a parentibus
suis ut illum ad eum locum sanctum non cunctanter
adferrent. Quo cum fuisset adlatus, oravit, atque
inde continuo pedibus suis salvus abscessit.

Victoriana dicitur villa, ab Hippone Regio minus
triginta milibus abest. Memoria martyrum ibi est
Mediolanensium Protasii et Gervasii. Portatus est
eo quidam adulescens qui cum die medio tempore
aestatis equum ablueret in fluminis gurgite daemonem incurrit. Ibi cum iaceret vel morti proximus
vel simillimus mortuo, ad vespertinos illuc hymnos et

---

[1] Soil from the Holy Land was much prized in Africa, as
appears from a number of inscriptions (Meer, 545).

the demons by his prayers. One of them went, and offered there the sacrifice of the body of Christ, praying as hard as he could that the affliction should cease, and by the mercy of God it did cease at once. This man had also received from a friend some holy earth brought from Jerusalem,[1] where Christ was buried and rose the third day, and this he had hung in his bedroom in case he, too, should suffer some harm from the demons. But when his house was purged of the invaders he pondered what to do with the earth, for out of reverence he was unwilling to keep it in his room any longer. It happened that I and my colleague Maximinus, then bishop of the church in Sinita, were at the time in the vicinity. He asked us to come, and we went. When he had told the whole story he also asked that the earth should be buried somewhere, and a place of prayer be built there, where Christians could assemble to celebrate the worship of God. We made no objection, and the thing was done. There was a young paralytic, a rustic, there, and when he heard the news from his parents, he asked them to carry him to the holy place without delay. When he had been brought, he prayed, and then at once departed on his own feet, completely healed.

There is a country place called Victoriana, less than thirty miles from Hippo Regius, with a shrine of the Milanese martyrs Protasius and Gervasius. A certain young man was carried thither, after he had met a demon while he was bathing his horse in a pool in the river at midday in the summer. While he was lying there nearly dead, or looking very much like one dead, the lady of the estate with her serving

orationes cum ancillis suis et quibusdam sancti-
monialibus ex more domina possessionis intravit
atque hymnos cantare coeperunt. Qua voce ille
quasi percussus excussus est, et cum terribili fremitu
altare adprehensum movere non audens sive non
valens, tamquam eo fuerit alligatus aut adfixus
tenebat, et cum grandi eiulatu parci sibi rogans
confitebatur ubi adulescentem et quando et quo
modo invaserit. Postremo se exiturum esse denun-
tians membra eius singula nominabat quae se
amputaturum exiens minabatur, atque inter haec
verba discessit ab homine. Sed oculus eius in
maxillam fusus tenui venula ab interiore quasi radice
pendebat, totumque eius medium, quod nigellum
fuerat, albicaverat. Quo viso qui aderant—con-
currerant autem etiam alii vocibus eius acciti et se
omnes in orationem pro illo straverant—quamvis eum
sana mente stare gauderent, rursus tamen propter
eius oculum contristati medicum quaerendum esse
dicebant. Ibi maritus sororis eius, qui eum illo
detulerat: " Potens est," inquit, " Deus sanctorum
orationibus, qui fugavit daemonem, lumen reddere."
Tum, sicut potuit, oculum lapsum atque pendentem
loco suo revocatum ligavit orario nec nisi post
septem dies putavit esse solvendum. Quod cum
fecisset, sanissimum invenit. Sanati sunt illic et alii,
de quibus dicere longum est.

Hipponiensem quandam virginem scio. Cum se
oleo perunxisset cui pro illa orans presbyter instil-
laverat lacrimas suas, mox a daemonio fuisse sanatam.

women and some nuns came in according to custom for their evening prayer and hymns, and began to sing. The demon was aroused by this sound, as if struck by a blow, and with a terrible roar grasped the altar. He did not dare, or was unable, to move it, but held it as if he were tied or nailed there. With a loud wail he asked them to spare him, and confessed where, and when, and how he had entered into the young man. Finally, he declared that he would leave him, but named one by one the limbs which he threatened to remove as he left, and while speaking thus he departed from the man. But his eye dropped out on his cheek and hung by a slender vein, like a root on the inside, and its pupil, which had been black, turned white. Others meantime had gathered, summoned by his cries, and all had prostrated themselves in prayer for him. When they saw what had happened, though they were glad that he was now standing in his right mind, they were nevertheless grieved for his eye, and said that a doctor should be summoned. Then the husband of his sister, who had brought him there, said: "God, who drove out the demon, is able through the prayers of the saints to restore his sight." Then, as best he could, he took the eye which had fallen and was hanging, put it back in its place and bound it up with a napkin. He reckoned that this should not be removed until seven days had passed. Then he took it off and found the eye entirely well. Others also were healed at that shrine, but it would take too long to tell of them.

I know a certain virgin at Hippo who anointed herself with oil in which the priest had let his tears fall while praying for her, and she was at once

Scio etiam episcopum semel pro adulescente quem
non vidit orasse illumque ilico daemone caruisse.

Erat quidam senex Florentius Hipponiensis noster,
homo religiosus et pauper. Sartoris se arte pascebat.
Casulam perdiderat et unde sibi emeret non habebat.
Ad viginti martyres, quorum memoria est apud nos
celeberrima, clara voce ut vestiretur oravit. Audierunt eum adulescentes qui forte aderant inrisores
eumque discedentem exagitantes prosequebantur,
quasi a martyribus quinquagenos folles unde vestimentum emeret petivisset. At ille tacitus ambulans
eiectum grandem piscem palpitantem vidit in litore,
eumque illis faventibus atque adiuventibus ad-
prehendit et cuidam coquo, Cattoso nomine, bene
Christiano, ad coquinam conditariam indicans quid
gestum sit trecentis follibus vendidit, lanam comparare inde disponens, ut uxor eius quo modo posset
ei quo indueretur efficeret. Sed coquus concidens
piscem anulum aureum in ventriculo eius invenit
moxque miseratione flexus et religione perterritus
homini eum reddidit dicens: " Ecce quo modo te
viginti martyres vestierunt."

Ad aquas Tibilitanas episcopo adferente Praeiecto
martyris gloriosissimi Stephani memoria veniebat

---

[1] The Twenty Martyrs of Hippo had a basilica of their own
where their feast day was celebrated (Meer, 397, 477 f.).

[2] The *follis* was a copper coin of small value.

[3] The relics of Stephen the first martyr (Acts 7.59) were discovered in Gaza in 415. When the coffin was opened the

healed of a demon. I also know that a bishop once prayed for a young man whom he had not seen, and he was immediately freed from a demon.

There was a certain old man, Florentius, in our city of Hippo. He was a pious man, and poor, and supported himself by the tailor's trade. He had lost his coat and did not have the money to buy another. So he went to the shrine of the Twenty Martyrs,[1] which is the most honoured in our city, and in a loud voice prayed that he might be clothed. Some scoffing youths who happened to be there heard him, and followed him with taunts, saying that he had asked fifty *folles* apiece from the martyrs with which to buy a coat. As he walked along in silence he saw a large fish stranded on the shore, still flopping about. With the encouragement and help of the youths he caught it, and, relating the story, sold it in a delicatessen shop to a cook named Cattosus, a good Christian, for three hundred *folles*.[2] He planned to buy wool with the money, so that his wife might make him a garment to wear, as best she could. But when the cook cut up the fish he found a gold ring in its stomach, and at once, moved with pity and full of the fear of God, returned it to the man, saying: " See how the Twenty Martyrs have clothed you! "

A relic of the most glorious martyr Stephen [3] was being brought to Aquae Tibilitanae by the bishop, Praeiectus, while a great throng accompanied him or

earth shook, it is said, and a fragrant odour was diffused by which seventy-three persons were restored to health. The fame of this event, and the relics themselves, were widely dispersed. Augustine's friend Orosius brought a portion of the relics to Africa. See *DCA* II, 1929 f.; Meer, 475.

magnae multitudinis concursu et occursu.[1] Ibi
caeca mulier ut ad episcopum portantem duceretur
oravit. Flores quos ferebat dedit, recepit, oculis
admovit—protinus vidit. Stupentibus qui aderant
praeibat exultans, viam carpens et viae ducem
ulterius non requirens.

Memorati memoriam martyris quae posita est in
castello Sinitensi, quod Hipponiensi coloniae vicinum
est, eiusdem loci Lucillus episcopus populo prae-
cedente atque sequente portabat. Fistula, cuius
molestia iam diu laboraverat et familiarissimi sui
medici, qui eum secaret, opperiebatur manus, illius
piae sarcinae vectatione repente sanata est; nam
deinceps eam in suo corpore non invenit.

Eucharius est presbyter ex Hispania, Calamae
habitat, vetere morbo calculi laborabat. Per memoriam supradicti martyris quam Possidius illo advexit
episcopus, salvus factus est. Idem ipse postea morbo
alio praevalescente mortuus sic iacebat ut ei iam
pollices ligarentur. Opitulatione memorati martyris,
cum de memoria eius reportata esset et super
iacentis corpus missa ipsius presbyteri tunica, susci-
tatus est.

Fuit ibi vir in ordine suo primarius, nomine Martialis, aevo iam gravis et multum abhorrens a religione
Christiana. Habebat sane fidelem filiam et generum
eodem anno baptizatum. Qui cum eum aegrotantem
multis et magnis lacrimis rogarent ut fieret Christianus, prorsus abnuit eosque a se turbida indigna-

---

[1] *The Benedictine editors, with some manuscript support, read:*
reliquias martyris gl. Stephani, ad eius memoriam veniebat
magnae multitudinis concursus et occursus.

came out to meet him. A blind woman of the place asked to be led to the bishop who was carrying the relic. She gave him the flowers which she was carrying, then, when he returned them, pressed them to her eyes, and immediately gained her sight. Proudly she led an admiring procession of those present, finding her own way, and no longer in need of a guide.

A relic of the same martyr which has been placed in Castellum Sinitense, near the Roman colony Hippo, was being carried by Lucillus, bishop of that place, preceded and followed by the populace. He had long suffered from a troublesome fistula, and was then waiting for his trusted physician to operate on it. But as he carried the holy burden, the ulcer was suddenly healed, for thereafter no trace of it was found on his body.

Eucharius, a Spanish priest who lives at Calama, had long been suffering from a gallstone, and was healed through a relic of Stephen which the bishop Possidius brought to the place. Later he was overcome by another sickness and was lying dead, so that they were tying up his thumbs. But by the help of the same martyr he was revived when his own tunic was brought back from the shrine and spread over his prostrate body.

In the same town lived a man, the first of his order, named Martialis, now burdened with age and hostile to the Christian religion. He had, however, a Christian daughter, and a son-in-law who had been baptized the same year. When he was sick, although they begged him with many tears to become a Christian, he absolutely refused, and drove them away with

tione submovit. Visum est genero eius ut iret ad memoriam sancti Stephani et illic pro eo quantum posset oraret ut Deus illi daret mentem bonam qua credere non differret in Christum. Fecit hoc ingenti gemitu et fletu et sinceriter ardente pietatis affectu. Deinde abscedens aliquid de altari florum quod occurrit tulit, eique cum iam nox esset ad caput posuit, tum dormitum est. Et ecce ante diluculum clamat ut ad episcopum curreretur, qui mecum forte tunc erat apud Hipponem. Cum ergo eum audisset absentem, venire presbyteros postulavit. Venerunt, credere se dixit, admirantibus atque gaudentibus omnibus baptizatus est. Hoc quamdiu vixit in ore habebat: " Christe, accipe spiritum meum," cum haec verba beatissimi Stephani, quando lapidatus est a Iudaeis, ultima fuisse nesciret. Quae huic quoque ultima fuerunt, nam non multo post etiam ipse defunctus est.

Sanati sunt illic per eundem martyrem etiam podagri duo cives, peregrinus unus—sed cives omni modo, peregrinus autem per revelationem quid adhiberet quando doleret audivit, et cum hoc fecerit dolor continuo conquiescit.

Audurus nomen est fundi ubi est ecclesia et in ea memoria martyris Stephani. Puerum quendam parvulum, cum in area luderet exorbitantes boves qui vehiculum trahebant rota obtriverunt, et confestim palpitavit expirans. Hunc mater abruptum ad eandem memoriam posuit, et non solum revixit, verum etiam inlaesus apparuit.

violent resentment. Then the son-in-law decided to go to the shrine of the holy Stephen and there pray for him with all his power, that God might grant him a heart set right, so as not to put off believing in Christ. He did this with great groaning and weeping, with a pure, burning flame of pious emotion. Then, as he left, he took part of the flowers from an altar that he encountered, and when night came he put them by the head of Martialis, then went to sleep. And lo, before dawn the sick man cried out to send for the bishop. He happened to be with me at Hippo, so when Martialis heard that he was gone, he asked the priests to come. They came, he confessed his faith, and while all marvelled and rejoiced, he was baptized. As long as he lived he had on his lips the words, " Christ, receive my spirit," though he did not know that these were the last words of the blessed Stephen, spoken when he was being stoned by the Jews. These were Martialis' last words, too, for he died not long after.

It was also through the help of the same martyr that two citizens and one foreigner were healed of gout. The citizens were healed completely, while the foreigner learned in a dream what remedy he should use when in pain, and when he did this the pain eased immediately.

Audurus is the name of an estate where there is a church, and in it a shrine of the martyr Stephen. While a small boy was playing in an open space, oxen drawing a waggon lunged from the road, crushed him under a wheel, and left him in dying convulsions. His mother picked him up and carried him to the shrine, and he not only revived, but was even found to be uninjured.

Sanctimonialis quaedam in vicina possessione, quae Caspaliana dicitur, cum aegritudine laboraret ac desperaretur, ad eandem memoriam tunica eius adlata est. Quae antequam revocaretur, illa defuncta est. Hac tamen tunica operuerunt cadaver eius parentes, et recepto spiritu salva facta est.

Apud Hipponem Bassus quidam Syrus ad memoriam eiusdem martyris orabat pro aegrotante et periclitante filia eoque secum vestem eius adtulerat, cum ecce pueri de domo cucurrerunt qui ei mortuam nuntiarent. Sed cum orante illo ab amicis eius exciperentur, prohibuerunt eos illi dicere, ne per publicum plangeret. Qui cum domum redisset iam suorum eiulatibus personantem, et vestem filiae quam ferebat super eam proiecisset, reddita est vitae.

Rursus ibidem apud nos Irenaei cuiusdam collectarii filius aegritudine extinctus est. Cumque corpus iaceret exanime atque a lugentibus et lamentantibus exequiae pararentur, amicorum eius quidam inter aliorum consolantium verba suggessit ut eiusdem martyris oleo corpus perungueretur. Factum est, et revixit.

Itemque apud nos vir tribunicius Eleusinus super memoriam martyrum quae in suburbano eius est, aegritudine exanimatum posuit infantulum filium, et post orationem, quam multis cum lacrimis ibi fudit, viventem levavit.

Quid faciam? Urget huius operis implenda promissio ut non hic possim omnia commemorare quae scio; et procul dubio plerique nostrorum, cum haec legent, dolebunt me praetermisisse tam multa quae

When a nun on a nearby estate, called Caspaliana, was desperately ill, her tunic was brought to the same shrine, but before it was brought back, she was gone. Her parents, however, covered her body with the tunic, and she recovered her breath and became well.

At Hippo, at the shrine of the same martyr, a Syrian named Bassus was praying for his daughter, who was dangerously ill, and whose garment he had brought with him. Slaves came running from his house to tell him that she was dead, but while he was praying they were intercepted by his friends and forbidden to tell him, lest he begin wailing in public. When he reached home, the house was echoing with the wails of his family, but he threw his daughter's garment which he was carrying, over her body, and she was restored to life.

Again, it was there in our city that the son of one Irenaeus, a tax-collector, fell sick and died. While the body was lying lifeless and his kindred were in mourning and lamentation and arranging the funeral, while others spoke words of consolation, one of his friends suggested that the body be anointed with oil from the martyr's shrine. It was done, and the man revived.

Likewise, in our city a former tribune, Eleusinus, had an infant son who grew ill and died. He laid the body on a shrine of the same martyr which was in the suburb where he lived, and after praying with many tears he took him up alive.

Now what shall I do? I must go on to finish this work, as I promised, so that I cannot here mention all that I know. Doubtless many of my friends will regret, as they read this, that I have passed over so

utique mecum sciunt. Quos iam nunc ut ignoscant rogo, et cogitent quam prolixi laboris sit facere quod me hic non facere suscepti operis necessitas cogit. Si enim miracula sanitatum, ut alia taceam, ea tantummodo velim scribere quae per hunc martyrem id est gloriosissimum Stephanum facta sunt in colonia Calamensi et in nostra, plurimi conficiendi sunt libri, nec tamen omnia colligi poterunt, sed tantum de quibus libelli dati sunt qui recitarentur in populis. Id namque fieri voluimus, cum videremus antiquis similia divinarum signa virtutum etiam nostris temporibus frequentari, et ea non debere multorum notitiae deperire. Nondum est autem biennium ex quo apud Hipponem regium coepit esse ista memoria, et multis, quod nobis certissimum est, non datis libellis de his quae mirabiliter facta sunt, illi ipsi qui dati sunt ad septuaginta ferme numerum pervenerant quando ista conscripsi. Calamae vero, ubi et ipsa memoria prius esse coepit et crebrius dantur, incomparabili multitudine superant.

Uzali etiam, quae colonia Uticae vicina est, multa praeclara per eundem martyrem facta cognovimus. Cuius ibi memoria longe prius quam apud nos ab episcopo Evodio constituta est. Sed libellorum dandorum ibi consuetudo non est vel potius non

---

[1] These reports, the *libelli miraculorum*, were read in church, and preserved as a permanent record. They were a kind of supplement to the Biblical miracles, serving both for the edification of believers and for the conversion of unbelievers. Augustine was an aggressive promoter of their use. It has been remarked that only after the relics of Stephen came to

many miracles which they know as well as I. I now beg them to excuse me, and consider how endless a task it would be to record them all—a thing which the plan of this work prevents me from doing here. For if I should omit all else, and undertake to write only the miracles of healing which were worked by the agency of this blessed martyr, the most glorious Stephen, in the colonies of Calama and Hippo, many books would have to be written. And even so it will not be possible to collect all the miracles, but only those concerning which reports have been published for public reading. For this is a thing that I decided should be done when I saw that signs of the power of God, like those of antiquity, were often repeated in our time as well, and I thought that they ought not to be allowed to fade from the knowledge of so many people. It is not yet two years that the relics have been in Hippo Regius, and though I am certain that there are many miraculous events of which no report has been published, those published at the time of my writing have almost reached the number of seventy.[1] But at Calama the relics were earlier in existence and reports are published more frequently, so that their number is far greater.

At Uzali also, a colony near Utica, I know that many glorious works have been wrought through the same martyr. His shrine there was set up by the bishop Evodius long before any in our city. But it is not the custom there to publish reports—or rather, it

Africa does he show a notable interest in such miracles. See Bardy in *BA* 37, 585, also 830 f., 835 f.; Meer, 532, 539 f. Stephen's shrine in Hippo was built in 425, and this account dates from 426–427.

fuit; nam fortasse nunc esse iam coepit. Cum
enim nuper illic essemus, Petroniam clarissimam
feminam quae ibi mirabiliter ex magno atque
diuturno in quo medicorum adiutoria cuncta de-
fecerant languore sanata est, hortati sumus, volente
supradicto loci episcopo, ut libellum daret qui
recitaretur in populo, et oboedientissime paruit. In
quo posuit etiam quod hic reticere non possum,
quamvis ad ea quae hoc opus urgent festinare com-
pellar. A quodam Iudaeo dixit sibi fuisse per-
suasum ut anulum capillacio vinculo insereret, quo
sub omni veste ad nuda corporis cingeretur, qui
anulus haberet sub gemma lapidem in renibus inventum bovis. Hoc alligata quasi remedio ad sancti
martyris limina veniebat. Sed profecta a Carthagine,
cum in confinio fluminis Bagradae in sua possessione
mansisset, surgens ut iter perageret ante pedes suos
illum iacentem anulum vidit et capillaciam zonam,
qua fuerat alligatus, mirata temptavit. Quam cum
omnino suis nodis firmissimis sicut erat comperisset
astrictam, crepuisse atque exiluisse anulum suspicata
est. Qui etiam ipse cum integerrimus fuisset inventus, futurae salutis quodam modo pignus de tanto
miraculo se accepisse praesumpsit, atque illud vinculum solvens simul cum eodem anulo proiecit in
flumen.

Non credant hoc, qui etiam Dominum Iesum per
integra matris virginalia enixum et ad discipulos

was not, for perhaps the custom has now been adopted. For when I was there recently I urged Petronia, a distinguished lady who was marvellously healed of a serious and prolonged illness in which all the resources of the doctors had failed, to publish her report for public reading. The bishop Evodius gave his approval and she most willingly obeyed. In it she set down a matter that I cannot refrain from telling here, even though I am pressed to hurry on to the proper theme of this book. She said that she had been persuaded by a Jew [1] to fasten a ring on a hair girdle, to wear under all her clothing, next to her body. The ring was to have under its gem a stone found in the kidney of an ox. Girdled with this supposed remedy she was on her way to the shrine of the holy martyr. She had left Carthage and stopped at her own estate near the river Bagrada, and then as she rose to continue her journey she saw the ring lying before her feet. In surprise she examined the hair girdle which she was wearing, but found it fastened, with all the knots tight, just as it was at first. She then supposed that the ring had broken and fallen off, but she found it also quite intact. So from this marvellous event she took it for granted that she had somehow received a pledge that she would be healed, and so she loosened the girdle and threw it into the river, along with the ring.

Let those refuse to believe this who refuse to believe that the Lord Jesus forced his way from his

---

[1] The Jews of antiquity were proverbially superstitious. Some were noted as fortune tellers, exorcists and the like. See Horace, *Satires* 1.5.100; Juvenal 6.544 and 14.96; Acts 19.13.

ostiis clausis ingressum fuisse non credunt. Sed hoc
certe quaerant et, si verum invenerint, illa credant.
Clarissima femina est, nobiliter nata, nobiliter nupta,
Carthagini habitat. Ampla civitas, ampla persona
rem quaerentes latere non sinit. Martyr certe ipse
quo inpetrante illa sanata est in filium permanentis
virginis credidit, in eum qui ostiis clausis ad discipulos
ingressus est credidit, postremo—propter quod omnia
ista dicuntur a nobis—in eum qui ascendit in caelum
cum carne in qua resurrexerat credidit. Et ideo
per eum tanta fiunt, quia pro ista fide animam posuit.[1]
Fiunt ergo etiam nunc multa miracula eodem Deo
faciente, per quos vult et quem ad modum vult,
qui et illa quae legimus fecit. Sed ista nec similiter
innotescunt neque, ut non excedant [2] animo quasi
glarea memoriae, crebra lectione tunduntur. Nam
et ubi diligentia est, quae nunc apud nos esse coepit
ut libelli eorum qui beneficia percipiunt recitentur in
populo, semel hoc audiunt qui adsunt pluresque non
adsunt, ut nec illi qui adfuerunt post aliquot dies quod
audierunt mente retineant, et vix quisque reperiatur
illorum qui ei quem non adfuisse cognoverit indicet
quod audivit.

[1] *The Benedictine editors, with some MS. support, add* suam.
[2] *Some editors and MSS. have* excidant.

---

[1] The belief in the perpetual virginity of Mary, miraculous
in the parturition as well as in the conception of Jesus, goes
back to an early apocryphal gospel, and was known to Cle-
ment of Alexandria (about A.D. 200). See M. R. James, *The
Apocryphal New Testament*, 46 f.; J. Quasten *Patrology* I,
120 f.

[2] John 20.19.

mother's womb, which was intact and in virgin state,[1] and that he entered a room whose doors were closed to join his disciples.[2] But let them at least investigate this marvel, and if they find it true, let them believe those other miracles. The woman is of high estate, of noble birth, married to a noble, and lives at Carthage. The renown of the city and of the woman ensure that the facts cannot be hidden from any who look into the matter. Certainly the martyr himself, by whose intercession she was healed, believed on the Son of a mother who remained always a virgin, and believed on him who came to his disciples through closed doors, and, to conclude, believed on him who ascended to heaven with the body in which he had risen again—and this is the point that occasioned all my argument. Furthermore, these miracles are worked through Stephen just because he laid down his life for this faith. So even now many miracles are wrought, as God works them through those whom he chooses and in the manner he chooses, the same God who did those things which we read in the Scriptures. But these later miracles are not as well known, nor are they, like gravel, pounded into the memory by frequent reading so as not to slip from the mind. For even where care is taken, as in Hippo today, to see that the reports of those who receive such favours are read to the people, those who are present hear it but once, and a larger number are not present. The result is that those who were present forget what they have heard after a few days, and you can hardly find anyone who reports what he has heard to anyone who he discovers was not there.

Unum est apud nos factum non maius quam illa
quae dixi, sed tam clarum atque inlustre miraculum
ut nullum arbitrer esse Hipponiensium qui hoc non
vel viderit vel didicerit, nullum qui oblivisci ulla
ratione potuerit. Decem quidam fratres (quorum
septem sunt mares, tres feminae) de Caesarea Cappa-
dociae, suorum civium non ignobiles maledicto matris,
recenti patris eorum obitu destitutae, quae iniuriam
sibi ab eis factam acerbissime tulit, tali poena sunt
divinitus coherciti ut horribiliter quaterentur omnes
tremore membrorum. In qua foedissima specie
oculos suorum civium non ferentes, quaqua versum
cuique ire visum est, toto paene vagabantur orbe
Romano. Ex his etiam ad nos venerunt duo, frater
et soror, Paulus et Palladia, multis aliis locis miseria
diffamante iam cogniti. Venerunt autem ante
Pascha ferme dies quindecim, ecclesiam cotidie et in
ea memoriam gloriosissimi Stephani frequentabant,
orantes ut iam sibi placaretur Deus et salutem
pristinam redderet. Et illic et quacumque ibant
convertebant in se civitatis aspectum. Nonnulli
qui eos alibi viderant causamque tremoris eorum
noverant aliis, ut cuique poterant, indicabant.

Venit et Pascha, atque ipso die dominico mane,
cum iam frequens populus praesens esset, et loci
sancti cancellos ubi martyrium erat idem iuvenis

---

[1] The story of Paulus and Palladia is the subject of a number of Augustine's sermons, and the official *libellus* is preserved
(*Sermons* 320–324; *Sermon* 322 is the *libellus*). For a full account see Meer, 549–553.

There is one miracle that has occurred among us, no greater than those I have mentioned, but so famous and illustrious that I think there is no one at Hippo who did not either see it or learn of it, and certainly no one could possibly forget it. There were ten children, seven sons and three daughters, belonging to Caesarea of Cappadocia, and distinguished among their fellow-citizens. They were cursed by their mother shortly after she was widowed by their father's death, for she bitterly resented a wrong they had done her. By divine power they were subjected to a punishment whereby they all shook with a fearful tremor of their limbs. In this most loathsome condition they could not bear to be seen by their fellow-citizens, and so wandered over almost all the Roman world, wherever each thought best to go. Two of them came to our city, a brother and sister named Paulus and Palladia, who were already well known in many other places since their wretched state spread a report of them.[1] They came about fifteen days before Easter, visiting the church every day, especially the shrine of the glorious Stephen that was there, and praying that God might be reconciled to them and restore them to their former health. Both there and wherever they went they drew the gaze of the city upon themselves. Some who had seen them elsewhere and had learned the cause of their tremor reported it to others as they had occasion.

Easter came, and early in the morning on the Lord's day a great throng was already there. While the young man was praying and holding the railing of the sacred place where the relics were, he suddenly

orans teneret, repente prostratus est et dormienti
simillimus iacuit, non tamen tremens, sicut etiam per
somnum solebant.[1] Stupentibus qui aderant atque
aliis paventibus, aliis dolentibus, cum eum quidam
vellent erigere, nonnulli prohibuerunt et potius
exitum expectandum esse dixerunt. Et ecce surrexit, et non tremebat, quoniam sanatus erat, et
stabat incolumis, intuens intuentes. Quis ergo se
tenuit a laudibus Dei? Clamantium gratulantium-
que vocibus ecclesia usquequaque completa est.
Inde ad me curritur, ubi sedebam iam processurus.
Inruit alter quisque post alterum, omnis posterior
quasi novum quod alius prior dixerat nuntiantes;
meque gaudente et apud me Deo gratias agente
ingreditur etiam ipse cum pluribus. Inclinatur ad
genua mea, erigitur ad osculum meum. Procedimus
ad populum, plena erat ecclesia, personabat vocibus
gaudiorum: Deo gratias, Deo laudes! nemine tacente
hinc atque inde clamantium. Salutavi populum, et
rursus eadem ferventiore voce clamabant. Facto
tandem silentio scripturarum divinarum sunt lecta
sollemnia. Ubi autem ventum est ad mei sermonis
locum, dixi pauca pro tempore et pro illius iucunditate
laetitiae. Magis enim eos in opere divino quandam
Dei eloquentiam non audire, sed considerare permisi.

Nobiscum homo prandit et diligenter nobis
omnem suae fraternaeque ac maternae calamitatis
indicavit historiam. Sequenti itaque die post ser-

---

[1] *The Benedictines, with some MSS., have* solebat, " *as he
was wont to do.*"

fell prostrate and lay still, very much as if he were asleep, but not shaking, as they were wont to do even in sleep. The bystanders were amazed, some in terror, some in sympathy. Some wished to lift him up, while others objected and said that they should rather wait to see how it would end. And lo, he arose, and was not shaking, for he was healed, and stood there well, looking at them as they looked at him. So who could refrain from praising God? The whole church was filled with cries of joy and thanksgiving. Then people ran to me where I was sitting, just ready to enter the church. One after another they came in, each arrival announcing as news what another had already told me. While I was rejoicing and silently thanking God the man himself came in with several others and knelt at my knees. I raised him up and kissed him, and we went in to the people. The church was full and was echoing with shouts of joy. No one was silent, but on this side and on that they were crying, " God be thanked," and " God be praised." I greeted the people, and again they cried out as before, and even more fervently. When at last there was silence, the appointed portions of the sacred writings were read. But when the time for my sermon came, I made only a few remarks appropriate to the time and the joy of that rejoicing. For I preferred to let them ponder the eloquence, so to speak, of God as he declared himself through his divine action instead of hearing about it.

The man dined with me and told me in detail the whole story of his calamity, and that of his mother, brothers and sisters. On the next day after the ser-

monem redditum narrationis eius libellum in cras-
tinum populo recitandum promisi. Quod cum ex
dominico Paschae die tertio fieret in gradibus exedrae
in qua de superiore loquebar loco, feci stare ambos
fratres cum eorum legeretur libellus. Intuebatur
populus universus sexus utriusque unum stantem
sine deformi motu, alteram membris omnibus contre-
mentem. Et qui ipsum non viderant, quid in eo
divinae misericordiae factum esset in eius sorore
cernebant. Videbant enim quid in illo gratulandum,
quid pro illa esset orandum. Inter haec recitato
eorum libello de conspectu populi eos abire praecepi,
et de tota ipsa causa aliquanto diligentius coeperam
disputare, cum ecce me disputante voces aliae de
memoria martyris novae gratulationis audiuntur.
Conversi sunt eo qui me audiebant coeperuntque
concurrere. Illa enim ubi de gradibus descendit in
quibus steterat ad sanctum martyrem orare per-
rexerat. Quae mox ut cancellos adtigit, conlapsa
similiter velut in somnum sana surrexit. Dum ergo
requireremus quid factum fuerit unde ille strepitus
laetus extiterit, ingressi sunt cum illa in basilicam
in qua eramus, adducentes eam sanam de martyris
loco. Tum vero tantus ab utroque sexu admirationis
clamor exortus est, ut vox continuata cum lacrimis
non videretur posse finiri. Perducta est ad eum
locum, ubi paulo ante steterat tremens. Exultabant
eam similem fratri cui doluerant remansisse dis-

---

[1] The *exedra* of the basilica was a recess provided with
chairs, of circular form, which later became the apse.

mon I promised that the report of his story would be
read aloud to the people on the following day.   While
this was being done, on the third day after Easter,
during the reading of the report I arranged for
brother and sister both to stand on the steps of the
exedra,[1] whence I was wont to address the people
from my place above them.   All the people, men and
women, watched the man standing without any
abnormal movement, while the girl shook in all her
limbs.   Those who had not seen him before could
perceive what the mercy of God had done for him by
comparing him with his sister, for they saw what to
give thanks for in his case and what to pray for in
hers.   Meanwhile, when the report was read I bade
them leave their place before the people, and began
to discuss the whole case somewhat more searchingly.
Suddenly, as I spoke, other cries of fresh congratula-
tion were heard from the shrine of the martyr.
Those who were listening to me turned and began to
rush to the spot.   For when the girl had gone down
from the steps where she stood, she had hurried to
pray at the holy martyr's shrine, and as soon as she
touched the railing she likewise fell down as if asleep,
and then rose healed.   So while I was inquiring what
had happened to cause the joyful noise, they came in
with her into the basilica where I was, bringing her
from the shrine of the martyr, sound and well.
Then indeed such a cry of wonder arose, from men
and women alike, that the persistent shouting and
weeping, it seemed, could never come to an end.
She was led to the place where she had stood shaking
a little while before.   They rejoiced that she was now
like her brother, where before they had grieved that

similem, et nondum fusas preces suas pro illa, iam tamen praeviam voluntatem tam cito exauditam esse cernebant. Exultabant in Dei laudem voce sine verbis, tanto sonitu quantum nostrae aures ferre vix possent. Quid erat in cordibus exultantium nisi fides Christi, pro qua Stephani sanguis effusus est?

IX

Quod universa miracula quae per martyres in Christi nomine fiunt ei fidei testimonium ferant qua in Christum martyres crediderunt.

Cui nisi huic fidei adtestantur ista miracula, in qua praedicatur Christus resurrexisse in carne et in caelum ascendisse cum carne? Quia et ipsi martyres huius fidei martyres, id est huius fidei testes, fuerunt; huic fidei testimonium perhibentes mundum inimicissimum et crudelissimum pertulerunt eumque non repugnando, sed moriendo vicerunt. Pro ista fide mortui sunt qui haec a Domino inpetrare possunt propter cuius nomen occisi sunt. Pro hac fide praecessit eorum mira patientia, ut in his miraculis tanta ista potentia sequeretur. Nam si carnis in aeternum resurrectio vel non praevenit in Christo, vel non ventura est sicut praenuntiatur a Christo vel sicut praenuntiata est a prophetis a quibus praenuntiatus est Christus, cur et mortui tanta possunt qui pro ea fide qua haec resurrectio praedicatur occisi sunt? Sive enim Deus ipse per se ipsum miro

---

[1] The Greek word *martyres* means "witnesses."

she had remained unlike him, and they perceived that although they had not yet offered their prayers for her, God had thus speedily heard their unexpressed desire. They cried out in praise of God, in shouts without words, a sound so loud that my ears could scarce endure it. What was in the hearts of the exulting people if it was not faith in Christ for which the blood of Stephen was shed?

IX

All the miracles that are worked through the martyrs in the name of Christ bear witness to the faith by which the martyrs believed in Christ.

WHAT is it that these miracles attest, except the faith which proclaims that Christ rose in the flesh and with it ascended to heaven? For the martyrs themselves were " martyrs " that is, witnesses, of this faith.[1] In giving their testimony to the faith they endured the enmity and cruelty of the world, and overcame it, not by fighting but by dying. For this faith they died, and now they are able to obtain favours from the Lord for whose name they were slain; for this faith they first suffered with marvellous patience, so that the mighty power seen in these miracles came as a result. For if the resurrection of the flesh for eternity did not take place first in Christ, or is not going to take place as foretold by Christ and by the prophets who foretold Christ's coming, then why can such miracles be wrought even by dead men who were slain for the faith that proclaims the resurrection? For it matters not whether

modo quo res temporales operatur aeternus, sive per
suos ministros ista faciat. Et eadem ipsa, quae per
ministros facit, sive quaedam faciat etiam per
martyrum spiritus sicut per homines adhuc in corpore
constitutos, sive omnia ista per angelos, quibus
invisibiliter, incorporaliter, inmutabiliter imperat,
operetur, ut quae per martyres fieri dicuntur eis
orantibus tantum et inpetrantibus, non etiam
operantibus fiant. Sive alia istis alia illis modis qui
nullo modo conprehendi a mortalibus possunt, ei
tamen adtestantur haec fidei in qua carnis in aeternum resurrectio praedicatur.

X

Quanto dignius honorentur martyres qui ideo multa
mira obtinent ut Deus verus colatur, quam
daemones qui ob hoc quaedam faciunt ut
ipsi dii esse credantur.

Hic forte dicturi sunt etiam deos suos aliqua mira
fecisse. Bene, si iam incipiunt deos suos nostris
mortuis hominibus comparare. An dicent etiam se
habere deos ex hominibus mortuis, sicut Herculem,
sicut Romulum, sicut alios multos quos in deorum
numerum receptos opinantur? Sed nobis martyres

God does these things in person, in the marvellous way in which the Eternal brings about events in time, or does them through his servants. Nor in the case of deeds done through his servants does it matter whether he does some deeds through the spirits of martyrs, just as he does some through men still living in the body, or does all these things through angels, to whom he gives commands in a manner invisible, incorporeal and immutable, so that the things said to be done through martyrs are done through their prayers and intercessions alone, and not by any action on their part. Or he may do some things in the ways I have stated while other things are wrought in such ways as cannot be understood at all by mortals; still these things that are done bear witness to that faith in which the resurrection of the dead for eternity is proclaimed.

X

That the martyrs, who obtain many miracles in order that the true God may be worshipped, are far more worthy of honour than the demons who do some miracles in order to make people believe that they themselves are gods.

HERE, perhaps, they will say that their gods also have done some marvellous deeds. Well done, if they now begin to compare their gods with our dead men. Or will they say that they, too, have gods from the ranks of dead men—like Hercules, Romulus and many others who, they suppose, have been admitted to the catalogue of gods? But for us martyrs

non sunt dii, quia unum eundemque Deum et
nostrum scimus et martyrum. Nec tamen miraculis
quae per memorias nostrorum martyrum fiunt ullo
modo sunt comparanda miracula quae facta per
templa perhibentur illorum. Verum si qua similia
videntur, sicut a Moyse magi Pharaonis, sic eorum dii
victi sunt a martyribus nostris.

Fecerunt autem illa daemones eo fastu inpurae
superbiae quo eorum dii esse voluerunt. Faciunt
autem ista martyres, vel potius Deus aut cooperan-
tibus aut orantibus eis, ut fides illa proficiat, qua eos
non deos nostros esse, sed unum Deum nobiscum
habere credamus. Denique illi talibus diis suis et
templa aedificaverunt et statuerunt aras et sacerdotes
instituerunt et sacrificia fecerunt. Nos autem
martyribus nostris non templa sicut diis, sed memorias, sicut hominibus mortuis quorum apud Deum
vivunt spiritus, fabricamus. Nec ibi erigimus altaria
in quibus sacrificemus martyribus, sed uni Deo et
martyrum et nostro. Ad quod sacrificium sicut
homines Dei qui mundum in eius confessione vicerunt
suo loco et ordine nominantur, non tamen a sacerdote
qui sacrificat invocantur. Deo quippe, non ipsis
sacrificat, quamvis in memoria sacrificet eorum, quia
Dei sacerdos est, non illorum. Ipsum vero sacri-

---

[1] Exodus 7.7–12; 8.18 f.
[2] From the time of Cyprian local martyrs were com-

are not gods, because we know that both we and the martyrs have one and the same God. And still the miracles that are reported to be worked in their temples are by no means worthy to be compared with those that are worked through the relics of our martyrs. And if any do seem similar, their gods have been defeated by our martyrs as the magicians of Pharaoh were defeated by Moses.[1]

Their acts were performed by demons in the arrogance of unholy pride, whereby they wished to become the gods of the people. Our miracles, on the other hand, are performed by martyrs—or rather by God, either because of the prayers or by the agency of the martyrs—in order that the faith may profit which teaches us that martyrs are not our gods, but have one God in company with us. Finally, the pagans have built temples, set up altars, instituted priesthoods and made sacrifices to such gods of their own, while we do not build temples to our martyrs as if they were gods, but construct memorial shrines for them as dead men whose spirits are living with God. And there we erect altars on which to offer sacrifices, not to the martyrs, but to the one God of the martyrs and ourselves. And at this sacrifice martyrs are named with their proper status and rank,[2] as men of God who have overcome the world by confessing his name, but they are not invoked by the priest who offers the sacrifice. For he is sacrificing to God, not to them, even though the sacrifice is made in their shrine, because he is God's priest, not theirs. In fact, the sacrifice is the

memorated in the liturgy, along with Biblical saints and others. Later a distinction was made, and each group assigned a fixed place. See *DCA* II, 1836 f.

ficium corpus est Christi, quod non offertur ipsis quia hoc sunt et ipsi.

Quibus igitur potius credendum est miracula facientibus? Eisne qui se ipsos volunt haberi deos ab his quibus ea faciunt, an eis qui ut in Deum credatur—quod et Christus est—faciunt quidquid mirabile faciunt? Eisne qui sacra sua etiam crimina sua esse voluerunt, an eis qui nec laudes suas volunt esse sacra sua, sed totum quod veraciter laudantur ad eius gloriam proficere in quo laudantur? In Domino quippe laudantur animae eorum. Credamus ergo eis et vera dicentibus et mira facientibus. Dicendo enim vera passi sunt, ut possint facere mira. In eis veris est praecipuum quod Christus resurrexit a mortuis et immortalitatem resurrectionis in sua carne primus ostendit, quam nobis adfuturam vel in principio novi saeculi vel in huius fine promisit.

XI

Contra Platonicos qui de naturalibus elementorum
ponderibus argumentantur terrenum corpus in
caelo esse non posse.

CONTRA quod magnum Dei donum ratiocinatores isti quorum *cogitationes novit Dominus quoniam vanae*

---

[1] Compare 19.23 (Vol. VI, 229 f.), and J. E. C. Welldon's essay, "Augustine's Theory of Sacrifice," in his edition of the *City of God* II, 670–675.

body of Christ, and is not offered to them, because they themselves are the mystic body of Christ.[1]

In whom, therefore, should we preferably put our trust, when they perform miracles? In those who wish themselves to be regarded as gods by the men whom they serve, or in those who do marvels only to produce faith in God—for Christ also is God? In those who decreed that even their crimes should be their sacred rites, or in those who do not wish even their praiseworthy deeds to be enacted as rites but wish all for which they are rightly praised to contribute to the glory of him in whose name they receive praise? For it is in the Lord's name that their souls receive honourable mention. Let us therefore put our trust in them, since they have both: words that are true and deeds that are wondrous. For they suffered because they spoke the truth, and so are able to do marvellous deeds. Foremost among those true words is this, that Christ rose from the dead and in his own flesh first displayed the immortality of the resurrection. And he has promised that we shall have such a resurrection at the beginning of the new age, or, if you prefer, at the end of this.

XI

Against the Platonists who argue from the natural weight of the elements that an earthly body cannot be in heaven.

AGAINST this great gift of God those reasoners "whose thoughts the Lord knoweth, that they are

257

sunt de ponderibus elementorum argumentantur; quoniam scilicet magistro Platone didicerunt mundi duo corpora maxima atque postrema duobus mediis, aere scilicet et aqua, esse copulata atque coniuncta. Ac per hoc, inquiunt, quoniam terra abhinc sursum versus est prima, secunda aqua super terram, tertius aer super aquam, quartum super aera caelum, non potest esse terrenum corpus in caelo. Momentis enim propriis ut ordinem suum teneant singula elementa librantur. Ecce qualibus argumentis omnipotentiae Dei humana contradicit infirmitas, quam possidet vanitas. Quid ergo faciunt in aere terrena tot corpora, cum a terra sit aer tertius? Nisi forte qui per plumarum et pennarum levitatem donavit avium terrenis corporibus ut portentur in aere, inmortalibus factis corporibus hominum non poterit donare virtutem qua etiam in summo caelo habitare valeant. Animalia quoque ipsa terrena quae volare non possunt, in quibus et homines sunt, sicut sub aqua pisces quae sunt aquarum animalia, ita sub terra vivere debuerunt. Cur ergo non saltem de secundo id est de aquis, sed de elemento tertio terrenum animal carpit hanc vitam? Quare, cum pertineat ad terram, in secundo quod super terram est elemento vivere si cogatur, continuo suffocatur, et ut vivat vivit in tertio? An errat hic ordo elementorum, vel potius non in natura rerum, sed in istorum argumentationibus deficit? Omitto dicere, quod iam in tertio decimo libro dixi, quam multa gravia terrena

---

[1] *Timaeus* 32 A–B.

vain," draw an argument from the weights of the
elements. They have learned from their master
Plato,[1] that the two greatest and outermost elements
are conjoined and united by two in the middle, that
is, air and water. Hence they say that since the
earth, going up from our level, is first, and water
above the earth second, and air above the water third,
and heaven above the air fourth, there can be no
earthly body in heaven. For the several elements
are held in equilibrium by their differences in weight,
so as to keep their proper order. There you see the
sort of arguments whereby human weakness, a prey
to vanity, contradicts the omnipotence of God!
What business have all these earthly bodies in the air,
when the air is third from the earth? Cannot he
who with feathers and wings gave lightness to the
earthly bodies of birds, that they might soar in the
air, bestow a special power on the bodies of men, when
he makes them immortal, that will enable them to
dwell even in the highest heaven? And the terrestrial animals also which cannot fly, including men,
should have dwelt under earth, just as fish, who are
water animals, live under water. Or why does not
the terrestrial animal at least depend for its life on
the second element, water, instead of on the air, the
third? Why is it, then, that though it belongs to
earth it is suffocated at once if it should be compelled
to live in the second element, next above the earth,
and in order to live at all, must live in the third? Is
there a mistake here in the order of the elements?
Or is the mistake in their arguments, rather than
in the nature of things? I will not repeat what I
have already said in the thirteenth book, how many

sint corpora, sicut plumbum, et formam tamen ab artifice accipiant qua natare valeant super aquam. Et ut accipiat qualitatem corpus humanum qua ferri in caelum et esse possit in caelo omnipotenti artifici contradicitur?

Iam vero contra illud quod iam dixi superius, etiam istum considerantes atque tractantes elementorum ordinem quo confidunt, non inveniunt omnino quod dicant. Sic est enim hinc sursum versus terra prima, aqua secunda, tertius aer, quartum caelum, ut super omnia sit animae natura. Nam et Aristoteles quintum corpus eam dixit esse et Plato nullum. Si quintum esset, certe superius esset ceteris. Cum vero nullum est, multo magis superat omnia. In terreno ergo quid facit corpore? In hac mole quid agit subtilior omnibus? In hoc pondere quid agit levior omnibus? In hac tarditate quid agit celerior omnibus? Itane per huius tam excellentis naturae meritum non poterit effici ut corpus eius levetur in caelum? Et cum valeat nunc natura corporum terrenorum deprimere animas deorsum, aliquando et animae levare sursum terrena corpora non valebunt?

Iam si ad eorum miracula veniamus quae facta a diis suis opponunt martyribus nostris, nonne etiam ipsa pro nobis facere et nobis reperientur omnino proficere? Nam inter magna miracula deorum suorum profecto magnum illud est quod Varro commemorat, Vestalem virginem, cum periclitaretur

---

[1] Cicero, *Academica* 1.7.26. Aristotle speaks, not of a fifth body (our " quintessence "), but of a soul-substance which is the first of the elements, above the other four. See *Generation of Animals* 2.3, 736–7, with note by A. L. Peck in the Loeb edition, p. 170 f.

earthly bodies there are, such as lead, which can nevertheless receive a shape from the artisan that will make them float on the water. Is the heavenly Artisan, then, denied the power to give the human body such properties as will make it soar heavenward and exist in that element?

Now against the argument that I have just used, no examination or discussion of the order of elements, in which they put their trust, affords any basis for a reply. For though the earth, beginning with our level, is first, water second, air third and heaven fourth, above all these is the natural substance of soul. Aristotle says that it is a fifth body,[1] Plato that it is not body at all. If it were a fifth, it would certainly be above the others. But since it is not a body, much more does it rise above them all. Then what is it doing in an earthly body? Finer than all, what is it doing in this coarse mass? Lighter than all, what is it doing in this dead weight? Swifter than all, what is it doing in this sluggish frame? Should not the virtue of its pre-eminent nature be able to accomplish the task of lifting its body to heaven? The substance of earthly bodies is able now to force souls downward by gravitation—will not souls one day be able to force earthly bodies upward by levitation?

Now if we turn to the miracles wrought by their gods, which they set against those wrought by our martyrs, will not these also be found to speak on our behalf, and contribute to our argument? For among the great marvels performed by their gods, certainly one that Varro relates is great. When a Vestal virgin was falsely suspected of unchastity she filled

de stupro falsa suspicione, cribrum implesse aqua de
Tiberi et ad suos iudices nulla eius perstillante parte
portasse.   Quis aquae pondus supra cribrum tenuit?
Quis tot cavernis patentibus nihil inde in terram
cadere permisit?   Responsuri sunt: " Aliquis deus
aut aliquis daemon."   Si deus, numquid maior est
Deo qui fecit hunc mundum?   Si daemon, numquid
potentior est angelo qui Deo servit a quo factus est
mundus?   Si ergo deus minor vel angelus vel daemon
potuit pondus umidi elementi sic suspendere ut
aquarum videatur mutata fuisse natura, itane Deus
omnipotens, qui omnia ipsa creavit elementa, terreno
corpori grave pondus auferre non poterit, ut in eodem
elemento habitet vivificatum corpus in quo voluerit
vivificans spiritus?

Deinde cum aera medium ponant inter ignem
desuper et aquam subter, quid est quod eum inter
aquam et aquam et inter aquam et terram saepe
invenimus?   Quid enim volunt esse aquosas nubes,
inter quas et maria aer medius reperitur?   Quonam,
quaeso, elementorum pondere atque ordine efficitur
ut torrentes violentissimi atque undosissimi, antequam sub aere in terris currant, super aera in nubibus
pendeant?   Cur denique aer est medius inter
summa caeli et nuda terrarum, quaqua versum orbis
extenditur, si locus eius inter caelum et aquas, sicut
aquarum inter ipsum et terras est constitutus?

Postremo si ita est elementorum ordo dispositus,
ut secundum Platonem duobus mediis id est aere et

---

[1] Compare 10.16 (Vol. III).

a sieve with water from the Tiber and carried it to
her judges without any part of it dripping through.[1]
Who kept the weight of water above the sieve?
While so many holes were open, who allowed nothing
to fall through them to the earth? They will answer,
"Some god, or some demon." If it is a god, is he
greater than the God who made this world? If a
demon, is he more powerful than an angel who serves
the God by whom the world was made? If, then, a
lesser god or angel or demon could support the weight
of the liquid element in such a way that the properties of water seemed changed, will not the almighty
God who created all the elements be able to take
away the heavy weight of the earthly body, so
that the life-endowed body may live in the element in which the life-endowing spirit would have it
live?

Secondly, since they put air in the middle, between
fire above and water below, why is it that we often
find air between water and water, or between water
and earth? Why do they maintain that clouds are
made of water, while air is found between them and
the sea? By what sort of comparative weight, I
ask, and order of elements, does it happen that
torrents of utmost violence and turbulence, before
they run in streams on the earth, below the air,
hang suspended in clouds above the earth? And why
does air fill the space between the uppermost heaven
and the bare surface of earth, wherever the land
surface extends, if its proper place is between heaven
and water, and that of water between air and earth?

Finally, if the order of the elements is so arranged,
as Plato says, that the two extremes of fire and earth

aqua, duo extrema id est ignis et terra, iungantur,
caelique obtineat ille summi locum, haec autem imi
velut fundaminis mundi, et ideo in caelo esse non
potest terra, cur est ipse ignis in terra? Secundum
hanc quippe rationem ita ista duo elementa in locis
propriis, imo ac summo, terra et ignis esse debuerunt
ut, quem ad modum nolunt in summo esse posse
quod imi est, ita nec in imo posset esse quod summi
est. Sicut ergo nullam putant vel esse vel futuram
esse terrae particulam in caelo, ita nullam particulam
videre debuimus ignis in terra. Nunc vero non
solum in terris, verum etiam sub terris ita est ut eum
eructent vertices montium, praeter quod in usibus
hominum et esse ignem in terra et eum nasci videmus
ex terra, quando quidem et de lignis et de lapidibus
nascitur, quae sunt corpora sine dubitatione terrena.
Sed ille, inquiunt, ignis est tranquillus, purus, in-
noxius, sempiternus, iste autem turbidus, fumeus,
corruptibilis atque corruptor. Nec tamen corrumpit
montes, in quibus iugiter aestuat, cavernasque
terrarum. Verum esto, sit illi iste dissimilis ut
terrenis habitationibus congruat. Cur ergo nolunt
ut credamus naturam corporum terrenorum aliquando
incorruptibilem factam caelo convenientem futuram,
sicut nunc ignis corruptibilis his convenit terris?
Nihil igitur afferunt ex ponderibus atque ordine
elementorum, unde omnipotenti Deo quominus faciat
corpora nostra talia ut etiam in caelo possint habitare
praescribant.

are linked by the two in the middle, air and water, and fire occupies its place in the highest heaven, while earth has its place in the lowest foundation of the world, so to speak, why is fire itself on the earth? For, according to this reasoning, the two elements of earth and fire should be in their proper places, the highest and the lowest. Thus, just as they argue that what belongs to the lowest element cannot be in the highest, so neither should that which belongs to the highest be in the lowest place. That is, just as they think that there is not and never will be any particle of earth in heaven, so we should have found no particle of fire on earth. But in fact fire is not only on the earth but even under the earth, so that the mountain peaks belch it forth. Moreover, we see that there is fire on earth when men make use of it, and that it comes from earth, since it is engendered both from sticks and stones, which are undoubtedly earthly bodies. But the heavenly fire, they say, is calm, pure, harmless and eternal, while this other is disordered, reeking, perishable and destructive. However, it does not destroy the mountains and caverns of earth in which it seethes continually. But granting that this fire below is unlike the other, so that it is suited to our dwelling-places on earth, why will they not allow us to believe that the substance of corporeal bodies will some day be made incorruptible and suited to heaven, just as now the corruptible fire is suited to this earth? From the comparative weight and order of the elements, therefore, they adduce no argument to prevent the almighty God from making our bodies such that they can dwell in heaven also.

XII

Contra calumnias infidelium quibus Christianos de credita carnis resurrectione inrident.

SED scrupulosissime quaerere, et fidem qua credimus resurrecturam carnem ita quaerendo adsolent inridere: utrum fetus abortivi resurgant; et quoniam Dominus ait: *Amen, dico vobis, capillus capitis vestri non peribit*, utrum statura et robur aequalia futura sint omnibus an diversae corporum quantitates. Si enim aequalitas erit corporum, unde habebunt quod hic non habuerunt in mole corporis illi abortivi, si resurgent et ipsi? Aut si non resurgent quia nec nati sunt sed effusi, eandem quaestionem de parvulis versant, unde illis mensura corporis quam nunc defuisse videmus accedat, cum in hac aetate moriuntur. Neque enim dicturi sumus eos non resurrecturos qui non solum generationis verum etiam regenerationis capaces sunt. Deinde interrogant quem modum ipsa aequalitas habitura sit. Si enim tam magni et tam longi erunt omnes quam fuerunt quicumque hic fuerunt maximi atque longissimi, non solum de parvulis sed de plurimis quaerunt unde illis accessurum sit quod hic defuit, si hoc quisque recipiat quod hic habuit.

Si autem, quod ait apostolus, occursuros nos omnes *in mensuram aetatis plenitudinis Christi*, et illud

---

[1] Luke 21.8.

[2] Ephesians 4.13, where English translations have " sta-

XII

*Against the taunts of unbelievers wherewith they
laugh Christians to scorn for believing in
the resurrection of the flesh.*

OUR adversaries are wont to question us very
closely, and in their questioning to ridicule our belief
in the resurrection of the flesh. They ask whether
abortive foetuses will rise again; they quote the
words of the Lord: " Verily I say unto you, not a
hair of your head shall perish," [1] then ask whether
all will have equal height and strength, or will have
different bodily sizes. For if the size of all bodies is
to be equal, how will those abortive births (if they,
too, are to rise again) have a bodily size which they
did not have before? Or, if they are not to rise,
since they were not properly born, but spilt, the same
question is raised of infants—when they die in infancy, how will they acquire the stature which we now
see is lacking? For we will not deny the resurrection
of any who are capable both of being born, and of
being born again in baptism. Then they ask what
will be the size of our bodies, if all are to be equal.
For if all are to be as large and as tall as the largest
and tallest have been here, the problem concerns not
only infants, but also the majority of men—from what
source will come the portion which was lacking here,
if each one is to receive what he had here.

The Apostle says that we shall all come " to the
measure of the age of the fullness of Christ," [2] and

ture " rather than " age." Augustine argues for the latter in
22.15, p. 277 below.

alterum: *Quos praedestinavit conformes ⟨ fieri ⟩ imaginis filii sui*, sic intellegendum est, ut statura et modus corporis Christi omnium qui in regno eius erunt humanorum corporum sit futurus: "Multis erit," inquiunt, "de magnitudine et longitudine detrahendum corporis. Et ubi iam erit: *capillus capitis vestri non peribit*, si de ipsa corporis quantitate tam multum peribit?" Quamvis et de ipsis capillis possit inquiri utrum redeat quidquid tondentibus decidit. Quod si rediturum est, quis non exhorreat illam deformitatem? Nam hoc et de unguibus videtur necessario secuturum, ut redeat tam multum quod corporis curatura desecuit. Et ubi erit decus, quod certe maius quam in ista esse corruptione potuit in illa iam inmortalitate esse debebit? Si autem non redibit, ergo peribit. Quo modo igitur, inquiunt, capillus capitis non peribit? De macie quoque vel pinguedine similiter disputant. Nam si aequales omnes erunt, non utique alii macri, alii pingues erunt. Accedet ergo aliis aliquid, aliis minuetur; ac per hoc non, quod erat, recipiendum, sed alicubi addendum est, quod non fuit, et alicubi perdendum, quod fuit.

De ipsis etiam corruptionibus et dilapsionibus corporum mortuorum, cum aliud vertatur in pulverem, in auras aliud exhaletur, sint quos bestiae, sint quos ignis absumit, naufragio vel quibuscumque aquis ita quidam pereant ut eorum carnes in umorem putredo dissolvat, non mediocriter permoventur

---

[1] Romans 8.29.

again, " whom he predestined to be conformed to
the image of his Son "[1]—if this means that the
stature and measure of Christ's body will be that of
the human bodies of all in his kindgom, they argue:
" It will be necessary in many cases to subtract something from the size or height of the body. Then where
will the promise be, ' Not a hair of your head shall
perish,' if so much will perish, even of the body's
mass? " And on the subject of the hair itself the
question can be raised whether what has fallen from
the barber's shears is to come back. If so, who
would not shudder at the horrid sight? For the same
rule would evidently apply to fingernails and toenails,
that everything must be restored which was trimmed
in grooming the body. And where will beauty be—
beauty which surely ought to be greater in that
immortal state than was possible in this state of corruption? But if trimmings of hair and nails are not
restored to the body, they perish; then how is it,
they say, that not a hair of the head will perish? A
similar argument is made about thinness and fatness,
for if all will be equal, certainly some will not be thin
while others are fat. Hence, some will put on flesh
while others lose it, and there is not to be a restoration of what once existed, but in one case the addition
of what did not exist, in another the loss of what did.

Objections are also made concerning the decay and
dissolution of dead bodies. One is changed into dust,
another evaporates into the air; some are consumed
by beasts, some by fire; some perish by shipwreck,
or drown by accident, so that their flesh rots and
dissolves into liquid. The objectors are no little
disturbed by this, and will not believe that all these

atque omnia ista recolligi in carnem et redintegrari posse non credunt. Consectantur etiam quasque foeditates et vitia, sive accidant sive nascantur, ubi et monstrosos partus cum horrore atque inrisione commemorant, et requirunt quaenam cuiusque deformitatis resurrectio sit futura. Si enim nihil tale redire in corpus hominis dixerimus, responsionem nostram de locis vulnerum cum quibus Dominum Christum resurrexisse praedicamus, se confutaturos esse praesumunt. Sed inter haec omnia quaestio difficillima illa proponitur, in cuius carnem reditura sit caro qua corpus alterius vescentis humana viscera fame compellente nutritur. In carnem quippe conversa est eius qui talibus vixit alimentis, et ea quae macies ostenderat detrimenta supplevit. Utrum ergo illi redeat homini cuius caro prius fuit, an illi potius cuius postea facta est, ad hoc percontantur ut fidem resurrectionis inludant, ac sic animae humanae aut alternantes sicut Plato veras infelicitates falsasque promittant beatitudines, aut post multas itidem per diversa corpora revolutiones aliquando tamen eam, sicut Porphyrius, finire miserias et ad eas numquam redire fateantur, non tamen corpus habendo inmortale, sed corpus omne fugiendo.

materials can be gathered up and renewed as human
flesh.   They also follow up every kind of monstrosi-
ties and defects, whether accidental or congenital;
with mingled horror and ridicule they mention monstrous births, and ask what will be the state of each
deformed creature in the resurrection.   For, if we say
that no such deformity will belong to the resurrected
body, they think that they will refute us by the marks
of the wounds with which the Lord Christ arose.
But among all these objections the most difficult
question proposed is: Into whose flesh will the flesh
return when under pressure of famine a man is kept
alive by eating human flesh?   For that flesh was
changed into the flesh of the eater, and replaced a
loss which was evident in his leanness.   Will the
flesh return to the man to whom it first belonged, or
to the one who acquired it afterwards?   They ask
the question in order to mock at our belief in the
resurrection, and in order, like Plato, either to promise the human soul an alternation of real unhappiness and false blessedness, or else, like Porphyry,
to admit that after many cycles of living again and
again in different bodies the soul at last ends its
miseries, and never returns to them, not, however,
that it has now an immortal body, but that it escapes
having any kind of body.[1]

---

[1] Compare 10.29 (Vol. III) where Augustine assigns the
same words (*omne corpus esse fugiendum*) to Porphyry's
treatise *On the Return of the Soul*.   A mention is also found in
chapter 26, p. 344 below.

XIII

*An abortivi non pertineant ad resurrectionem, si
pertinent ad numerum mortuorum.*

AD haec ergo quae ab eorum parte contraria me
digerente mihi videntur opposita misericordia Dei
meis nisibus opem ferente respondeam. Abortivos
fetus, qui cum iam vixissent in utero ibi sunt mortui,
resurrecturos ut adfirmare ita negare non audeo;
quamvis non videam quo modo ad eos non pertineat
resurrectio mortuorum, si non eximuntur de numero
mortuorum. Aut enim non omnes mortui resurgent
et erunt aliquae humanae animae sine corporibus in
aeternum quae corpora humana quamvis intra viscera
materna gestarunt; aut si omnes animae humanae
recipient resurgentia sua corpora quae habuerunt,
ubicumque viventia et morientia reliquerunt, non
invenio quem ad modum dicam ad resurrectionem
non pertinere mortuorum quoscumque mortuos etiam
in uteris matrum. Sed utrumlibet de his quisque
sentiat, quod de iam natis infantibus dixerimus, hoc
etiam de illis intellegendum est, si resurgent.

XIV

*An infantes in ea sint resurrecturi habitudine corporis
quam habituri erant aetatis accessu.*

QUID ergo de infantibus dicturi sumus, nisi quia
non in ea resurrecturi sunt corporis exiguitate qua

XIII

Whether abortive births have a part in the resurrection, if they are counted among the dead.

To these objections on their side I will reply in the order in which I have arranged them, as God's mercy grants help to my efforts. I do not dare either to affirm or to deny that abortive offspring, who lived and died in the womb, will rise from the dead. Yet I do not see how they fail to share in the resurrection of the dead unless they are not counted in the number of the dead. For then, either not all the dead will rise, leaving some human souls without bodies forever, that had once had human bodies, though only in their mother's womb; or if all human souls are to receive in the resurrection the bodies which they had, wherever they had them while living and wherever they left them when dying, I find no reason to say that such dead have no part in the resurrection, even those who died in their mother's womb. But each may choose whichever of these views he likes. Then, if they are to rise, one must understand as referring to abortive offspring whatever we shall say concerning infants already born.

XIV

Whether infants will be raised with the form of body which they would have had in maturity.

WELL, what are we to say about infants, except that they will not be raised with the small size in

mortui, sed quod eis tardius accessurum erat tempore, hoc sunt illi Dei opere miro atque celerrimo recepturi? In sententia quippe Domini, qua ait: *Capillus capitis vestri non peribit*, dictum est non defuturum esse quod fuit, non autem negatum est adfuturum esse quod defuit. Defuit autem infanti mortuo perfecta quantitas sui corporis. Perfecto quippe infanti deest utique perfectio magnitudinis corporalis, quae cum accesserit statura iam longior esse non possit. Hunc perfectionis modum sic habent omnes ut cum illo concipiantur atque nascantur; sed habent in ratione, non mole, sicut ipsa membra omnia iam sunt latenter in semine, cum etiam natis nonnulla adhuc desint, sicut dentes ac si quid eius modi. In qua ratione uniuscuiusque materiae indita corporali iam quodam modo, ut ita dicam, liciatum videtur esse, quod nondum est, immo quod latet, sed accessu temporis erit vel potius apparebit. In hac ergo infans iam brevis aut longus est qui brevis longusve futurus est. Secundum hanc rationem profecto in resurrectione corporis detrimenta corporis non timemus, quia—etsi aequalitas futura esset omnium ita ut omnes usque ad giganteas magnitudines pervenirent, ne illi qui maximi fuerunt minus haberent aliquid in statura, quod eis contra sententiam Christi periret, qui dixit nec capillum capitis esse periturum—Creatori utique qui creavit cuncta de nihilo quo modo deesse posset unde adderet quod addendum esse mirus artifex nosset?

which they died, but by a miracle of God will receive
in a moment the form which would have accrued to
them at a later time? For in the saying of the Lord:
" A hair of your head will not perish," [1] it is stated
that nothing which once was will be lacking, but it is
not denied that there may be something more which
once was lacking. But the dead infant lacked the
full growth of his body. Though a perfect infant he
certainly lacks the perfection of bodily size, beyond
which, when it has accrued, his stature can no longer
increase. All men have this limit of perfection; they
are conceived and born with it, but they have it in
design, not in actual mass, just as all the members
already potentially exist in the seed, and even after
birth some things are still lacking, such as teeth and
the like. In this design which is impressed on the
corporeal substance of each one the parts which as yet
do not exist, or rather, are not seen, seem already
somehow threaded in, if I may speak so, and with the
passage of time they will come into being, or rather,
into view. So by this design the infant who is going
to be short or tall is already short or tall. In accordance with this design we assuredly do not fear any
diminution of the body in the resurrection. For even
if the equality of all required all to reach gigantic size,
so that those who were very large need lose nothing
in stature and thus belie the saying of Christ that not
even a hair of the head would perish, how could the
Creator who made all things from nothing lack
material to add whatever as marvellous designer he
knows should be added?

[1] Luke 21.18.

XV

An ad dominici corporis modum omnium mortuorum
resurrectura sint corpora.

SED utique Christus in ea mensura corporis in qua
mortuus est resurrexit, nec fas est dicere cum
resurrectionis omnium tempus venerit accessuram
corpori eius eam magnitudinem, quam non habuit
quando in ea discipulis in qua illis erat notus apparuit,
ut longissimis fieri possit aequalis. Si autem
dixerimus ad dominici corporis modum etiam quorumque maiora corpora redigenda, peribit de multorum
corporibus plurimum, cum ipse nec capillum periturum esse promiserit. Restat ergo ut suam recipiat
quisque mensuram quam vel habuit in iuventute
etiamsi senex est mortuus, vel fuerat habiturus si est
ante defunctus, atque illud quod commemoravit
apostolus de mensura aetatis plenitudinis Christi aut
propter aliud intellegamus dictum esse, id est, ut illi
capiti in populis Christianis accedente omnium per-
fectione membrorum aetatis eius mensura compleatur aut, si hoc de resurrectione corporum dictum
est, sic accipiamus dictum ut nec infra nec ultra
iuvenalem formam resurgant corpora mortuorum, sed
in eius aetate et robore usque ad quam Christum hic
pervenisse cognovimus—circa triginta quippe annos
definierunt esse etiam saeculi huius doctissimi
homines iuventutem; quae cum fuerit spatio proprio
terminata, inde iam hominem in detrimenta vergere
gravioris ac senilis aetatis—et ideo non esse dictum

---

[1] Ephesians 4.13.

XV

Whether the bodies of all the dead will rise with the same size as the Lord's body.

BUT in any case Christ rose with the same bodily size as that with which he died, and it is wrong to say that when the time of the general resurrection comes his bodily size will increase, so that he will be equal to the tallest, though he had no such size in the body when he appeared to his disciples with the size in which he was known to them. But if we say that all larger bodies must be reduced to the size of the Lord's body, much will have to be taken from the bodies of many, though he promised that not a hair would perish. Hence it follows that each one is to receive his own measure, either the size that he had in youth, if he died an old man, or if he died in childhood, the size that he would have reached. And we must understand that what the Apostle says about " the measure of the age of the fullness of Christ "[1] was spoken for another purpose, that is, that the measure of his age will be completed when to him as head all Christian people are added to complete his members. Or, if this had reference to the resurrection of bodies, we should understand that the dead do not rise with bodies either older or younger than the state of youth, but have bodies of the age and strength that we know Christ reached here. For even the learned of this world have defined youth as reaching to thirty years, stating that when that limit is reached, then man begins to decline into the worse conditions of a burdensome and senile age. Hence it was not said " into the

in mensuram corporis vel in mensuram staturae, sed *in mensuram aetatis plenitudinis Christi.*

XVI

Qualis intellegenda sit sanctorum conformatio ad imaginem filii Dei.

Illud etiam quod ait praedestinatos *conformes fieri imaginis filii Dei,* potest et secundum interiorem hominem intellegi, unde nobis alio loco dicit: *Nolite conformari huic saeculo, sed reformamini in novitate mentis vestrae;* ubi ergo reformamur, ne conformemur huic saeculo, ibi conformamur Dei filio. Potest et sic accipi ut, quem ad modum nobis ille mortalitate, ita nos illi efficiamur inmortalitate conformes, quod quidem et ad ipsam resurrectionem corporum pertinet. Si autem etiam in his verbis qua forma resurrectura sint corpora sumus admoniti, sicut illa mensura, ita et ista conformatio non quantitatis intellegenda est, sed aetatis. Resurgent itaque omnes tam magni corpore quam vel erant vel futuri erant aetate iuvenali; quamvis nihil oberit, etiamsi erit infantilis vel senilis corporis forma, ubi nec mentis nec ipsius corporis ulla remanebit infirmitas. Unde etiam si quis in eo corporis modo in quo defunctus est resurrecturum unumquemque contendit, non est cum illo laboriosa contradictione pugnandum.

measure of the body," or " into the measure of the height," but " into the measure of the age of the fullness of Christ."

XVI

What is to be understood by the conformity of the saints to the image of the Son of God.

THE passage also which says that the elect are conformed to the image of the Son of God can be understood of the inner man.   On this point another passage says: " Be not conformed to this world, but be ye reformed in the renewing of your mind." [1] So where we are reformed in order not to be conformed to this world, there we are conformed to the Son of God.   It can also be taken to mean that as he was conformed to us in his mortality, so we should be to him in his immortality, and this belongs to the time of the bodily resurrection.   But if by these words we are taught in what form bodies will rise, as in the case of the " measure," so in this " conformation," not size, but age, must be understood.   And so all will arise with bodies as large as before, or as large as they would have had in full-grown youth. Yet no harm will be done if the form be that of an infant or old man, in a life where no weakness either of mind or body will remain.   So if any one maintains that each one will rise with the same size of body with which he died, there is no need of engaging in toilsome controversy with him.

[1] Romans 12.2.

XVII

*An in suo sexu resuscitanda atque mansura sint
corpora feminarum.*

NONNULLI propter hoc, quod dictum est: *Donec
occurramus omnes in virum perfectum, in mensuram
aetatis plenitudinis Christi*, et: *Conformes imaginis filii
Dei*, nec in sexu femineo resurrecturas feminas
credunt, sed in virili omnes aiunt, quoniam Deus
solum virum fecit ex limo, feminam ex viro. Sed mihi
melius sapere videntur qui utrumque sexum resur-
rectum esse non dubitant. Non enim libido ibi erit
quae confusionis est causa. Nam priusquam peccas-
sent nudi erant et non confundebantur vir et femina.
Corporibus ergo illis vitia detrahentur, natura serva-
bitur. Non est autem vitium sexus femineus, sed
natura, quae tunc quidem et a concubitu et a partu
inmunis erit. Erunt tamen membra feminea non
adcommodata usui veteri sed decori novo, quo non
alliciatur aspicientis concupiscentia quae nulla erit,
sed Dei laudetur sapientia atque clementia qui et
quod non erat fecit et liberavit a corruptione quod
fecit.

Ut enim in exordio generis humani de latere viri
dormientis costa detracta femina fieret, Christum et

---

[1] Ephesians 4.13.
[2] Romans 8.29.
[3] Jerome quotes Origen as believing that there would be no
female sex in heaven, and was charged by Rufinus with

XVII

Whether the bodies of women will be raised and remain with their own sex.

THE Scriptures say: " Till we all come to a perfect man, to the measure of the age of the fullness of Christ," [1] and: " Conformed to the image of the Son of God." [2] On account of these sayings some believe that women will not rise in female sex, but that all will be males, since God made only man from clay, and the woman from the man.[3] But I think that those are wiser who do not doubt that both sexes will rise. For there will be no lust there, which is the cause of shame. For before they sinned they were naked, and the man and woman were not ashamed. So all defects will be taken away from those bodies, but their natural state will be preserved. The female sex is not a defect, but a natural state, which will then know no intercourse or childbirth. There will be female parts, not suited to their old use, but to a new beauty, and this will not arouse the lust of the beholder, for there will be no lust, but it will inspire praise of the wisdom and goodness of God, who both created what was not, and freed from corruption what he made.

For as in the beginning of the human race a woman was made from a rib taken from the side of the sleeping man,[4] it was fitting that by such a deed even

holding that view himself. But Jerome disclaims that view. See his *Apology against Rufinus* 1.28 in *NPNF* second series III, 497, also (same series) VI, 155, 208, 374.

[4] Genesis 2.21.

ecclesiam tali facto iam tunc prophetari oportebat.
Sopor quippe ille viri mors erat Christi, cuius exani-
mis in cruce pendentis latus lancea perforatum est
atque inde sanguis et aqua defluxit, quae sacramenta
esse novimus quibus aedificatur ecclesia.¹ Nam hoc
etiam verbo scriptura usa est, ubi non legitur
" formavit" aut " finxit," sed: *Aedificavit eam in
mulierem;* unde et apostolus aedificationem dicit
corporis Christi, quod est ecclesia.² Creatura est ergo
Dei femina sicut vir. Sed ut de viro fieret unitas
commendata, ut autem illo modo fieret, Christus ut
dictum est et ecclesia figurata est.³ Qui ergo utrumque sexum instituit utrumque restituet.

Denique ipse Iesus interrogatus a Sadducaeis, qui
negabant resurrectionem, cuius septem fratrum erit
uxor quam singuli habuerunt, dum quisque eorum
vellet defuncti semen sicut lex praeceperat excitare:
Erratis, inquit, *nescientes scripturas, neque virtutem Dei.*⁴
Et cum locus esset ut diceret: " De qua enim me
interrogatis, vir erit etiam ipsa, non mulier," non
hoc dixit, sed dixit: *In resurrectione enim neque nubent
neque uxores ducent, sed sunt sicut angeli Dei in caelo*⁵—
aequales utique angelis inmortalitate ac felicitate,
non carne, sicut nec resurrectione qua non indi-
guerunt angeli, quoniam nec mori potuerunt.
Nuptias ergo Dominus futuras esse negavit in resurrectione, non feminas. Et ibi negavit ubi talis
quaestio vertebatur ut eam negato sexu muliebri
celeriore facilitate dissolveret, si eum ibi praenosceret

---

¹ John 19.34.   ² Genesis 2.22.
³ Ephesians 4.12.   ⁴ Matthew 22.29.
⁵ Matthew 22.30.

then Christ and the church should be foreshadowed. For that sleep of the man was the death of Christ, and when he was hanging lifeless on the cross, his side was pierced with a spear, and from it flowed blood and water,[1] which we know are the sacraments through which the church is built. For the Scripture used this very word, saying not "formed" or "fashioned," but "he built it into a woman." [2] Hence the Apostle also speaks of the building of the body of Christ, which is the church.[3] So woman is a creature of God, just as man is; but by her being made from the man, unity was commended, while by her being made in that manner, as we have said, Christ and the church were symbolized. Therefore he who created both sexes will restore both.

Finally, Jesus himself was asked by the Sadducees, who denied the resurrection, whose wife the woman would be whom seven brothers had married in turn, inasmuch as each of them wished to raise up seed to his deceased brother, as the law had enjoined. "Ye err," he said, "not knowing the Scriptures nor the power of God." [4] And though here was an occasion to say: "As for your question, she will be a man herself, not a woman," he did not say this, but said: "In the resurrection women will not marry nor men take wives, but they will be as the angels of God in heaven." [5] They will be equal to angels in immortality and happiness, not in flesh, nor indeed in resurrection, which the angels had no need of, since they could not die. So the Lord said that there would be no marriage in the resurrection, not that there would be no women. And at the time a question was under consideration that he could have settled

non futurum. Immo etiam futurum esse firmavit dicendo: *Non nubent*, quod ad feminas pertinet, *nec uxores ducent*, quod ad viros. Erunt ergo, quae vel nubere hic solent, vel ducere uxores, sed ibi non facient.

XVIII

De viro perfecto, id est Christo, et corpore eius, id est ecclesia, quae est ipsius plenitudo.

PROINDE quod ait apostolus, occursuros nos omnes in virum perfectum, totius ipsius circumstantiam lectionis considerare debemus, quae ita se habet: *Qui descendit*, inquit, *ipse est et qui ascendit super omnes caelos ut adimpleret omnia. Et ipse dedit quosdam quidem apostolos, quosdam autem prophetas, quosdam vero evangelistas, quosdam autem pastores et doctores ad consummationem sanctorum in opus ministerii, in aedificationem corporis Christi, donec occurramus omnes in unitatem fidei et agnitionem filii Dei, in virum perfectum, in mensuram aetatis plenitudinis Christi; ut ultra non simus parvuli iactati et circumlati omni vento doctrinae, in inlusione hominum, in astutia ad machinationem erroris, veritatem autem facientes in caritate augeamur in illo per omnia, qui est caput Christus; ex quo totum corpus conexum et compactum per omnem tactum subministrationis secundum operationem in mensuram unius-*

more quickly by denying the presence of females, if he foreknew that there would be none there. Instead, he showed that there would be some when he said: "They will not marry," which is said of women, "nor take wives," which is said of men. So those who either marry husbands or take wives here will be present there, but will not do those things there.

XVIII

On the perfect man, Christ, and his body the church,
which is his fullness.

THEN, as for the Apostle's saying that we shall all attain "to the perfect man," we must consider the whole context of the passage, which is as follows: " He who descended is also the one who ascended above all the heavens, that he might fulfil all things. And he himself gave some men as apostles, some as prophets, some as evangelists, and some as pastors and teachers, in order to perfect the saints for the work of ministering and for building up the body of Christ, until we all attain to the unity of the faith and the full knowledge of the Son of God, to mature manhood, to the measure of the age of the fullness of Christ, so that we may no longer be children, tossed about and carried around by every wind of doctrine through the cunning of men and their cleverness in inventing error. But rather by practising the truth in love we must grow up in every way in him who is the head, Christ. On him the whole body depends, being connected and united by each contact with his bounty, as each part is active in its due measure.

cuiusque partis incrementum corporis facit in aedifica-
tionem sui in caritate.

Ecce qui est vir perfectus, caput et corpus, quod
constat omnibus membris quae suo tempore comple-
buntur, cotidie tamen eidem corpori accedunt, dum
aedificatur ecclesia, cui dicitur: *Vos autem estis corpus*
Christi et membra, et alibi: *Pro corpore,* inquit, *eius*
quod est ecclesia, itemque alibi: *Unus panis, unum*
corpus multi sumus. De cuius corporis aedificatione
et hic dictum est: *Ad consummationem sanctorum in*
opus ministerii, in aedificationem corporis Christi ac
deinde subiectum unde nunc agimus: *Donec occur-*
ramus omnes in unitatem fidei et agnitionem filii Dei, in
virum perfectum, in mensuram aetatis plenitudinis Christi,
et cetera; donec eadem mensura in quo corpore intellegenda esset ostenderet dicens: *Augeamur in illo*
per omnia qui est caput Christus. *Ex quo totum corpus*
conexum et compactum per omnem tactum subministra-
tionis secundum operationem in mensuram uniuscuiusque
partis. Sicut ergo est mensura uniuscuiusque partis,
ita totius corporis quod omnibus suis partibus constat
est utique mensura plenitudinis, de qua dictum est:
In mensuram aetatis plenitudinis Christi. Quam pleni-
tudinem etiam illo commemoravit loco ubi ait de
Christo: *Et ipsum dedit caput super omnia ecclesiae,*[1]
quae est corpus eius, plenitudo eius qui omnia in omnibus
impletur.

---

[1] *Part of the Manuscripts follow the Vulgate in reading*
omnem ecclesiam.

---

[1] Ephesians 4.10–16.   [2] 1 Corinthians 12.27.
[3] Colossians 1.24.   [4] 1 Corinthians 10.17.
[5] Ephesians 1.22–23.   The verb *impletur* must be taken as

From him the body derives its increase, so as to build itself up in love." [1]

Here is described the perfect man—the Head and the body which consists of all the members whose number will be made up at the proper time. Now, however, members are daily being added to that body. Thus the Church is being built, to which the Scripture says: " But ye are the body and members of Christ," [2] and in another passage: " For his body, which is the church," [3] and again likewise: " We, being many, are one bread, one body." [4] Concerning the building of this body the passage we have quoted also says: " In order to perfect the saints for the work of ministering and for building up the body of Christ." Then follow the words we are discussing: " Until we all attain to the unity of the faith and the full knowledge of the Son of God, to mature manhood, to the measure of the age of the fullness of Christ," and so on, till he shows to what body the measure belongs by saying: " We must grow up in every way in him who is the head, Christ. On him the whole body depends, being connected and united by each contact with his bounty, as each part is active in due measure." Hence, just as there is a due measure of each part, so there is surely a measure of the fullness of the whole body, which consists of all its members, and of this it is said, " to the measure of the age of the fullness of Christ." This fullness is mentioned also in the place where he says of Christ: " And him he gave as head over all things to the church, which is his body, the fullness of him who fills all in all." [5]

a Graecism, following the original πληρουμένου, a middle voice not much differing from an active in sense.

Verum si hoc ad resurrectionis formam in qua erit
unusquisque referendum esset, quid nos impediret
nominato viro intellegere et feminam, ut virum pro
homine positum acciperemus, sicut in eo quod dictum
est: *Beatus vir qui timet Dominum*, utique ibi sunt et
feminae quae timent Dominum?[1]

XIX

*Quod omnia corporis vitia quae in hac vita humano
contraria sunt decori in resurrectione non sint
futura, ubi manente naturali substantia in
unam pulchritudinem et qualitas concurret
et quantitas.*

QUID iam respondeam de capillis atque unguibus?
Semel quippe intellecto ita nihil periturum esse de
corpore ut deforme nihil sit in corpore, simul intellegitur ea quae deformem factura fuerant enormi-
tatem massae ipsi accessura esse, non locis in quibus
membrorum forma turpetur. Velut si de limo vas
fieret, quod rursus in eundem limum redactum totum
de toto iterum fieret, non esset necesse ut illa pars
limi quae in ansa fuerat ad ansam rediret, aut quae
fundum fecerat ipsa rursus faceret fundum, dum
tamen totum reverteretur in totum, id est, totus ille
limus in totum vas nulla sui perdita parte remearet.

---

[1] Psalms 112.1.

But even if the words, " mature manhood," should be taken as a reference to the shape each one will have in the resurrection, what would prevent us from understanding the woman also when the man is named, taking " man " to mean " human being," as in the passage, " Blessed is the man who fears the Lord," [1] which surely includes also the women who fear the Lord ?

XIX

That none of the bodily defects which in this life detract from man's beauty will exist in the resurrection; for then man's natural substance will remain, but both its quality and quantity will conform to one pattern of beauty.

Now what answer shall I make about the hair and the nails ? Once it is understood that in order to save the body from deformity nothing will be allowed to perish, it is at the same time understood that those things which might cause a monstrous enormity will be restored, not to the places where they would cause an ugly disproportion, but to the total mass of the body. For example, if a vase were made of clay, then the whole reduced to the original lump of clay and formed into a vase a second time, it would not be necessary for that part of the clay which was in the handle to return to the new handle, or what was in the base to form a base again, but only for all to be turned into all, that is, all the clay into all the vase with no part lost. Accordingly, if the hair shorn

Quapropter si capilli totiens tonsi unguesve desecti
ad sua loca deformiter redeunt, non redibunt. Nec
tamen cuique resurgenti peribunt, quia in eandem
carnem, ut quemcumque ibi locum corporis teneant,
servata partium congruentia materiae mutabilitate
vertentur.

Quamvis quod ait Dominus: *Capillus capitis vestri
non peribit,* non de longitudine, sed de numero
capillorum dictum multo aptius possit intellegi.
Unde et alibi dicit: *Capilli capitis vestri numerati sunt
omnes.* Neque hoc ideo dixerim, quod aliquid
existimem corpori cuique periturum quod naturaliter
inerat, sed quod deforme natum fuerat (non utique
ob aliud nisi ut hinc quoque ostenderetur quam sit
poenalis condicio ista mortalium), sic esse rediturum
ut servata integritate substantiae deformitas pereat.
Si enim statuam potest artifex homo, quam propter
aliquam causam deformem fecerat, conflare et pulcherrimam reddere, ita ut nihil inde substantiae
sed sola deformitas pereat, ac si quid in illa figura
priore indecenter extabat nec parilitate partium
congruebat, non de toto unde fecerat amputare atque
separare, sed ita conspergere universo atque miscere
ut nec foeditatem faciat nec minuat quantitatem,
quid de omnipotenti artifice sentiendum est?
Ergone non poterit quasque deformitates humanorum
corporum, non modo usitatas verum etiam raras
atque monstrosas quae huic miserae vitae congruunt,

---

time after time, and the nails which are trimmed off, produce ugliness by returning to their old place, they will not return. Yet when men are raised they will not perish, for they will return to the same flesh with a change of substance so as to occupy whatever place they may in the body, as long as the due proportion of parts is preserved.

However, what the Lord says: " A hair of your head shall not perish," [1] can be understood much more aptly, not of the length, but of the number of hairs. Hence he says elsewhere: " The hairs of your head are all numbered." [2] I do not say this to imply that anything which naturally belongs to the body will perish for anyone. But when some ugliness is innate—and this certainly could happen for no other reason than to show from this also how this present state of mortals is one of punishment—the restoration will be such that the deformity will disappear while the substance will be preserved intact. A human artist can melt down a statue which for some reason he had cast with a deformity, and recast it in perfect beauty, so that none of its substance is lost, but only its deformity. If anything in the first figure stood out unbecomingly and disturbed the equality of the parts, he need not cut it off from the whole which he formed and separate it, but he can so scatter it and mix it with the whole that he neither creates an ugly thing nor does he lessen the amount of substance. If the human artist can do this, what must we think of the almighty Artist? Will he not be able to remove and destroy all the deformities of human bodies, not only the common ones, but also the rare and monstrous? These have their place in this wretched life, but are

abhorrent autem ab illa futura felicitate sanctorum, sic auferre ac perdere ut, quascumque earum faciunt etsi naturalia, tamen indecora excrementa substantiae corporalis, nulla eius deminutione tolluntur?[1]

Ac per hoc non est macris pinguibusque metuendum ne ibi etiam tales sint quales si possent nec hic esse voluissent. Omnis enim corporis pulchritudo est partium congruentia cum quadam coloris suavitate. Ubi autem non est partium congruentia, aut ideo quid offendit quia pravum est, aut ideo quia parum, aut ideo quia nimium. Proinde nulla erit deformitas quam facit incongruentia partium ubi et quae prava sunt corrigentur, et quod minus est quam decet unde Creator novit inde supplebitur, et quod plus est quam decet materiae servata integritate detrahetur. Coloris porro suavitas quanta erit, ubi iusti fulgebunt sicut sol in regno Patris sui![1]

Quae claritas in Christi corpore cum resurrexit ab oculis discipulorum potius abscondita fuisse quam defuisse credenda est. Non enim eam ferret humanus atque infirmus aspectus, quando ille a suis ita deberet adtendi ut posset agnosci. Quo pertinuit etiam ut contrectantibus ostenderet suorum vulnerum cicatrices, ut etiam cibum potumque sumeret, non alimentorum indigentia, sed ea qua et hoc poterat potestate. Cum autem aliquid non videtur quamvis adsit a quibus alia quae pariter adsunt videntur, sicut illam claritatem dicimus

---

[1] *Many manuscripts and some editors have the subjunctive* tollantur, *thus conforming to classical Latin grammar.*

---

[1] Matthew 13.43.

inconsistent with that future happiness of the saints. Thus any of these deformities caused by the natural but unseemly growth of bodily substance are removed without diminishing the body.

Therefore those who are too gaunt or too fat need not fear to find themselves there too in a condition that they would not have chosen here, if they had had a choice. For all bodily beauty is the harmony of parts, with a certain agreeable effect of colour. But when there is no harmony of parts a thing offends either because it is misshapen, or too small or too large. Accordingly, there will be no deformity caused by disharmony of the parts there where even misshapen parts will be straightened, and where the lack of what is seemly will be supplied from a source known to the Creator, and the excess beyond the seemly will be taken away without destroying the material substance. And how agreeable will the colours be when the righteous shall shine like the sun in the kingdom of their Father! [1]

This brightness, we must believe, in the case of Christ's risen body after his resurrection, was hidden from the eyes of the disciples rather than non-existent. For the weak sight of men would not have endured it, when the due moment came that required his disciples to observe him with such attention that they could recognize him. It was with the same purpose also that he showed the scars of his wounds which they handled, and that he also took food and drink, not because he needed sustenance but because of his power that made this too possible for him. When something present is invisible to those who see other equally present objects, as was the case with that

adfuisse non visam a quibus alia videbantur, ἀορασία
Graece dicitur, quod nostri interpretes Latine dicere
non valentes in libro geneseos caecitatem interpretati
sunt. Hanc enim sunt passi Sodomitae quando
quaerebant ostium iusti viri nec poterant invenire.
Quae si fuisset caecitas qua fit ut nihil possit videri
non ostium qua ingrederentur, sed duces itineris a
quibus inde abducerentur, inquirerent.

Nescio quo autem modo sic afficimur amore martyrum beatorum ut velimus in illo regno in eorum
corporibus videre vulnerum cicatrices quae pro
Christi nomine pertulerunt, et fortasse videbimus.
Non enim deformitas in eis sed dignitas erit, et
quaedam quamvis in corpore non corporis sed virtutis
pulchritudo fulgebit. Nec ideo tamen si aliqua
martyribus amputata et ablata sunt membra, sine
ipsis membris erunt in resurrectione mortuorum
quibus dictum est: *Capillus capitis vestri non peribit.*
Sed si hoc decebit in illo novo saeculo ut indicia
gloriosorum vulnerum in illa inmortali carne cer-
nantur, ubi membra ut praeciderentur percussa vel
secta sunt, ibi cicatrices, sed tamen eisdem membris
redditis non perditis, apparebunt. Quamvis itaque
omnia quae acciderunt corpori vitia tunc non erunt,
non sunt tamen deputanda vel appellanda vitia
virtutis indicia.

---

[1] This word can mean "failure to see," as well as "blindness." In his earlier *Questions on the Heptateuch*, 1.43,
Augustine had invented the word *avidentia* to express his view

brightness, unseen by those who saw other objects, it is called in Greek *aorasia*.[1] Our translators could not find a Latin equivalent, and in the book of Genesis translated it *caecitas*, or "blindness." For this is what the men of Sodom suffered when they were looking for the door of the righteous man and could not find it.[2] If it had been the blindness in which nothing can be seen, they would not have been looking for the door to enter, but for guides to take them away from there.

Our love for the blessed martyrs somehow leads us to wish in that kingdom to see in their bodies the scars of the wounds which they have suffered for the name of Christ, and perhaps we shall see them. For it will not be a deformity in them, but an honour, and in their body will shine a certain beauty, not of the body, but of virtue. Still, if limbs have been cut off or torn away from the martyrs, they will not for this reason be without those limbs in the resurrection. For it was said to them: "A hair of your head shall not perish."[3] But if in that new age it is fitting that the marks of their glorious wounds be seen in that immortal flesh, then in the place where the limbs were struck off or cut away that they might be separated, there will be seen scars, but the limbs will nevertheless be restored, not destroyed. And so though all the defects that may have befallen the body will then be gone, the marks of virtue are not to be considered or spoken of as defects.

of the Greek. Apparently, however, all translators take the Hebrew to mean "blindness."

[2] Genesis 19.11.

[3] Luke 21.18.

SAINT AUGUSTINE

XX

*Quod in resurrectione mortuorum natura corporum
quibuslibet modis dissipatorum in integrum
undecumque revocanda sit.*

ABSIT autem ut ad resuscitanda corpora vitaeque
reddenda non possit omnipotentia Creatoris omnia
revocare quae vel bestiae vel ignis absumpsit vel in
pulverem cineremve conlapsum vel in umorem solu-
tum vel in auras est exhalatum. Absit ut sinus ullus
secretumque naturae ita recipiat aliquid subtractum
sensibus nostris ut omnium Creatoris aut cognitionem
lateat aut effugiat potestatem. Deum certe volens,
sicut poterat, definire Cicero, tantus auctor ipsorum:
" Mens quaedam est," inquit, " soluta et libera,
secreta ab omni concretione mortali, omnia sentiens
et movens ipsaque praedita motu sempiterno." Hoc
autem repperit in doctrinis magnorum philosophorum. Ut igitur secundum ipsos loquar, quo
modo aliquid vel latet omnia sentientem vel in-
revocabiliter fugit omnia moventem?

Unde iam etiam quaestio illa solvenda est quae
difficilior videtur ceteris, ubi quaeritur, cum caro
mortui hominis etiam alterius fit viventis caro, cui
potius eorum in resurrectione reddatur. Si enim
quispiam confectus fame atque compulsus vescatur
cadaveribus hominum, quod malum aliquotiens

---

[1] *Tusculan Disputations* 1.27.66.

XX

*That in the resurrection bodies scattered in any
manner will be summoned from whatever place
they occupy, and be made whole.*

MOREOVER, let it never be said that the almighty
Creator, in his purpose of raising up bodies and
restoring them to life, is unable to recall all the substance which beasts or fire have consumed, or which
has crumbled to dust or ashes, or has been dissolved
in water or gone with the winds. Let it never be
said that there is any recess or hidden place in nature
where anything, though removed from our perceptions, can hide from the knowledge or escape the
power of the Creator of all. When Cicero, the
renowned writer of the pagans, wished to define God
precisely, as well as he could, he said: " He is a kind
of mind, unfettered and free, severed from all
perishable matter, conscious of all and moving all
things, and self-endowed with unending motion." [1]
This definition he found in the teachings of the great
philosophers. Then, to speak in their language,
how is anything hid from him who perceives all
things, or how does it escape beyond recall from him
who moves all things?

This leads me also to answer the question which
seems still more difficult than the others, that is,
when the flesh of a dead man becomes also the flesh
of another living man, to which of them will it return
in the resurrection? For if a man, exhausted and
driven by hunger, should eat the bodies of men—an
evil which has sometimes happened both according

297

accidisse et vetus testatur historia et nostrorum temporum infelicia experimenta docuerunt, num quisquam veridica ratione contendet totum digestum fuisse per imos meatus, nihil inde in eius carnem mutatum atque conversum, cum ipsa macies quae fuit et non est satis indicet quae illis escis detrimenta suppleta sint? Iam itaque aliqua paulo ante praemisi quae ad istum quoque nodum solvendum valere debebunt. Quidquid enim carnium exhausit fames, utique in auras est exhalatum, unde diximus omnipotentem Deum posse revocare quod fugit. Reddetur ergo caro illa homini in quo esse caro humana primitus coepit. Ab illo quippe altero tamquam mutuo sumpta deputanda est, quae sicut aes alienum ei redhibenda est unde sumpta est. Sua vero illi quem fames exinanierat, ab eo qui potest etiam exhalata revocare reddetur. Quamvis etsi omnibus perisset modis nec ulla eius materies in ullis naturae latebris remansisset, unde vellet eam repararet Omnipotens. Sed propter sententiam Veritatis, qua dictum est: *Capillus capitis vestri non peribit*, absurdum est ut putemus, cum capillus hominis perire non possit, tantas carnes fame depastas atque consumptas perire potuisse.

Quibus omnibus pro nostro modulo consideratis

---

[1] Augustine speaks of a long famine during the siege of Rome in 410 (1.10, Vol. I, 55), but nowhere states that cannibalism took place, unless this passage be taken as proof. Jerome in a letter from Bethlehem relates the shock brought by the news, which included the report that a mother had

to the testimony of ancient history and in the unhappy experiences of our times [1]—will anyone by honest reasoning contend that the whole is digested and passes out through the rear, and nothing of it is changed and converted into the flesh of the eater? The very change from his former emaciation shows well enough what were the losses made up by such food. I have already set down a little while ago some arguments which should duly serve to solve this problem as well. For whatever flesh is lost in hunger is undoubtedly gone out into the air, and we have said that almighty God can summon from the air what has escaped. So that flesh will be restored to the man in whom it first took shape as human flesh. For it must be reckoned as borrowed, so to speak, by the second man, and, like any debt, must be repaid to the one from whom it was borrowed. And to the man who was consumed with hunger, his own flesh will be restored by him who can recall even what vanished into the air. Even if it had utterly perished, and no substance of his remained in any of nature's hiding-places, the Almighty would restore it from any source he might choose. But since we have the statement of the Truth where it says: "A hair of your head shall not perish," [2] it is absurd to think that while a man's hair cannot perish, so much flesh wasted and consumed by hunger could perish.

Now that all these objections have been considered

---

eaten her own child. Jerome's highly rhetorical letter may well be taking this theme from Josephus, *Jewish War* 6.201–213. Augustine again refers to cannibalism in Chapter XXII, p. 313.

[2] Luke 21.18.

atque tractatis haec summa conficitur, ut in resurrectione carnis in aeternum eas mensuras habeat corporum magnitudo quas habebat perficiendae sive perfectae cuiusque indita corpori ratio iuventutis, in membrorum quoque omnium modulis congruo decore servato. Quod decus ut servetur, si aliquid demptum fuerit indecenti alicui granditati in parte aliqua constitutae, quod per totum spargatur, ut neque id pereat et congruentia partium ubique teneatur, non est absurdum ut aliquid inde etiam staturae corporis addi posse credamus, cum omnibus partibus ut decorem custodiant id distribuitur quod, si enormiter in una esset, utique non deceret. Aut si contenditur in ea quemque statura corporis resurrecturum esse, in qua defunctus est, non pugnaciter resistendum est; tantum absit omnis deformitas, omnis infirmitas, omnis tarditas omnisque corruptio, et si quid aliud illud non decet regnum, in quo resurrectionis et promissionis filii aequales erunt angelis Dei, si non corpore, non aetate, certe felicitate.

XXI

De novitate corporis spiritalis, in quam sanctorum caro mutabitur.

RESTITUETUR ergo quidquid de corporibus vivis vel post mortem de cadaveribus periit, et simul cum eo quod in sepulcris remansit in spiritalis corporis novitatem ex animalis corporis vetustate mutatum resurget incorruptione atque inmortalitate vestitum.

---

[1] Matthew 22.30.

and dealt with according to our small ability, the conclusion is that in the resurrection of the flesh for eternity the body will have those dimensions which the body of each one reached, or would have reached, in full-grown youth, with harmony and beauty preserved in the proportions of all the members. If, to preserve this beauty something is taken from the unseemly size of one part, to be spread over the whole, so as not to perish but keep the harmony of the parts everywhere, it is not unreasonable to think that some of this matter should be added also to the height of the body. For to preserve beauty the flesh, which would certainly be unseemly if abnormally concentrated in one part, is distributed over all. But if someone contends that every man will rise with the same height of body with which he died, there is no need to oppose him contentiously. Only let every deformity be excluded, every weakness, impediment or decay, and whatever else is not suited to a kingdom in which the sons of the resurrection and the promise will be equal to the angels of God [1]— if not in body, or age, at least in happiness.

XXI

On the new spiritual body, into which the flesh of the saints will be changed.

WHATEVER, therefore, has perished from living bodies or corpses after death will be restored, and, along with that which has remained in the tombs, will rise changed from the old animal body into a new spiritual body, clothed with incorruption and immor-

Sed etsi vel casu aliquo gravi vel inimicorum inmanitate totum penitus conteratur in pulverem atque in auras vel in aquas dispersum, quantum fieri potest, nusquam esse sinatur omnino, nullo modo subtrahi poterit omnipotentiae Creatoris, sed capillus in eo capitis non peribit. Erit ergo spiritui subdita caro spiritalis, sed tamen caro, non spiritus, sicut carni subditus fuit spiritus ipse carnalis, sed tamen spiritus, non caro. Cuius rei habemus experimentum in nostrae poenae deformitate. Non enim secundum carnem, sed utique secundum spiritum carnales erant, quibus ait apostolus: *Non potui vobis loqui quasi spiritalibus, sed quasi carnalibus*; et homo spiritalis sic in hac vita dicitur, ut tamen corpore adhuc carnalis sit et videat aliam legem in membris suis repugnantem legi mentis suae. Erit autem etiam corpore spiritalis, cum eadem caro sic resurrexerit, ut fiat quod scriptum est: *Seminatur corpus animale, resurget corpus spiritale*.

Quae sit autem et quam magna spiritalis corporis gratia, quoniam nondum venit in experimentum, vereor ne temerarium sit omne quod de illa profertur eloquium. Verum tamen quia spei nostrae gaudium propter Dei laudem non est tacendum et de intimis ardentis sancti amoris medullis dictum est: *Domine, dilexi decorem domus tuae*, de donis eius quae in hac aerumnosissima vita bonis malisque largitur ipso adiuvante coniciamus, ut possumus, quantum sit illud quod nondum experti utique digne eloqui non valemus. Omitto enim, quando fecit hominem

---

[1] 1 Corinthians 3.1.   [2] Romans 7.23.
[3] 1 Corinthians 15.44.   [4] Psalms 26.8.

tality. Nay, even if by some dire misfortune or by the savagery of foes the whole should be utterly ground to dust and scattered in the air or water so that, as far as possible, it may be allowed no existence at all, it can by no means be removed from the omnipotence of the Creator. No, not a hair of its head will perish. Hence the spiritual flesh will be subject to spirit, but it will still be flesh, not spirit; just as the carnal spirit was subject to the flesh, but was still spirit, not flesh. Of this we have an example in the deformity of our penal state. For those men to whom the Apostle says: " I could not speak to you as unto spiritual, but as unto carnal," [1] were carnal not in flesh but in spirit. And the man who is called spiritual in this life is still carnal in respect to his body, and sees another law in his members fighting against the law of his mind.[2] But he will be spiritual in respect to his body as well when the same flesh is raised so as to fulfil the Scripture: " It is sown an animal body, it will rise a spiritual body." [3]

But since we have had no experience as yet to tell us what this spiritual body is, or how great its beauty is, I suspect that all utterance published concerning it is rash. Nevertheless, the joy of our hope must be expressed for the glory of God, and from the inmost marrow of burning, holy love come the words: " Lord, I have loved the beauty of Thy house." [4] Hence, from the gifts which he bestows on the good and the evil in this most troubled life, with his help let us estimate, as best we can, how great is that which we have not yet experienced, and surely are not able worthily to utter. For I will not speak of the time when God made man upright, nor of that

rectum—omitto vitam illam duorum coniugum in paradisi fecunditate felicem, quoniam tam brevis fuit ut ad nascentium sensum nec ipsa pervenerit. In hac quam novimus, in qua adhuc sumus, cuius temptationes, immo quam totam temptationem, quamdiu in ea sumus, quantumlibet proficiamus, perpeti non desinimus, quae sint indicia circa genus humanum bonitatis Dei, quis poterit explicare?

XXII

De miseriis ac malis quibus humanum genus merito
primae praevaricationis obnoxium est et a quibus
nemo nisi per Christi gratiam liberatur.

Nam quod ad primam originem pertinet, omnem mortalium progeniem fuisse damnatam, haec ipsa vita, si vita dicenda est, tot et tantis malis plena testatur. Quid enim aliud indicat horrenda quaedam profunditas ignorantiae ex qua omnis error existit qui omnes filios Adam tenebroso quodam sinu suscepit,[1] ut homo ab illo liberari sine labore dolore timore non possit? Quid amor ipse tot rerum vanarum atque noxiarum et ex hoc mordaces curae, perturbationes, maerores, formidines, insana gaudia, discordiae, lites, bella, insidiae, iracundiae, inimicitiae, fallacia, adulatio, fraus, furtum, rapina, perfidia, superbia, ambitio, invidentia, homicidia, parricidia, crudelitas, saevitia, nequitia, luxuria, petulantia, inpudentia, inpudicitia, fornicationes, adulteria, incesta et contra naturam utriusque sexus tot

---

[1] *The Benedictines, along with some manuscripts, have the present tense* suscipit.

happy life of husband and wife in the fruitful garden, since it was so brief that it did not last even till their offspring should have any experience of it. But in this life which we know, in which we still live, whose trials—or rather trial, for there is nothing else—we do not cease to endure, no matter how long we are here and no matter what progress we make, who can set forth the marks of the goodness of God towards the human race?

XXII

Of the miseries and evils to which the human race is subject as a result of the first sin, and from which no one is freed except through the grace of Christ.

THIS very life, if life it can be called, pregnant with so many dire evils, bears witness that from its very beginning all the progeny of mankind was damned. For what else is the meaning of the dreadful depth of ignorance, from which all error arises, which has taken to its bosom, so to speak, all the sons of Adam in its dark embrace, so that man cannot be freed from that embrace without toil, pain and fear? What is the meaning of the love of so many vain and harmful things, from which come gnawing cares, passions, griefs, fears, mad joys, discords, strifes, wars, plots, wraths, enmities, deceits, flattery, fraud, theft, robbery, perfidy, pride, ambition, envy, murder, parricide, cruelty, ferocity, vileness, riotous living, disorderly conduct, impudence, shamelessness, fornication, adultery, incest and so many outrageous and

305

stupra atque inmunditiae, quas turpe est etiam
dicere, sacrilegia, haereses, blasphemiae, periuria,
oppressiones innocentium, calumniae, circumven-
tiones, praevaricationes, falsa testimonia, iniqua
iudicia, violentiae, latrocinia et quidquid talium
malorum in mentem non venit et tamen de vita ista
hominum non recedit? Verum haec hominum sunt
malorum, ab illa tamen erroris et perversi amoris
radice venientia cum qua omnis filius Adam nascitur.
Nam quis ignorat cum quanta ignorantia veritatis,
quae iam in infantibus manifesta est, et cum quanta
abundantia vanae cupiditatis, quae in pueris incipit
apparere, homo veniat in hanc vitam, ita ut, si
dimittatur vivere ut velit et facere quidquid velit, in
haec facinora et flagitia quae commemoravi et quae
commemorare non potui vel cuncta vel multa
perveniat?

Sed divina gubernatione non omni modo deserente
damnatos et Deo non continente in ira sua miserationes suas, in ipsis sensibus generis humani pro-
hibitio et eruditio contra istas cum quibus nascimur
tenebras vigilant et contra hos impetus opponuntur,
plenae tamen etiam ipsae laborum et dolorum.
Quid enim sibi volunt multimodae formidines quae
cohibendis parvulorum vanitatibus adhibentur? Quid
paedagogi, quid magistri, quid ferulae, quid lora,
quid virgae, quid disciplina illa qua scriptura sancta
dicit dilecti filii latera esse tundenda, ne crescat
indomitus domarique iam durus aut vix possit aut
fortasse nec possit? Quid agitur his poenis omnibus,

---

[1] Psalms 77.9.
[2] Ecclesiasticus 30.12. Compare Augustine's *Confessions*

foul forms of unnatural vice in each sex which it is
indecent even to mention, sacrilege, heresies,
blasphemies, perjuries, oppressions of the innocent,
calumnies, deceptions, duplicities, false witness, unjust verdicts, violence, brigandage and all the other
evils which come not to mind, but still do not pass from
this life of men? Yes, these are misdeeds of bad
men, for they spring from that root of error and per-
verse love with which every son of Adam is born.
Indeed, who does not know with what ignorance of
truth, manifest already in infancy, and with what
excess of vain desire, which begins to appear in childhood, man comes into this life, so that if he is allowed
to live and do as he likes, he falls into all, or many,
of these misdeeds and crimes which I have rehearsed,
and others which I was unable to rehearse?

But since divine providence does not entirely forsake the condemned, and since God does not in
anger shut up his mercies,[1] even in the perceptions
of mankind prohibition and instruction keep watch
against those dark evils with which we are born
and oppose their attacks. Still, even this instruction
abounds in toil and pain. For what is the meaning
of the manifold threats that are employed to restrain
the foolishness of children? What of the attendants,
the masters, the ferule, the thongs, the rods and that
discipline whereby Holy Scripture says the sides of
the beloved son should be beaten, lest he grow up
unbroken?[2] For when he is once hardened, he can
be tamed with difficulty, or perhaps not at all. What
is the purpose of all these penalties, except to over-

1.9.14 ff. for recollection of his miserable school days; see
also 21.14, p. 81 with note.

nisi ut debelletur inperitia et prava cupiditas in-
frenetur, cum quibus malis in hoc saeculum venimus?
Quid est enim quod cum labore meminimus, sine
labore obliviscimur cum labore discimus, sine labore
nescimus; cum labore strenui, sine labore inertes
sumus? Nonne hinc apparet in quid velut pondere
suo proclivis et prona sit vitiosa natura, et quanta
ope ut hinc liberetur indigeat? Desidia, segnitia,
pigritia, neglegentia vitia sunt utique quibus labor
fugitur, cum labor ipse, etiam qui est utilis, poena sit.

Sed praeter pueriles poenas, sine quibus disci non
potest quod maiores volunt—qui vix aliquid utiliter
volunt—quot et quantis poenis genus agitetur
humanum, quae non ad malitiam nequitiamque
iniquorum, sed ad condicionem pertinent miseriam-
que communem, quis ullo sermone digerit? quis
ulla cogitatione conprehendit? Quantus est metus,
quanta calamitas ab orbitatibus atque luctu, a
damnis et damnationibus, a deceptionibus et men-
daciis hominum, a suspicionibus falsis, ab omnibus
violentis facinoribus et sceleribus alienis! quando
quidem ab eis et depraedatio et captivitas, et vincla
et carceres, et exilia et cruciatus, et amputatio
membrorum et privatio sensuum, et oppressio corporis ad obscenam libidinem opprimentis explendam
et alia multa horrenda saepe contingunt.

Quid? ab innumeris casibus quae forinsecus corpori formidantur—aestibus et frigoribus, tempesta-
tibus imbribus adluvionibus, coruscatione tonitru,
grandine fulmine, motibus hiatibusque terrarum,

come ignorance and restrain base desire, which are evils with which we come into this world? Why is it that we remember with effort but forget without effort? That we learn with effort but stay ignorant without effort? That we are active with effort, and lazy without effort? Is it not clear from this which way our depraved nature runs downhill and is ready to fall, as it were, by its own weight, and how great the help it needs in order to escape from this predicament? Idleness, sluggishness, laziness, carelessness are certainly vices that make us shun work, yet work, even useful work, is itself a punishment.

But besides the punishment of children, without which they will not learn what their parents wish—and parents rarely wish what is useful—how many and how great are the penalties that trouble mankind—penalties that appertain, not to the wickedness and wantonness of unrighteous men, but to the common condition and misery of all! Who can sum them up in any discourse? Or who can grasp them in any act of thought? How great is the fear and the disaster of bereavement and grief, of losses and condemnations, of men's deceptions and lies, of false suspicions, of all violent deeds and crimes of other men! For from them come plundering and captivity, chains and prison, exile and torture, the severing of limbs and destruction of the means of sensation, the seizure of the body to gratify the obscene lust of the rapist and many other shocking deeds often done.

What fear there is of the countless accidents that threaten the body from without—of heat and cold, storms, rain, floods, lightning, thunder, hail, the bolt that strikes, earthquakes and chasms in the earth,

oppressionibus ruinarum, ab offensionibus et pavore
vel etiam malitia iumentorum, a tot venenis fruticum
aquarum, aurarum bestiarum, a ferarum vel tantummodo molestis vel etiam mortiferis morsibus, a rabie
quae contingit ex rabido cane, ut etiam blanda et
amica suo domino bestia nonnumquam vehementius
et amarius quam leones draconesque metuatur
faciatque hominem, quem forte adtaminaverit, con-
tagione pestifera ita rabiosum, ut a parentibus
coniuge filiis peius omni bestia formidetur! Quae
mala patiuntur navigantes! quae terrena itinera
gradientes! Quis ambulat ubicumque non inopinatis
subiacens casibus? De foro quidam rediens domum
sanis pedibus suis cecidit, pedem fregit et ex illo
vulnere finivit hanc vitam. Quid videtur sedente
securius? De sella, in qua sedebat, cecidit Heli
sacerdos et mortuus est. Agricolae, immo vero
omnes homines, quot et quantos a caelo et terra
vel a perniciosis animalibus casus metuunt agrorum
fructibus! Solent tamen de frumentis tandem
collectis et reconditis esse securi. Sed quibusdam,
quod novimus, proventum optimum frumentorum
fluvius inprovisus fugientibus hominibus de horreis
eiecit atque abstulit.

Contra milleformes daemonum incursus quis
innocentia sua fidit? Quando quidem, ne quis
fideret, etiam parvulos baptizatos, quibus certe nihil
est innocentius, aliquando sic vexant, ut in eis
maxime Deo ista sinente monstretur huius vitae
flenda calamitas et alterius desideranda felicitas.
Iam vero de ipso corpore tot existunt morborum

---

[1] 1 Samuel 4.18.

of being crushed by falling buildings, or run down by frightened or even by vicious domestic animals, of the numerous poisons in shrubs, bodies of water, currents of air, and animals, of the merely painful or even deadly bites of wild beasts, of the madness that is contracted from a mad dog, when even an animal that fawns and is friendly to its owner is sometimes feared more strongly and more bitterly than lions and snakes, and the man who happens to be infected with the deadly virus is driven so mad that he is feared by parents, wife and children more than any wild beast! What ills sailors endure, and those who travel by land! Who goes anywhere and is not liable to unexpected accidents? A man returning home from the forum with sound limbs fell, broke his leg and died from the wound. Who seems safer than a man seated? Yet Eli the priest fell from the chair in which he was sitting, and died.[1] Farmers, or rather, all men fear danger to their crops from sky and earth and hurtful animals, but they commonly feel safe when the grain is finally gathered and stored. Yet we know men who have lost an excellent crop of grain, when it was suddenly expelled from the granaries and carried away by a flood, while men fled. How many, how great are these accidents!

Who can rely on his innocence for protection against the thousand wiles of demons? No one dare feel safe, for they sometimes vex baptized infants (and nothing is more innocent than they!) so that in them above all it appears, with God's permission, what a lamentable misfortune this life is and how much we must needs desire the happiness of the future life. In fact, from the body itself arise so many diseases

311

mala ut nec libris medicorum cuncta conprehensa
sint; in quorum pluribus ac paene omnibus etiam
ipsa adiumenta et medicamenta tormenta sunt, ut
homines a poenarum exitio poenali eruantur auxilio.
Nonne ad hoc perduxit sitientes homines ardor
inmanis, ut urinam quoque humanam vel etiam suam
biberent? Nonne ad hoc fames, ut a carnibus
hominum se abstinere non possent nec inventos
homines mortuos, sed propter hoc a se occisos, nec
quoslibet alienos, verum etiam filios matres incredibili
crudelitate, quam rabida esuries faciebat, absu-
merent? Ipse postremo somnus, qui proprie quietis
nomen accepit, quis verbis explicet, saepe somniorum
visis quam sit inquietus et quam magnis licet falsarum
rerum terroribus, quas ita exhibet et quodam modo
exprimit ut a veris eas discernere nequeamus,
animam miseram sensusque perturbet? Qua falsi-
tate visorum etiam vigilantes in quibusdam morbis et
venenis miserabilius agitantur, quamvis multimoda
varietate fallaciae homines etiam sanos maligni
daemones nonnumquam decipiant talibus visis ut,
etiamsi eos per haec ad sua traducere non potuerint,
sensus tamen eorum solo appetitu qualitercumque
persuadendae falsitatis inludant.

Ab huius tam miserae quasi quibusdam inferis vitae
non liberat nisi gratia Salvatoris Christi, Dei ac
Domini nostri (hoc enim nomen est ipse Iesus;
interpretatur quippe Salvator), maxime ne post hanc

---

[1] Matthew 1.21.

that not even the books of the doctors contain them all, and in the case of most of them, or almost all of them, the treatments and drugs themselves are painful. Thus men are rescued from a penal destruction by a penal remedy. Has not fierce heat brought thirsty men to the point that they would drink even human urine, and that too their own? Has not hunger brought them to the point where they could not refrain from eating human flesh? And not merely dead bodies that they found, but human beings slain for this purpose; not merely strangers, but sons eaten by their mothers with an incredible barbarity caused by ravening hunger. Finally, there is sleep itself, which has as its own name a word meaning rest— who can tell the tale in words how restless it often is because of what is seen in dreams, and with what terrors it alarms the unhappy soul and senses? The terrible things that we see are unreal, but they are somehow made to appear so vividly that we cannot distinguish them from realities. In certain diseases and under the influence of certain drugs men even when awake are afflicted with such false apparitions, and sometimes malignant demons by their many different tricks deceive even well men by such appearances. Even if they are unable by these means to bring men into subjection, they nevertheless deceive their senses with no object in view but somehow or other to make them believe what is false.

From the hell, as it were, of this wretched life no one is freed except by the grace of our Saviour Christ, our God and Lord (for his very name " Jesus " means " Saviour ").[1] The chief purpose of salvation is that

miserior ac sempiterna suscipiat, non vita, sed mors.
Nam in ista quamvis sint per sancta et sanctos
curationum magna solacia, tamen ideo non semper
etiam ipsa beneficia tribuuntur petentibus, ne
propter hoc religio quaeratur. Quae propter aliam
magis vitam ubi mala non erunt omnino ulla quae-
renda est, et ad hoc meliores quosque in his malis
adiuvat gratia, ut quanto fideliore, tanto fortiore
corde tolerentur. Ad quam rem etiam philo-
sophiam prodesse dicunt docti huius saeculi, quam
dii quibusdam paucis, ait Tullius, veram dederunt,
nec hominibus, inquit, ab his aut datum est donum
maius aut potuit ullum dari. Usque adeo et ipsi
contra quos agimus quoquo modo compulsi sunt in
habenda non quacumque, sed vera philosophia
divinam gratiam confiteri. Porro si paucis divinitus
datum est verae philosophiae contra miserias huius
vitae unicum auxilium, satis et hinc apparet humanum
genus ad luendas miseriarum poenas esse damnatum.
Sicut autem hoc, ut fatentur, nullum divinum maius
est donum, sic a nullo deo dari credendum est nisi ab
illo quo et ipsi qui multos deos colunt nullum dicunt
esse maiorem.

we may not after this life enter a worse state, an eternal state which is not life, but death. For though in this life there are great consolations when cures are wrought by holy objects and holy saints, still even these benefits are not always granted to those who ask, lest religion be sought for their sake. Religion is rather to be sought for the sake of another life, where there will be no evils at all, and to that end even in the midst of these present evils all good men are helped by grace, so that, as they endure them with greater faith, they may find their courage so much the greater. The learned of this world say that philosophy also helps to achieve truth. The gods have given the true philosophy, as Cicero says, to a select few, nor have they given, nor could they have given, says he, any greater gift to men.[1] To this extent even our opponents are compelled somehow to admit the need of divine grace in finding, not just any philosophy, but the true philosophy. But if the gods give only to a few the true philosophy, which is the one help against the miseries of this life, it is clear enough from this too that mankind has been condemned to endure those miseries as a penalty. Moreover, just as by their admission there is no greater divine gift than this, so we must believe that it is the gift of no other god than that God who is declared the greatest of all, even by the worshippers of many gods.

[1] Cicero, *Academica* 1.2.7.

SAINT AUGUSTINE

XXIII

*De his quae praeter illa mala quae bonis malisque
communia sunt, ad iustorum laborem specialiter
pertinent.*

PRAETER haec autem mala huius vitae bonis malisque communia habent in ea iusti etiam proprios
quosdam labores suos quibus adversus vitia militant
et in talium proeliorum temptationibus periculisque
versantur. Aliquando enim concitatius, aliquando
remissius, non tamen desinit caro concupiscere
adversus spiritum et spiritus adversus carnem, ut non
ea quae volumus faciamus, omnem malam concupiscentiam consumendo, sed eam nobis quantum
divinitus adiuti possumus non ei consentiendo sub-
damus, vigiliis continuis excubantes ne opinio veri
similis fallat, ne decipiat sermo versutus, ne se
tenebrae alicuius erroris offundant, ne quod bonum
est malum, aut quod malum est bonum esse credatur,
ne ab his quae agenda sunt metus revocet, ne in ea
quae agenda non sunt cupido praecipitet, ne super
iracundiam sol occidat, ne inimicitiae provocent ad
retributionem mali pro malo, ne absorbeat inhonesta
vel inmoderata tristitia, ne inpertiendorum bene-
ficiorum ingerat mens ingrata torporem, ne maledicis
rumoribus bona conscientia fatigetur, ne temeraria
de alio [1] suspicio nos nostra decipiat, ne aliena de
nobis falsa nos frangat, ne regnet peccatum in nostro
mortali corpore ad oboediendum desideriis eius, ne

---

[1] *Some MSS. and editors omit the words* de alio *and* nos.

XXIII

Of the troubles which (in addition to the evils common to the good and the bad) belong especially to the distress of the righteous.

BESIDES the evils of this life which are common to the good and the bad, the righteous have also certain troubles of their own amid their struggle against vices, and amid the trials and dangers of that struggle. For though the conflict grows more violent or more slack from time to time, yet it never ceases, as the flesh lusts against the spirit and the spirit against the flesh, so that we do not do the things we wish,[1] by destroying evil desire. Rather, so far as we can with the help of God, we conquer desire by refusing our consent. We are always alert at our post lest the appearance of truth deceive, lest ingenious arguments ensnare us, lest some cloud of error befog us, lest we assume that good is evil, or evil good, lest fear make us refrain from what should be done, or desire plunge us headlong into what should not be done, lest the sun go down upon our wrath,[2] lest enmities provoke us to return evil for evil, lest undue or immoderate sorrow overwhelm us, lest ingratitude make us slow in sharing benefits, lest a good conscience grow weary when report spreads evil rumours, lest unfounded suspicion deceive us concerning another, lest the mistaken suspicion of others concerning us crush us, lest sin reign in our mortal body that we should obey its desires, lest our members be

---

[1] Galatians 5.17.
[2] Ephesians 4.26.

membra nostra exhibeantur iniquitatis arma peccato,
ne oculus sequatur concupiscentiam, ne vindicandi
cupiditas vincat, ne in eo quod male delectat vel
visio vel cogitatio remoretur, ne inprobum aut
indecens verbum libenter audiatur, ne fiat quod non
licet etiamsi libet, ne in hoc bello laborum peri-
culorumque plenissimo vel de viribus nostris speretur
facienda victoria vel viribus nostris facta tribuatur,
sed eius gratiae de quo ait apostolus: *Gratias autem
Deo, qui dat nobis victoriam per Dominum nostrum
Iesum Christum;* qui et alio loco: *In his,* inquit,
omnibus supervincimus per eum qui dilexit nos—sciamus
tamen, quantalibet virtute proeliandi vitiis re-
pugnemus vel etiam vitia superemus et subiugemus,
quamdiu sumus in hoc corpore nobis deesse non posse
unde dicamus Deo: *Dimitte nobis debita nostra.* In
illo autem regno, ubi semper cum corporibus inmortalibus erimus, nec proelia nobis erunt ulla nec
debita. Quae nusquam et numquam essent, si
natura nostra sicut recta creata est permaneret.
Ac per hoc etiam noster iste conflictus, in quo peri-
clitamur et de quo nos victoria novissima cupimus
liberari, ad vitae huius mala pertinet, quam tot
tantorumque testimonio malorum probamus esse
damnatam.

given up to sin as instruments of iniquity,[1] lest our eye follow after lust, lest the desire for vengeance overcome us, lest sight or thought linger on that which gives sinful delight, lest a vile or unbecoming word be heard with pleasure, lest we do what is forbidden even if it pleases us, lest in this warfare that is full of toils and dangers we hope to gain the victory by our own strength, or lest we attribute the victory we have won to our own strength and not to the grace of him of whom the Apostle says: " Thanks be to God, who gives us the victory through our Lord Jesus Christ," [2] and in another place: " In all these things we are more than conquerors through him who loved us." [3] We must know, therefore, that however bravely we struggle against vices, or even overcome and subjugate them, as long as we are in this body we shall never lack reason to say to God. " Forgive us our debts." [4] But in that kingdom where we shall live for ever with immortal bodies we shall have no battles and no debts. These would never have existed anywhere if our nature had still remained upright as it was created. Hence also this conflict of ours, on which depends our salvation, and from which we desire to be freed in final victory, is one of the evils of this life. And so by the evidence of these evils, so many and so great, we prove that this life is one of condemnation.

[1] Romans 6.12–13. [2] 1 Corinthians 15.57.
[3] Romans 8.37. [4] Matthew 6.12.

SAINT AUGUSTINE

XXIV

*De bonis quibus etiam hanc vitam damnationi obnoxiam
Creator implevit.*

Iam nunc considerandum est, hanc ipsam miseriam
generis humani in qua laudatur iustitia punientis,
qualibus et quam multis impleverit bonis eiusdem
bonitas cuncta quae creavit administrantis.   Primum
benedictionem illam quam protulerat ante peccatum
dicens: *Crescite et multiplicamini et implete terram*, nec
post peccatum voluit inhibere, mansitque in stirpe
damnata donata fecunditas, nec illam vim mirabilem
seminum, immo etiam mirabiliorem qua efficiuntur et
semina, inditam corporibus humanis et quodam
modo intextam peccati vitium potuit auferre, quo
nobis inpacta est etiam necessitas mortis. Sed
utrumque simul currit isto quasi fluvio atque torrente
generis humani, malum quod a parente trahitur,
et bonum quod a creante tribuitur. In originali
malo duo sunt, peccatum atque supplicium; in
originali bono alia duo, propagatio et conformatio.
Sed quantum ad praesentem pertinet intentionem
nostram, de malis, quorum unum de nostra venit
audacia id est peccatum, alterum de iudicio Dei id est

XXIV

*Of the good things with which the Creator has filled
even this condemned life.*[1]

Now we must consider how even this wretched
state of mankind, by which the justice of his punishment is glorified, has been blessed, and how rich and
numerous are the blessings due to the same God's
goodness, as he guides all things which he created.
First, he chose not to withdraw after the sin that blessing which he granted before the sin, when he said:
" Increase and multiply and fill the earth." [2] So the
fecundity once granted remained in the condemned
race, nor could the flaw of sin by which even the
necessity of death is imposed upon us take away
the marvellous power of seed, or rather the still more
marvellous power by which seeds are made, that was
conferred on human bodies and somehow interwoven
in our texture.   But in this rushing stream of human
life two currents, as it were, flow together, the evil
derived from Adam and the good bestowed by the
Creator.   In the original evil there are two parts,
sin and punishment.   So in the original good there
are two parts, propagation and conformation.[3]   For
our present purpose we have said enough about the
evils, of which one (that is, sin) comes from our presumption, the other (that is, punishment) comes from

book of his work. Characteristically, Cicero gives the last
word to his sceptic, while Augustine reverses the order.

[2] Genesis 1.28.

[3] This *conformatio*, as Augustine explains below, p. 323, is
the process which maintains the proper form of each species.

supplicium, iam satis diximus. Nunc de bonis Dei,
quae ipsi quoque vitiatae damnataeque naturae
contulit sive usque nunc confert, dicere institui.
Neque enim damnando aut totum abstulit quod
dederat, alioquin nec esset omnino; aut eam removit
a sua potestate, etiam cum diabolo poenaliter sub-
didit, cum nec ipsum diabolum a suo alienarit
imperio. Quando quidem, ut ipsius quoque diaboli
natura subsistat, ille facit qui summe est et facit esse
quidquid aliquo modo est.

Duorum igitur illorum, quae diximus bona etiam in
naturam peccato vitiatam supplicioque damnatam de
bonitatis eius quodam veluti fonte manare, propaga-
tionem in primis mundi operibus benedictione largitus
est, a quibus operibus die septimo requievit; conformatio vero in illo eius est opere quo usque nunc
operatur. Efficacem quippe potentiam suam si rebus
subtrahat, nec progredi poterunt et suis dimensis
motibus peragere tempora nec prorsus in eo quod
creatae sunt aliquatenus permanebunt. Sic ergo
creavit hominem Deus, ut ei adderet fertilitatem
quandam qua homines alios propagaret, congenerans
eis etiam ipsam propagandi possibilitatem, non
necessitatem. Quibus tamen voluit hominibus abstulit eam Deus, et steriles fuerunt; non tamen
generi humano abstulit semel datam primis duobus
coniugibus benedictione generali. Haec ergo pro-

---

[1] John 5.17.

the judgement of God. Now I plan to speak of the good gifts of God which he has conferred, or still is conferring, even on our corrupted and condemned nature. For in condemning he did not take away from that nature everything which he had given, otherwise it would not exist at all. Nor did he release it from his power, even when he subjected it to the devil as a punishment—for not even the devil himself is banished from his rule. For the very existence of the devil is the work of him who exists in the highest sense and gives existence to whatever exists in any sense.

So there are those two goods that we have said flow, as it were, from the spring of his goodness, even into our nature corrupted by sin and condemned to punishment. The first of these, propagation, he bestowed as a blessing during the original work of creation, from which he rested on the seventh day. The second, however, conformation, belongs to that part of his work which he is still carrying on.[1] Indeed if he should withdraw his efficient power from our world, the heavenly bodies would not be able to move forward and complete their appointed times in measured motion, nor would they remain at all in the state in which they were created. Hence God created man in such a way as to give him a fertility by which he might propagate others, begetting in them the same possibility, but not necessity, of propagating. For from some men, as he has willed, God has taken the power away, and they have been sterile. But he has not taken from mankind the general blessing which he once gave to the first couple. Although this power of propagating was

pagatio quamvis peccato non fuerit ablata, non tamen
etiam ipsa talis est qualis fuisset si nemo peccasset.
Ex quo enim homo in honore positus, postea quam
deliquit comparatus est pecoribus, similiter generat.
Non in eo tamen penitus extincta est quaedam velut
scintilla rationis, in qua factus est ad imaginem Dei.

Huic autem propagationi si conformatio non ad-
hiberetur, nec ipsa in sui generis formas modosque
procederet. Si enim non concubuissent homines et
nihilo minus Deus vellet implere terras hominibus,
quo modo creavit unum sine commixtione maris et
feminae, sic posset omnes. Concumbentes vero nisi
illo creante generantes esse non possunt. Sicut ergo
ait apostolus de institutione spiritali qua homo ad
pietatem iustitiamque formatur: *Neque qui plantat,
est aliquid, neque qui rigat, sed qui incrementum dat
Deus,* ita etiam hic dici potest: " Nec qui concumbit
nec qui seminat, est aliquid, sed qui format Deus.
Nec mater quae conceptum portat et partum nutrit
est aliquid, sed qui incrementum dat Deus." Ipse
namque operatione qua usque nunc operatur facit ut
numeros suos explicent semina, et a quibusdam
latentibus atque invisibilibus involucris in formas
visibiles huius quod aspicimus decoris evolvant.
Ipse incorpoream corpoream que naturam illam
praepositam istam subiectam miris modis copulans et

---

[1] Psalms 49.12.
[2] 1 Corinthians 3.7.
[3] The seed contains the form, or pattern of the body which
is to be, and the essence of the form is "number." This

not lost by sin, still it is not such as it would have been if no one had sinned. For after man fell from the place of honour in which he was created, he was made like the beasts,[1] and begets young like them. However, the spark of reason with which he was made in the image of God was not entirely extinguished in him.

But if conformation were not joined to this propagation, the latter would not maintain the form and type of each species. If man and woman had not mated, and God nevertheless wished to fill the earth with men, just as he created one without the union of male and female, so he could have created all. But the act of mating cannot produce offspring unless God creates. The Apostle says of the spiritual instruction by which a man is shaped in piety and righteousness: "Neither is he who plants anything, nor he who waters, but God who gives the increase."[2] Just so in this case it can be said: "Neither is he who mates nor he who plants his seed, anything, but God who gives the form. Neither is the mother who carries what is conceived, and suckles her offspring, anything, but God who gives the growth." For God himself, by the work which he still carries on, causes seeds to develop from their numbers,[3] and from certain hidden and invisible folds to evolve into the visible forms of this beauty that we see. God himself in wondrous wise unites the incorporeal and corporeal nature, the first to rule, the second to be ruled, and

thought is developed frequently by Augustine, especially in the treatise *On Free-Will* 2.16.42. The adjustment, or "harmony" of the body depends on numbers (pp. 333, 373 below).

conectens animantem facit. Quod opus eius tam
magnum et mirabile est ut non solum in homine
quod est animal rationale et ex hoc cunctis terrenis
animantibus excellentius atque praestantius, sed in
qualibet minutissima muscula bene consideranti
stuporem mentis ingerat laudemque pariat Creatoris.

Ipse itaque animae humanae mentem dedit, ubi
ratio et intellegentia in infante sopita est quodam
modo, quasi nulla sit, excitanda scilicet atque
exerenda aetatis accessu, qua sit scientiae capax
atque doctrinae et habilis perceptioni veritatis et
amoris boni. Qua capacitate hauriat sapientiam
virtutibusque sit praedita, quibus prudenter, fortiter,
temperanter et iuste adversus errores et cetera
ingenerata vitia dimicet, eaque nullius rei desiderio
nisi boni illius summi atque inmutabilis vincat.
Quod etsi non faciat, ipsa talium bonorum capacitas
in natura rationali divinitus instituta quantum sit
boni, quam mirabile Omnipotentis opus, quis com-
petenter effatur aut cogitat? Praeter enim artes
bene vivendi et ad inmortalem perveniendi felicitatem, quae virtutes vocantur et sola Dei gratia
quae in Christo est filiis promissionis regnique
donantur, nonne humano ingenio tot tantaeque artes
sunt inventae et exercitae, partim necessariae partim
voluptariae, ut tam excellens vis mentis atque
rationis in his etiam rebus quas superfluas immo et
periculosas perniciosasque appetit, quantum bonum

by mating and joining them makes a living creature. This work of his is so great and marvellous that not only in the case of man—a rational animal, hence more excellent and outstanding than all earthly animals—but even in the case of the tiniest little fly, it fills with amazement one who considers well, and calls forth praise of the Creator.

God himself, therefore, gave a mind to the human soul. In the infant, reason and intelligence somehow slumber, as if non-existent, but ready to be roused and developed with the increase of age, so as to become capable of knowledge and learning, and competent to perceive truth and love the good. Thanks to these faculties it may imbibe wisdom and be endowed with the virtues so as to struggle with prudence, fortitude, temperance, and justice against errors and the other inborn vices, and conquer them by desiring nothing except that supreme, immutable Good. Even if it does not do this, who can properly say or conceive how great a good, how marvellous a work of the Almighty, is the mere capacity for such good things, implanted by God in the rational nature? For besides the arts of living rightly and at last attaining immortal happiness—which are called virtues, and are given only by the grace of God that is in Christ to the sons of the promise and of the kingdom—has not human ingenuity discovered and exploited all our numerous and important techniques, some of which supply our needs, while others are for mere pleasure? And is not this mental, this rational drive, even when it seeks satisfaction in things superfluous, nay more, in things dangerous and suicidal, a witness to the excellence of its natural endowment,

habeat in natura unde ista potuit vel invenire vel
discere vel exercere, testetur?

Vestimentorum et aedificiorum ad opera quam
mirabilia, quam stupenda industria humana pervenerit; quo in agricultura, quo in navigatione pro-
fecerit; quae in fabricatione quorumque vasorum vel
etiam statuarum et picturarum varietate excogitaverit et impleverit; quae in theatris mirabilia
spectantibus, audientibus incredibilia facienda et
exhibenda molita sit; in capiendis occidendis
domandis inrationabilibus animantibus quae et
quanta reppererit; adversus ipsos homines tot
genera venenorum, tot armorum, tot machina-
mentorum, et pro salute mortali tuenda atque
reparanda quot medicamenta atque adiumenta conprehenderit; pro voluptate faucium quot condimenta
et gulae inritamenta reppererit; ad indicandas et
suadendas cogitationes quam multitudinem varie-
tatemque signorum, ubi praecipuum locum verba et
litterae tenent; ad delectandos animos quos elocu-
tionis ornatus, quam diversorum carminum copiam;
ad mulcendas aures quot organa musica, quos
cantilenae modos excogitaverit; quantam peritiam
dimensionum atque numerorum, meatusque et
ordines siderum quanta sagacitate conprehenderit;
quam multa rerum mundanarum cognitione se
impleverit, quis possit eloqui, maxime si velimus non
acervatim cuncta congerere, sed in singulis in-
morari?

In ipsis postremo erroribus et falsitatibus defen-
dendis quam magna claruerint ingenia philosophorum

thanks to which it had the ability, whether to discover, to be taught, or to exploit these arts?

What marvellous, stupendous results has human industry achieved in the production of clothing and buildings! What progress in agriculture and in navigation! What imagination and elaboration it has employed in producing all kinds of vases, and also in the varieties of statues and paintings! How marvellous, in theatres, to those who sit as spectators, how incredible to those who merely hear the report, are the compositions and performances contrived by men! What great inventions for capturing, killing and taming irrational animals! Against even human beings all the many kinds of poison, weapons, engines of war! And how many drugs and remedies it has discovered to preserve and restore men's health! How many seasonings and appetizers it has found to increase the pleasure of eating! What a number, what variety of signs for conveying thought and persuading men, among which words and letters are most important! What ornaments of speech to delight the mind, what abundance of all kinds of poetry! What musical instruments, what modes of song have been devised to soothe the ears! What skill in measuring and reckoning! With what acuteness have the courses and laws of the heavenly bodies been grasped! With what enormous knowledge of worldly things have men filled their minds! Who could describe this, especially if we wished not to gather everything in one pile, but to dwell on each several topic?

Finally, who could estimate the great talent of philosophers and heretics displayed in defending

atque haereticorum, quis aestimare sufficiat? Loquimur enim nunc de natura mentis humanae qua ista
vita mortalis ornatur, non de fide atque itinere veritatis qua illa inmortalis adquiritur. Huius tantae
naturae conditor cum sit utique Deus verus et
summus, ipso cuncta quae fecit administrante et
summam potestatem summamque habente iustitiam,
numquam profecto in has miserias decidisset atque
ex his praeter eos solos qui liberabuntur in aeternas
esset itura, nisi nimis grande peccatum in homine
primo, de quo ceteri exorti sunt, praecessisset.

Iam vero in ipso corpore, quamvis nobis sit cum
beluis mortalitate commune multisque earum reperiatur infirmius, quanta Dei bonitas, quanta providentia tanti Creatoris apparet! Nonne ita sunt in
eo loca sensuum et cetera membra disposita species-
que ipsa ac figura et statura totius corporis ita modificata ut ad ministerium animae rationalis se indicet
factum? Non enim ut animalia rationis expertia
prona esse videmus in terram ita creatus est homo,
sed erecta in caelum corporis forma admonet eum
quae sursum sunt sapere. Porro mira mobilitas,
quae linguae ac manibus adtributa est, ad loquendum
et scribendum apta atque conveniens et ad opera
artium plurimarum officiorumque complenda, nonne
satis ostendit quali animae ut serviret tale sit corpus
adiunctum?

Quamquam et detractis necessitatibus operandi ita
omnium partium congruentia numerosa sit et pulchra

---

[1] Colossians 3.12. The significance of man's erect posture
is a Stoic commonplace; see Cicero, *On the Nature of the Gods*
2.56.140.

errors and untruth? For we are speaking now about the natural capacity of the human mind with which this mortal life is endowed, not about the faith and way of truth by which that immortal life is obtained. Since the creator of this nature, great as it is, is surely the true and supreme God, who himself governs what he has made, and has supreme power and supreme justice, mankind would surely never have fallen to this wretched state, would never have been doomed—except for those who shall be set free—to go from present into eternal wretchedness unless there had come first an all too great sin in the case of the first man from whom the others sprang.

But even in our body, though it shares the mortality of the beasts, and is weaker than many of them, how great the goodness of God appears! How great the providence of our great Creator! Are not the sense organs and other members so arranged in it, and the appearance, shape and stature of the whole body so adapted that it shows clearly that it was designed to serve a rational soul? For man was not created as we see the irrational animals, looking towards the earth. No, his bodily shape, being raised up towards heaven, warns us that he has a sense of the things which are above.[1] Then does not the marvellous mobility which is given to the tongue and the hands, suited to speaking and writing, and adapted to the performance of what belongs to many arts and many duties, make it as clear as can be to what sort of soul such a body has been joined for its service?

And yet, even disregarding necessary adaptation to the requirements of operations to be performed, the harmony of all the parts is so well proportioned

sibi parilitate respondeat, ut nescias utrum in eo condendo maior sit utilitatis habita ratio quam decoris. Certe enim nihil videmus creatum in corpore utilitatis causa quod non habeat etiam decoris locum. Plus autem nobis id appareret, si numeros mensurarum quibus inter se cuncta conexa sunt et coaptata nossemus. Quos forsitan data opera in his quae foris eminent, humana posset vestigare sollertia. Quae vero tecta sunt atque a nostris remota conspectibus, sicuti est tanta per- plexitas venarum atque nervorum et viscerum secreta vitalium, invenire nullus potest. Quia etsi medicorum diligentia nonnulla crudelis, quos anato- micos appellant, laniavit corpora mortuorum sive etiam inter manus secantis perscrutantisque morien- tium atque in carnibus humanis satis inhumane abdita cuncta rimata est, ut quid et quo modo quibus locis curandum esset addisceret, numeros tamen de quibus loquor, quibus coaptatio, quae ἁρμονία Graece dicitur, tamquam cuiusdam organi, extrinsecus atque in- trinsecus totius corporis constat, quid dicam. Nemo valuit invenire, quos nemo ausus est quaerere ? Qui si noti esse potuissent, in interioribus quoque visceribus, quae nullum ostentant decus, ita delec- taret pulchritudo rationis ut omni formae apparenti quae oculis placet ipsius mentis quae oculis utitur praeferretur arbitrio.

Sunt vero quaedam ita posita in corpore ut tantum-

and their balance so beautiful as to make it uncertain whether in designing the body the consideration of utility counted for more, or that of beauty. In any case, we see nothing created in the body for the sake of utility that does not also have the effect of beauty. This would appear to us more clearly if we knew the numerical proportions by which all things are united and joined to each other. Perhaps human intelligence could by directing its research to such things as appear on the surface discover those proportions, but no one can find the things that are hid and removed from our sight, such as the network of veins and nerves and internal organs, and the secrets of the vital parts. To be sure, some doctors called anatomists with a cruel zeal for science have dissected bodies of dead men and even of men who died while the doctor was cutting and examining them. Thus they have not humanely, but in human flesh, explored every secret place in order to gain new information about such parts and the kind of treatment to employ, and in what spot. However, as for the numbers of which I am speaking, on which depends the adjustment of each organ, which the Greeks call *harmonia*, and of the whole body, within and without —what am I to say? That no one has been able to discover what no one has ventured to seek? If these numbers could be known, the beauty of proportion in the inner organs too, which make no display of beauty, would produce such delight that it would be preferred to every visible form that pleases the eyes, if decision were left to the mind itself that uses the eyes.

But there are certain parts so placed in the body

modo decorem habeant, non et usum, sicut habet
pectus virile mamillas, sicut facies barbam, quam non
esse munimento, sed virili ornamento indicant purae
facies feminarum, quas utique infirmiores muniri
tutius conveniret. Si ergo nullum membrum, in
his quidem conspicuis, unde ambigit nemo, quod ita
sit alicui operi accommodatum ut non etiam sit
decorum, sunt autem nonnulla quorum solum decus
et nullus est usus, puto facile intellegi in conditione
corporis dignitatem necessitati fuisse praelatam.
Transitura est quippe necessitas tempusque venturum quando sola invicem pulchritudine sine ulla
libidine perfruamur. Quod maxime ad laudem
referendum est Conditoris, cui dicitur in psalmo:
Confessionem et decorem induisti.

Iam cetera pulchritudo et utilitas creaturae, quae
homini, licet in istos labores miseriasque proiecto
atque damnato, spectanda atque sumenda divina
largitate concessa est—quo sermone terminari potest ?
In caeli et terrae et maris multimoda et varia pulchritudine, in ipsius lucis tanta copia tamque mirabili
specie, in sole ac luna et sideribus, in opacitatibus
nemorum, in coloribus et odoribus florum, in diversitate ac multitudine volucrum garrularum atque
pictarum, in multiformi specie tot tantarumque
animantium, quarum illae plus habent admirationis
quae molis minimum (plus enim formicularum et
apicularum opera stupemus quam inmensa corpora
ballaenarum), in ipsius quoque maris tam grandi
spectaculo, cum sese diversis coloribus velut vestibus
induit et aliquando viride atque hoc multis modis,

---

[1] Psalms 104.1.

as to have beauty only, and no use. For example, a man's chest has nipples, and his face a beard. That the beard is no protection but a male adornment, is proved by the smooth faces of women, for since they are weaker, they should be better protected. If therefore there is no member—at least among those which are visible, about which no one is in doubt—which is intended for some service but is not also beautiful, while there are some that have beauty alone and no use, I find it easy to deduce that in creating the body a noble mien was put before practical need. For need is bound to pass away, and the time will come when we shall enjoy nothing but one another's beauty, without any lust. This especially should redound to the praise of the Creator, to whom the Psalmist says: " Thou art robed with praise and beauty." [1]

And now, all the remaining beauty and utility of God's creation, which by the bounty of God man is allowed to view and share, though he is condemned and cast forth into these toils and miseries—with what words can it be properly described? Behold the manifold and varied beauty of heaven and earth and sea, the abundance and marvellous quality of light, sun and moon and stars, shady woods, the colours and odours of flowers, the many kinds of birds who sing and display their bright-coloured plumage, the diverse kinds of so many animals of all sizes—and the smallest are most admired, for we are more amazed at the work of tiny ants and bees than at the huge bodies of whales. Behold also the grandiose spectacle of the sea when it clothes itself with varied colours as with garments, and sometimes is green, and that too with many variations, some-

335

aliquando purpureum, aliquando caeruleum est.
Quam porro delectabiliter spectatur etiam quandocumque turbatur, et fit inde maior suavitas quia sic
demulcet intuentem ut non iactet et quatiat navi-
gantem! Quid ciborum usquequaque copia contra
famem? Quid saporum diversitas contra fastidium,
naturae diffusa divitiis, non coquorum arte ac labore
quaesita? Quid in tam multis rebus tuendae aut
recipiendae salutis auxilia! Quam grata vicissitudo
diei alternantis et noctis! Aurarum quam blanda
temperies! In fruticibus et pecoribus indumentorum
conficiendorum quanta materies! Omnia commemorare quis possit? Haec autem sola quae a me velut
in quendam sunt aggerem coartata, si vellem velut
conligata involucra solvere atque discutere, quanta
mihi mora esset in singulis quibus plurima conti-
nentur! Et haec omnia miserorum sunt damnator-
umque solacia, non praemia beatorum.

Quae igitur illa sunt, si tot et talia ac tanta sunt
ista? Quid dabit eis quos praedestinavit ad vitam,
qui haec dedit etiam eis quos praedestinavit ad
mortem? Quae bona in illa beata vita faciet eos
sumere, pro quibus in hac misera unigenitum suum
filium voluit usque ad mortem mala tanta perferre?
Unde apostolus de ipsis in illud regnum prae-
destinatis loquens: *Qui proprio*, inquit, *filio non*

---

[1] Lucretius 2.1-4.

[2] This text, along with others, is cited by Calvin in claiming
Augustine as a supporter of "double predestination." See
J. Cadier, "Calvin et Saint Augustin," in *Augustinus Magister*,

times is crimson, sometimes is blue. And what a
pleasant sight it is also whenever it is raised by a
storm! From that the pleasure is greater because
it charms the spectator without tossing and shaking
him on shipboard.[1] What of the abundance of foods
to satisfy hunger on every occasion? What of the
diversity of flavours to win over the jaded palate—
a diversity poured out from the riches of nature, not
invented by the skill and toil of the cook? What of
the means for keeping and recovering health, found
in so many things? How welcome is the alternation
of day and night! How pleasant the coolness of the
breeze! How great a supply of material for the
manufacture of clothing is furnished by plants and
animals! Who can rehearse them all? If I should
take only these things that I have tied up, as it were,
in bundles and undo the bundles for examination,
what a long time it would take me to describe the
several items in each category! And all these are
the comforts of men unhappy and condemned, not
the rewards of the blessed.

Then what are those rewards, if these are so many
and so varied and so great? What will God give to
those whom he has predestined to life, when he has
given these things even to those predestined to
death?[2] What good things in that happy life will
he cause those to enjoy, for whom in this wretched
life he chose that his only begotten Son should bear
such sufferings even unto death? Hence the Apostle
says, speaking of those predestined to that kingdom:
" He who spared not his own Son, but gave him up

1039–1056, especially 1048–50; also F. J. Thonnard in *BA* 37,
851–853.

pepercit, sed pro nobis omnibus tradidit eum, quo modo non et cum illo omnia nobis donabit? Cum haec promissio complebitur, quid erimus! Quales erimus! Quae bona in illo regno accepturi sumus, quando quidem Christo moriente pro nobis tale iam pignus accepimus! Qualis erit spiritus hominis nullum omnino habens vitium, nec sub quo iaceat, nec cui cedat, nec contra quod saltem laudabiliter dimicet, pacatissima virtute perfectus! Rerum ibi omnium quanta, quam speciosa, quam certa scientia, sine errore aliquo vel labore, ubi Dei sapientia de ipso suo fonte potabitur, cum summa felicitate, sine ulla difficultate! Quale erit corpus, quod omni modo spiritui subditum et eo sufficienter vivificatum nullis alimoniis indigebit! Non enim animale, sed spiritale erit, habens quidem carnis, sed sine ulla carnali corruptione substantiam.

XXV

De pervicacia quorundam qui resurrectionem carnis, quam sicut praedictum est totus mundus credit, inpugnant.

VERUM de animi bonis quibus post hanc vitam beatissimus perfruetur, non a nobis dissentiunt philosophi nobiles. De carnis resurrectione contendunt, hanc quantum possunt negant. Sed credentes multi negantes paucissimos reliquerunt et

---

[1] Romans 8.32.

for us all, how shall he not also with him give us all things?"[1] When this promise is fulfilled, what shall we be! And what shall we be like! What good things shall we receive in that kingdom, when we have already received such a pledge in Christ who died for us! What will man's spirit be when he has no vice at all—no vice to which he is subject, or to which he yields, or against which he struggles, in however praiseworthy a manner—but is perfect in the mastery of virtue! How great, how beautiful, how sure will be the knowledge of all things there, without any error or toil, when we shall drink the knowledge of God from its proper source, with the greatest happiness, without any difficulty! What will the body be like, a body that will be in every way subject to the spirit, and being abundantly made alive by it, will need no food to nourish it! For it will not be an animal body but a spiritual body, having indeed the substance of flesh, but without any fleshly corruption.

XXV

On the stubbornness of some who dispute the resurrection of the flesh, though all the world, as was predicted, accepts it.

Now concerning the goods of the soul which it will enjoy in perfect bliss after this life, the great philosophers do not disagree with us, but they argue about the resurrection of the flesh and deny it with all their might. Yet the many who believe have left few to deny. Learned and unlearned, the wise of this world

ad Christum, qui hoc quod istis videtur absurdum in
sua resurrectione monstravit, fideli corde conversi
sunt, docti et indocti, sapientes mundi et insipientes.
Hoc enim credidit mundus quod praedixit Deus,
qui etiam hoc praedixit, quod hanc rem mundus
fuerat crediturus. Neque enim Petri maleficiis ea
cum laude credentium tanto ante praenuntiare compulsus est. Ille est enim Deus quem, sicut iam dixi
aliquotiens nec commonere[1] me piget, confitente
Porphyrio atque id oraculis deorum suorum probare
cupiente, ipsa numina perhorrescunt, quem sic
laudavit ut eum et Deum patrem et regem vocaret.
Absit enim ut sic intellegenda sint quae praedixit
quo modo volunt hi qui hoc cum mundo non crediderunt quod mundum crediturum esse praedixit.
Cur enim non potius ita sicut crediturus tanto ante
praedictus est mundus, non sicut paucissimi garriunt
qui hoc cum mundo, quod crediturus praedictus est,
credere noluerunt?

Si enim propterea dicunt alio modo esse credenda
ne, si dixerint vana esse conscripta, iniuriam faciant
illi Deo cui tam magnum perhibent testimonium,
tantam prorsus ei vel etiam graviorem faciunt
iniuriam, si aliter dicunt esse intellegenda, non sicut
mundus ea credidit, quem crediturum ipse laudavit,
ipse promisit, ipse complevit. Utrum enim non

---

[1] *The Benedictines along with some MSS. have* commemorare.

---

[1] See 18.53 (Vol. VI, 78–83) regarding the oracle which
declared that Peter by his magic arts would cause Christ to be
worshipped for 365 years.

and the foolish, they have believed with their heart
and been converted to Christ, for he by his own
resurrection demonstrated the thing which seems
absurd to our opponents. The world has believed
what God predicted, and he also predicted that the
world was going to believe it. And it was surely
not any sorcery of Peter's,[1] displayed while believers
praised him, which compelled God so long in advance
to predict these things. For he is the God before
whom the gods of the nations tremble, as I have said
a number of times and am not weary of saying, and
as Porphyry admits and seeks to prove by quoting
the oracles of his own gods.[2] He goes so far in his
praise as to call him both God the Father, and King.
Far be it from us to understand his predictions as do
those who have not believed with the rest of the
world what he predicted that the world would believe. Why should they not be understood as he
predicted that all the world would understand them,
and not as a few babblers understand them—men
who did not consent to believe with the rest of the
world what it was predicted that the world would
believe?

Will they say that these things must be believed
in another way, in order not to do an injustice by
ascribing foolish writings to that God to whom they
bear such strong witness? Then truly they do as
great an injustice to him, or even greater, if they say
that it should be understood otherwise than as the
world has believed, for God has praised the faith of
the world, foretold it and brought it to pass. Is he

---

[2] On this oracle reported by Porphyry see 19.23 and 20.24
(Vol. VI, 217 f.), also Chapter III, p. 185 above.

potest facere ut resurgat caro et vivat in aeternum, an propterea credendum non est id eum esse facturum quia malum est atque indignum Deo? Sed de omnipotentia eius qua tot et tanta facit incredibilia iam multa diximus. Si volunt invenire quod omnipotens non potest, habent prorsus, ego dicam: mentiri non potest. Credamus ergo quod potest non credendo quod non potest. Non itaque credentes quod mentiri possit credant esse facturum quod se facturum esse promisit, et sic credant sicuti credidit mundus, quem crediturum esse praedixit, quem crediturum esse laudavit, quem crediturum esse promisit, quem credidisse iam ostendit. Hoc autem malum esse unde demonstrant? Non erit illic ulla corruptio, quod est corporis malum. De ordine elementorum iam disputavimus, de aliis hominum coniecturis satis diximus. Quanta sit futura in corpore incorruptibili facilitas motus, de praesentis bonae valetudinis temperamento quae utique nullo modo illi comparanda est inmortalitati, in libro tertio decimo satis, ut opinor, ostendimus. Legant superiora operis huius, qui vel non legerunt vel volunt recolere quod legerunt.

not able to cause the flesh to rise again and live for ever? Or must we refuse to believe that he will do this, for the reason that it is evil and unworthy of God? We have already said much concerning his omnipotence, by which he does so many incredible things. If they wish to discover what the Almighty cannot do, they have it forthwith—he cannot lie. Then let us believe what he can do, by not believing the thing which he cannot do. So by not believing that he can lie let them believe that he will do what he has promised to do. And let them believe as the world has believed, for he predicted that they would believe, praised their faith, promised it and now shows it accomplished. And how will they show that this is an evil? There will be no corruption there, which is the evil of the body. We have already discussed the order of the elements,[1] and have said enough about other difficulties which men propose. In the thirteenth book [2] I think we have shown well enough how great will be the ease of movement in the incorruptible body, by a comparison with the present body in the state of health—though even in that state it is not by any means comparable with the immortal body. Let those read the earlier parts of this work who either have not yet done so or wish to meditate again on what they have read.

[1] Chapter XI, p. 259 above.
[2] 13.18 (Vol. IV, 203).

XXVI

Quo modo Porphyrii definitio, qua beatis animis putat corpus omne fugiendum, ipsius Platonis sententia destruatur, qui dicit summum Deum diis promisisse ut numquam corporibus exuerentur.

SED Porphyrius ait, inquiunt, ut beata sit anima, corpus esse omne fugiendum. Nihil ergo prode est [1] quia incorruptibile diximus futurum corpus, si anima beata non erit nisi omne corpus effugerit. Sed iam et hinc in libro memorato quantum oportuit disputavi, verum hic unum inde tantum commemorabo. Emendet libros suos istorum omnium magister Plato et dicat eorum deos, ut beati sint, sua corpora fugituros, id est esse morituros, quos in caelestibus corporibus dixit inclusos; quibus tamen Deus, a quo facti sunt, quo possent esse securi, inmortalitatem, id est in eisdem corporibus aeternam permansionem, non eorum natura id habente, sed suo consilio praevalente, promisit. Ubi etiam illud evertit quod dicunt, quoniam est inpossibilis, ideo resurrectionem carnis non esse credendam. Apertissime quippe iuxta eundem philosophum, ubi diis a se factis promisit Deus non factus inmortalitatem, quod inpossibile est se dixit esse facturum. Sic enim eum locutum narrat Plato: " Quoniam estis orti,

---

[1] *The Benedictine editors have* prodest.

---

[1] From Porphyry's *On the Return of the Soul*; see Chapter XII, p. 271 above, with note.

XXVI

*How the rule of Porphyry, that the souls of the
blessed must shun every kind of body, is refuted by
the opinion of Plato himself who says that the
supreme God has promised the gods that they
will never be deprived of bodies.*

But, they say, Porphyry declares that for the soul
to be happy it must shun every kind of body.[1] So
it is no help to say that the body will be incorruptible,
if the soul will not be happy unless it has escaped from
body completely. I have already discussed this
topic sufficiently in the thirteenth book,[2] mentioned
above, but here I will mention just one point of that
discussion. Let Plato, the teacher of them all,
correct his own books and say that their gods, in
order to be happy, will escape from their bodies, that
is, will die. I refer to the gods who, as he says, are
shut up in celestial bodies. The God who made them,
however, gave them, in order to reassure them, a
promise of immortality, that is, that they would
remain for ever in the same bodies, not because it
was their nature, but because God's will overruled
all else. Here Plato also overthrows the argument
that the resurrection of the flesh is impossible, and
so must not be believed. For clearly, according to
the same philosopher, when the uncreated God
promised immortality to gods created by him, he
said that he would do what is impossible. For
Plato says that he spoke as follows: " Since you have

[2] 13.16 (Vol. IV, 189 f.).

345

inquit, inmortales esse et indissolubiles non potestis;
non tamen dissolvemini neque vos ulla mortis fata
periment nec erunt valentiora quam consilium meum,
quod maius est vinculum ad perpetuitatem vestram
quam illa quibus estis conligati." Si non solum
absurdi, sed surdi non sunt qui haec audiunt, non
utique dubitant diis factis ab illo Deo qui eos fecit
secundum Platonem quod est inpossibile fuisse pro-
missum. Qui enim dicit: "Vos quidem inmortales
esse non potestis, sed mea voluntate inmortales
eritis," quid aliud dicit quam "id quod fieri non
potest me faciente tamen eritis?"

Ille igitur carnem incorruptibilem, inmortalem,
spiritalem resuscitabit, qui iuxta Platonem id quod
inpossibile est se facturum esse promisit. Quid adhuc, quod promisit Deus, quod Deo promittenti
credidit mundus, qui etiam ipse promissus est
crediturus, esse inpossibile clamant, quando quidem
nos Deum, qui etiam secundum Platonem facit
inpossibilia, id facturum esse clamamus? Non ergo,
ut beatae sint animae, corpus est omne fugiendum,
sed corpus incorruptibile recipiendum. Et in quo
convenientius incorruptibili corpore laetabuntur,
quam in quo corruptibili gemuerunt? Sic enim non
in eis erit illa dira cupiditas, quam posuit ex Platone
Vergilius, ubi ait:

Rursus et incipiant in corpora velle reverti;

sic, inquam, cupiditatem revertendi ad corpora non
habebunt, cum corpora, in quae reverti cupiunt,

---

[1] *Timaeus* 41 B, quoted also 13.16 (Vol. IV, 189).
[2] *Aeneid* 6.751.

an origin in time, you cannot be immortal and indissoluble. Nevertheless, you will not be dissolved,
nor will any mortal fate extinguish you or prove more
powerful than my will. It is a stronger bond to
assure your continued survival than the bonds wherewith you were bound together."[1] Unless the hearers
have ears as deaf to sense as their reasoning is devoid
of sense, they surely cannot doubt that according
to Plato the created gods were promised what is
impossible by the God who created them. For
when he says: " You cannot be immortal, but by
my will you shall be immortal," what else does he
say except: " You will be something which is impossible, since despite everything I will accomplish
it " ?

So he who has, according to Plato, promised that
he will do the impossible, will raise up our flesh to be
incorruptible, immortal, spiritual. Therefore, when
we proclaim that this will be done by God—who, even
according to Plato, does the impossible—why do they
still proclaim that what God has promised is impossible ? It is a thing that the world believed, on
God's promise, the world's future belief being a part
of his promise. So in order to be happy souls need
not flee from every kind of body, but must receive an
incorruptible body. And in what incorruptible body
will they more fittingly rejoice than in the one in
which they groaned while it was corruptible ? Thus
they will not have that dire longing which Vergil,
following Plato, ascribes to them when he says: " And
once more begin to want to go back into bodies."[2]
Thus, I say, they will have no longing for return to
bodies, since they will possess the bodies into which

secum habebunt et sic habebunt ut numquam non
habeant, numquam ea prorsus vel ad exiguum
quamlibet tempus ulla morte deponant.

XXVII

*De contrariis definitionibus Platonis atque Porphyrii,
in quibus si uterque alteri cederet, a veritate neuter
deviaret.*

SINGULI [1] quaedam dixerunt Plato atque Porphyrius, quae si inter se communicare potuissent,
facti essent fortasse Christiani. Plato dixit sine
corporibus animas in aeternum esse non posse. Ideo
enim dixit etiam sapientum animas post quamlibet
longum tempus, tamen ad corpora redituras. Porphyrius autem dixit animam purgatissimam, cum
redierit ad Patrem, ad haec mala mundi numquam
esse redituram. Ac per hoc, quod verum vidit
Plato, si dedisset Porphyrio, etiam iustorum atque
sapientum purgatissimas animas ad humana corpora
redituras, rursus quod verum vidit Porphyrius,
dedisset Platoni, numquam redituras ad miserias
corruptibilis corporis animas sanctas ut non singuli
haec singula, sed ambo et singuli utrumque dicerent,
puto quod viderent esse iam consequens, ut et
redirent animae ad corpora et talia reciperent corpora in quibus beate atque inmortaliter viverent.
Quoniam secundum Platonem etiam sanctae animae
ad humana corpora redibunt; secundum Porphyrium
ad mala mundi huius sanctae animae non redibunt.
Dicat itaque cum Platone Porphyrius: " Redibunt

---

[1] *Most MSS. and editors have* singula.

they want to return, and possess them in such a way that they can never lose them, never put them aside in death, even for the smallest moment of time.

XXVII

Of the conflicting teaching of Plato and Porphyry, in which if each yielded to the other, neither would miss the truth.

PLATO and Porphyry severally made certain statements, and if they could have shared these with each other, perhaps they would have become Christians. Plato said that souls could not live for ever without bodies. Hence he said that even the souls of wise men, after some long period, would at last return to bodies. But Porphyry said that a soul fully cleansed, when it has returned to the Father, will never return to the evils of this world. And, hence, if Plato had given Porphyry the truth which he saw, that is, that the souls of the just and wise when fully cleansed will return to human bodies, and again, if Porphyry had given Plato the truth which he saw, that holy souls would never return to the wretched state of a corruptible body, so that one man no longer held just one view, but both men held the two views together, I think that they would have seen the logical conclusion, that souls return to bodies and that they receive bodies in which they can live happy and immortal. For according to Plato even holy souls will return to human bodies, while according to Porphyry holy souls will not return to the evils of this world. So let Porphyry say with Plato, " They will return

349

ad corpora," dicat Plato cum Porphyrio: " Non
redibunt ad mala," et ad ea corpora redire con-
sentient in quibus nulla patiantur mala. Haec
itaque non erunt nisi illa quae promittit Deus,
beatas animas in aeternum cum sua aeterna carne
victuras.[1] Hoc enim, quantum existimo, iam facile
nobis concederent ambo, ut qui faterentur ad in-
mortalia corpora redituras animas esse sanctorum ad
sua illas redire permitterent in quibus mala huius
saeculi pertulerunt, in quibus Deum, ut his malis
carerent, pie fideliterque coluerunt.

XXVIII

*Quid ad veram resurrectionis fidem vel Plato vel Labeo
vel etiam Varro conferre sibi potuerint, si opiniones
eorum in unam sententiam convenissent.*

Nonnulli nostri propter quoddam praeclarissimum
loquendi genus et propter nonnulla quae veraciter
sensit, amantes Platonem dicunt eum aliquid simile
nobis etiam de mortuorum resurrectione sensisse.
Quod quidem sic tangit in libris de re publica Tullius
ut eum lusisse potius quam quod id verum esse
adfirmet dicere voluisse. Inducit enim hominem
revixisse et narrasse quaedam quae Platonicis
disputationibus congruebant. Labeo etiam duos

---

[1] *Most MSS. and editors have* facturus; *others have* victurus,
facturum, facturas, *or* futuras.

---

[1] *Republic* 6.4.

to bodies," and let Plato say with Porphyry, " They will not return to evils," and they will agree that they return to bodies in which they can suffer no evils. So these bodies will be none other than those which God promises, when he says that blessed souls will live for ever with their own eternal flesh. For I think that both would readily grant that those who agreed that the souls of holy men would return to immortal bodies, would permit them to return to their own, in which they endured the evils of this world, and in which they piously and faithfully served God in order to escape these evils.

XXVIII

What Plato, Labeo and even Varro might have contributed to produce a true faith in the resurrection, if their views had coalesced to form a single expression of opinion.

THERE are some Christians who, because they love Plato for his distinguished literary style of speaking and for some true judgements of his, declare that he adopted a view similar to ours concerning the resurrection of the dead. Cicero, in his treatment of this point in his *Republic*,[1] declares that Plato was rather in a playful mood than in earnest when he said that the doctrine was true. For he represents a man as having come back to life and having told a story that agreed with the views of Plato.[2] Labeo [3]

---

[2] Plato, *Republic*, 10.614 to end, gives the report of Er, who returned from the dead.

[3] Labeo is previously cited 2.11 (Vol. I, 178).

dicit uno die fuisse defunctos et occurrisse invicem in
quodam compito, deinde ad corpora sua iussos fuisse
remeare et constituisse inter se amicos se esse
victuros, atque ita esse factum donec postea morerentur. Sed isti auctores talem resurrectionem
corporis factam fuisse narrarunt quales fuerunt
eorum quos resurrexisse novimus et huic quidem
redditos vitae, sed non eo modo ut non morerentur
ulterius. Mirabilius autem quiddam Marcus Varro
ponit in libris, quos conscripsit de gente populi
Romani, cuius putavi verba ipsa ponenda. " Genethliaci quidam scripserunt, inquit, esse in renascendis
hominibus quam appellant παλιγγενεσίαν Graeci;
hac scripserunt confici in annis numero quadringentis
quadraginta ut idem corpus et eadem anima quae
fuerint coniuncta in homine aliquando eadem rursus
redeant in coniunctionem."

Iste Varro quidem sive illi genethliaci nescio qui
(non enim nomina eorum prodidit, quorum commemoravit sententiam) aliquid dixerunt quod licet
falsum sit (cum enim semel ad eadem corpora quae
gesserunt animae redierint, numquam ea sunt postea
relicturae), tamen multa illius inpossibilitatis qua
contra nos isti garriunt argumenta convellit et
destruit. Qui enim hoc sentiunt sive senserunt,
non eis visum est fieri non posse ut dilapsa cadavera
in auras in pulverem, in cinerem in umores, in corpora
vescentium bestiarum vel ipsorum quoque hominum
ad id rursus redeant quod fuerunt. Quapropter
Plato et Porphyrius, vel potius quicumque illos
diligunt et adhuc vivunt, si nobis consentiunt etiam

also says that two men died in one day and met each other at a certain crossroad, then were bidden to return to their bodies. They determined to live as friends, and so it was done, as long as they lived thereafter. But these writers described a resurrection of the body such as we know occurred in the case of men restored to this life, not a resurrection such that they never died thereafter. Moreover, in the books which he wrote *On the Race of the Roman People* Marcus Varro sets down a more marvellous thing.[1] I think his words should be quoted: " Certain astrologers have written that there is a rebirth of men which the Greeks call *palingenesia*, by which in four hundred forty years the same body and soul which were once joined in a man come back to be joined once more."

Now this Varro, or the astrologers, whoever they were, whose view he mentions without giving their names, made a statement which is certainly false, for when souls have returned to the same bodies which they once had they will never leave them thereafter. Nevertheless, he shatters and destroys many arguments used to support the supposed impossibility on which they like to harp away to put us down. For those who hold, or once held, this view did not think it impossible for corpses which had been dispersed into air, dust, ashes, or liquids, or into the bodies of beasts that devoured them, or even men, to return again to their previous state. Therefore, as for Plato and Porphyry, or rather, as for those living men who admire them, if they agree with us that even

[1] Fragment 4 of Varro's work, in Peter, *Historicorum Romanorum Fragmenta*, frg. 229.

sanctas animas ad corpora redituras, sicut ait Plato,
nec tamen ad mala ulla redituras, sicut ait Porphyrius, ut ex his fiat consequens, quod fides prae-
dicat Christiana, talia corpora recepturas in quibus
sine ullo malo in aeternum feliciter vivant, adsumant
etiam hoc de Varrone, ut ad eadem corpora redeant
in quibus antea fuerunt, et apud eos tota quaestio de
carnis in aeternum resurrectione solvetur.

XXIX

De qualitate visionis qua in futuro saeculo sancti Deum videbunt.

NUNC iam quid acturi sint in corporibus inmortalibus atque spiritalibus sancti, non adhuc eorum
carne carnaliter, sed spiritaliter iam vivente, quantum Dominus dignatur adiuvare videamus. Et illa
quidem actio vel potius quies atque otium quale
futurum sit, si verum velim dicere, nescio. Non
enim hoc umquam per sensus corporis vidi. Si
autem mente, id est intellegentia, vidisse me dicam,
quantum est aut quid est nostra intellegentia ad
illam excellentiam? Ibi est enim *pax Dei, quae,*
sicut dicit apostolus, *superat omnem intellectum.* Quem
nisi nostrum, aut fortasse etiam sanctorum angelorum? Non enim et Dei. Si ergo sancti in Dei
pace victuri sunt, profecto in ea pace victuri sunt
quae superat omnem intellectum. Quoniam nostrum
quidem superat, non est dubium; si autem superat et

---

[1] Philippians 4.7.

holy souls will return to bodies (as Plato says), and still will not return to any evils (as Porphyry says), and thus arrive at the conclusion maintained by the Christian faith that souls will receive bodies in which they can live happily for ever without any evil, let them also add thereto this truth from Varro, that souls will return to the same bodies in which they lived before. Then in their own words the whole question about the resurrection of the flesh for eternity will be solved.

XXIX

Of the nature of the vision by which in the next world the saints will see God.

Now, with the help God grants, let us see what will be the activity of the saints in their immortal and spiritual bodies, when their flesh lives no longer carnally, but spiritually. But, to tell the truth, I do not know what that activity, or rather, that peace and rest, will be like, for I have never experienced it through my bodily senses. And if I should say that I have perceived it in my mind, or understanding, what is our understanding in comparison with that excellence? For in that region is found the peace of God which, as the Apostle says, passes all understanding.[1] What understanding does it surpass, except ours, or perhaps even that of the holy angels? For it does not surpass God's understanding also. If, therefore, the saints are to live in the peace of God, assuredly they will live in that peace which passes all understanding. That it passes our understanding there

355

angelorum ut nec ipsos excepisse videatur qui ait
omnem intellectum, secundum hoc dictum esse debemus
accipere quia pacem Dei, qua Deus ipse pacatus est,
sicut Deus novit, non eam nos sic possumus nosse nec
ulli angeli. *Superat* itaque *omnem intellectum*, non
dubium quod praeter suum.

Sed quia et nos pro modo nostro pacis eius participes facti scimus summam in nobis atque inter nos
et cum ipso pacem, quantum nostrum summum est
isto modo pro suo modo sciunt eam sancti angeli.
Homines autem nunc longe infra, quantumlibet
provectu mentis excellant. Considerandum est enim
quantus vir dicebat: *Ex parte scimus et ex parte
prophetamus, donec veniat quod perfectum est;* et:
*Videmus nunc per speculum in aenigmate, tunc autem
faciem ad faciem.* Sic iam vident sancti angeli, qui
etiam nostri angeli dicti sunt, quia eruti de potestate
tenebrarum et accepto spiritus pignore translati ad
regnum Christi ad eos angelos iam coepimus pertinere, cum quibus nobis erit sancta atque dulcissima,
de qua iam tot libros scripsimus, Dei civitas ipsa
communis. Sic sunt ergo angeli nostri, qui sunt
angeli Dei, quem ad modum Christus Dei Christus
est noster. Dei sunt, quia Deum non reliquerunt;
nostri sunt, quia suos cives nos habere coeperunt.
Dixit autem Dominus Iesus: *Videte ne contemnatis
unum de pusillis istis. Dico enim vobis quia angeli
eorum in caelis semper vident faciem patris mei, qui in*

---

[1] 1 Corinthians 13.9–12.   [2] Colossians 1.13.

is no doubt; if it passes that of angels, so that he who said " all understanding " did not except even the angels, then we must take the saying to mean that neither we nor any angels can know the peace of God which belongs to God himself, as God knows it. So it passes all understanding, except his own of course.

But since, when made partakers of his peace according to our capacity, we too know the highest peace in ourselves and with each other and with him, whatever our " highest " is, so likewise according to their capacity the holy angels know God's peace. But men's knowledge is now much lower, however outstanding their mental progress is. For we must consider how great a man it was who said: " We know in part and we prophesy in part, until that which is perfect shall come," and: " Now we see in a mirror dimly, but then face to face." [1] The holy angels see in that way now, who are also called our angels. For, since we have been delivered from the power of darkness and translated into the kingdom of Christ,[2] after receiving the pledge of the Spirit, we have already begun to be joined to those angels with whom we will one day share the holy and most delightful City of God, the subject of these many books that I have written. So God's angels are our angels in the same way that God's Christ is our Christ. They are God's because they have not left God, and they are ours because they have begun to have us as their fellow-citizens. But the Lord Jesus said: " See that ye despise not one of these little ones. For I say to you that their angels in heaven always see the face of my Father who is in

caelis est. Sicut ergo illi vident, ita et nos visuri sumus; sed nondum ita videmus. Propter quod ait apostolus, quod paulo ante dixi: *Videmus nunc per speculum in aenigmate, tunc autem faciem ad faciem.* Praemium itaque fidei nobis visio ista servatur, de qua et Iohannes apostolus loquens: *Cum apparuerit,* inquit, *similes ei erimus, quoniam videbimus eum sicuti est.* Facies autem Dei manifestatio eius intellegenda est, non aliquod tale membrum, quale nos habemus in corpore atque isto nomine nuncupamus.

Quapropter cum ex me quaeritur, quid acturi sint sancti in illo corpore spiritali, non dico quod iam video, sed dico quod credo, secundum illud quod in psalmo lego: *Credidi, propter quod et locutus sum.* Dico itaque: Visuri sunt Deum in ipso corpore; sed utrum per ipsum, sicut per corpus nunc videmus solem, lunam, stellas, mare ac terram et quae sunt in ea, non parva quaestio est. Durum est enim dicere quod sancti talia corpora tunc habebunt ut non possint oculos claudere atque aperire cum volent; durius autem quod ibi Deum quisquis oculos clauserit non videbit. Si enim propheta Helisaeus puerum suum Giezi absens corpore vidit accipientem munera, quae dedit ei Naeman Syrus, quem propheta memoratus a leprae deformitate liberaverat, quod servus nequam domino suo non vidente latenter se fecisse putaverat, quanto magis in illo corpore spiritali videbunt sancti omnia, non solum si oculos claudant, verum etiam unde sunt corpore absentes! Tunc enim erit perfectum illud, de quo loquens

---

[1] Matthew 18.10.   [2] 1 John 3.2.
[3] Psalms 116.10 LXX.   [4] 2 Kings 5.21–26.

heaven."[1] Therefore as they now see him, so we
shall see him, but as yet we do not see him so.
Hence the words of the Apostle, which I quoted a
moment ago: " Now we see in a mirror dimly, but
then face to face." So that vision is kept for us as
the reward of faith, concerning which John the
apostle also spoke: " When he shall have appeared
we shall be like him, for we shall see him as he is."[2]
By God's " face " we must understand his manifes-
tation, not any such bodily features as we have and
call by the name of " face."

Hence, when I am asked what will be the activity
of the saints in that spiritual body, I do not say what
I already see, but I say what I believe, according to
the words of the Psalm: " I have believed, and therefore I have also spoken."[3] Therefore I say, they are
going to see God in the body itself, but whether by
means of the body—as now by means of the body
we see sun, moon, stars, sea, the earth and the things
that are in it—is no easy question. For it is hard
to say that the saints will then have such bodies
that they cannot close and open their eyes when
they choose, but still harder to say that whoever
closes his eyes there, will not see God. For the
prophet Elisha, though absent in body, saw his
servant Gehazi receiving gifts from Naaman the
Syrian, whom the prophet cited had freed from the
deformity of leprosy.[4] The wicked servant thought
that he had done this deed in secret, without his
master seeing him. How much more in that spiritual
body will the saints see everything, not only when
they close their eyes, but even where they are absent
in body! For then will be fulfilled that of which the

apostolus: *Ex parte*, inquit, *scimus et ex parte pro-*
phetamus; cum autem venerit quod perfectum est, quod
ex parte est evacuabitur. Deinde ut quo modo posset
aliqua similitudine ostenderet, quantum ab illa quae
futura est distet haec vita, non qualiumcumque
hominum, verum etiam qui praecipua hic sanctitate
sunt praediti: *Cum essem*, inquit, *parvulus, quasi*
parvulus sapiebam, quasi parvulus loquebar, quasi
parvulus cogitabam; cum autem factus sum vir, evacuavi
ea quae parvuli erant. Videmus nunc per speculum
in aenigmate, tunc autem faciem ad faciem. Nunc
scio ex parte, tunc autem cognoscam sicut et cognitus
sum.

Si ergo in hac vita, ubi hominum mirabilium
prophetia ita comparanda est illi vitae, quasi parvuli
ad iuvenem, vidit tamen Helisaeus accipientem
munera servum suum, ubi ipse non erat, itane cum
venerit quod perfectum est nec iam corpus corrupti-
bile adgravabit animam, sed incorruptibile nihil
impediet, illi sancti ad ea quae videnda sunt oculis
corporeis, quibus Helisaeus absens ad servum suum
videndum non indiguit, indigebunt? Nam secundum
interpretes septuaginta ista sunt ad Giezi verba
prophetae: *Nonne cor meum iit tecum, quando con-*
versus est vir de curru in obviam tibi et accepisti pecuniam?
et cetera; sicut autem ex Hebraeo interpretatus est
presbyter Hieronymus: *Nonne cor meum*, inquit, *in*
praesenti erat, quando reversus est homo de curru suo in
occursum tui? Corde suo ergo se dixit hoc vidisse
propheta, adiuto quidem mirabiliter nullo dubitante
divinitus. Sed quanto amplius tunc omnes munere

---

[1] 1 Corinthians 13.11–12.

Apostle spoke: "We know in part and we prophesy in part, but when that which is perfect has come, that which is in part shall be done away." Then, in order to show as best he could by a comparison how different this life is from that which is to come—not the life of the average man, but even the life of those here endowed with outstanding holiness, he says: "When I was a child I understood as a child, I spoke as a child, I thought as a child, but when I became a man, I put away childish things. Now we see in a mirror dimly, but then face to face. Now I know in part, but then I shall know just as I also am known."[1]

If then, in this life, where the miraculous gift of prophecy must be compared to the future life as the life of a child to full-grown youth, yet Elisha by such miraculous power saw his servant receiving gifts when he was absent, then, when that which is perfect has come and the soul no longer is dragged down by a corruptible body, but has an incorruptible body that offers no hindrance, will the saints need bodily eyes to see what is to be seen, though Elisha did not need them to see his servant when absent? For according to the Septuagint these are the words of the prophet to Gehazi: "Did not my heart go with you when the man turned from his chariot to meet you, and you received the money?" and so on. But as the presbyter Jerome has translated it from the Hebrew: "Was not my heart present when the man returned from his chariot to encounter you?" So the prophet says that he saw this with his heart, marvellously aided by God, as no one doubts. But how much more will all then have that gift abundantly, when

isto abundabunt, cum Deus erit omnia in omnibus!
Habebunt tamen etiam illi oculi corporei officium
suum et in loco suo erunt, uteturque illis spiritus per
spiritale corpus. Neque enim et ille propheta, quia
non eis indiguit ut videret absentem, non eis usus est
ad videnda praesentia; quae tamen spiritu videre
posset, etiamsi illos clauderet, sicut vidit absentia,
ubi cum eis ipse non erat. Absit ergo, ut dicamus
illos sanctos in illa vita Deum clausis oculis non
visuros, quem spiritu semper videbunt.

Sed utrum videbunt et per oculos corporis cum eos
apertos habebunt, inde quaestio est. Si enim
tantum poterunt in corpore spiritali eo modo utique
ipsi oculi etiam spiritales quantum possunt isti quales
nunc habemus, procul dubio per eos Deus videri non
poterit. Longe itaque alterius erunt potentiae, si
per eos videbitur incorporea illa natura quae non
continetur loco sed ubique tota est. Non enim quia
dicimus Deum et in caelo esse et in terra (ipse quippe
ait per prophetam: *Caelum et terram ego impleo*),
aliam partem dicturi sumus eum in caelo habere et in
terra aliam; sed totus in caelo est, totus in terra,
non alternis temporibus, sed utrumque simul, quod
nulla natura corporalis potest. Vis itaque prae-
pollentior oculorum erit illorum, non ut acrius videant
quam quidam perhibentur videre serpentes vel
aquilae—quantalibet enim acrimonia cernendi eadem
quoque animalia nihil aliud possunt videre quam
corpora—sed ut videant et incorporalia. Et fortasse

---

[1] 1 Corinthians 15.28.   [2] Jeremiah 23.24.

God himself shall be all in all![1] However, those bodily eyes also will have their function and will be in their place, and the spirit will use them as part of the spiritual body. For while the prophet did not need his eyes to see one who was absent, he did not therefore cease to use them to see things present. And yet he would have been able to see those things with the spirit even if he had closed his eyes, just as he saw things absent when he himself was not with them. Far be it from us then to say that those saints will not in that life with their eyes closed see God, whom they will always see in spirit.

But whether they will see with the eyes of the body also, when they have them open, is the question. For if in the spiritual body the eyes, which will of course be spiritual also, can see no more than these eyes which we have now, undoubtedly we shall not be able to see God with them. Hence they will have a very different power, if we are then to see with them that incorporeal nature which is not contained in a place, but is everywhere entirely present. For when we say that God is both in heaven and on earth (he himself says through the prophet: " I fill heaven and earth "),[2] we are not going to say next that he has one part in heaven and another on earth. Rather, he is wholly in heaven and wholly on earth, not at different times, but both at the same time, which is impossible for any bodily substance. Therefore the power of those eyes will be greater, not to see more sharply than some serpents or eagles are said to see (for however great their keenness of vision, these animals can see nothing but bodies), but to see incorporeal things as well. And perhaps this mighty

ista virtus magna cernendi data fuerit ad horam etiam
in isto mortali corpore oculis sancti viri Iob, quando
ait ad Deum: *In obauditu auris audiebam te prius,
nunc autem oculus meus videt te; propterea despexi
memet ipsum et distabui et existimavi me terram et
cinerem;* quamvis nihil hic prohibeat oculum cordis
intellegi, de quibus oculis ait apostolus: *Inluminatos
oculos* habere *cordis vestri.* Ipsis autem videri Deum,
cum videbitur, Christianus ambigit nemo qui fideliter
accipit quod ait Deus ille magister: *Beati mundi-
cordes, quoniam ipsi Deum videbunt.* Sed utrum etiam
corporalibus ibi oculis videatur, hoc in ista quaestione
versamus.

Illud enim quod scriptum est: *Et videbit omnis caro
salutare Dei,* sine ullius nodo difficultatis sic intellegi
potest ac si dictum fuerit: " Et videbit omnis homo
Christum Dei," qui utique in corpore visus est et in
corpore videbitur, quando vivos et mortuos iudicabit.
Quod autem ipse sit salutare Dei, multa sunt et alia
testimonia scripturarum; sed evidentius venerandi
illius senis Simeonis verba declarant, qui cum infan-
tem Christum accepisset in manus suas: *Nunc,*
inquit, *dimittis, Domine, servum tuum secundum verbum
tuum in pace, quoniam viderunt oculi mei salutare tuum.*
Illud etiam quod ait supra memoratus Iob, sicut in
exemplaribus quae ex Hebraeo sunt invenitur: *Et in
carne mea videbo Deum,* resurrectionem quidem carnis
sine dubio prophetavit, non tamen dixit: " Per

---

[1] Job 42.5–6. [2] Ephesians 1.18.
[3] Matthew 5.8. [4] Luke 3.6.

power of discernment was given for a season in this
mortal body to the eyes of the holy man Job, when
he said to God: " With the hearing of the ear I
heard of thee before, but now my eye sees thee.
Therefore I have despised myself and have melted
away and have thought myself dust and ashes." [1]
And yet nothing prevents us from understanding here
the eye of the heart, of which eyes the Apostle says:
" Having the eyes of your heart enlightened." [2]
And that God will be seen with those eyes, when he
comes to be seen, no Christian doubts, if he accepts
in faith what our God and Teacher says: " Blessed
are the pure in heart, for they shall see God." [3]
But whether he is seen there by the eyes of the body
also is the question that concerns us.

The Scripture, " And all flesh shall see the salvation of God," [4] can be understood without difficulty,
as if it were said: " And every man shall see God's
Christ," for he was, of course, seen in the body, and
will be seen in the body when he shall judge the living
and the dead. And there are many other Scripture
proofs that he is the salvation of God, but it is most
plainly indicated by the words of that venerable, aged
Simeon, who said, when he had taken the infant
Christ in his arms: " Now, O Lord, thou lettest thy
servant depart, according to thy word, in peace,
since my eyes have seen thy salvation." [5] And the
words of Job, whom I mentioned above, as found in
the copies translated from the Hebrew: " And in
my flesh I shall see God," [6] undoubtedly foretell the
resurrection of the flesh. Still, he did not say,

[5] Luke 2.29–30.
[6] Job 19.26 Vulgate.

carnem meam." Quod quidem si dixisset, posset
Deus Christus intellegi, qui per carnem in carne
videbitur; nunc vero potest et sic accipi: *In carne
mea videbo Deum*, ac si dixisset: "In carne mea ero,
cum videbo Deum." Et illud, quod ait apostolus:
Faciem ad faciem, non cogit ut Deum per hanc faciem
corporalem, ubi sunt oculi corporales, nos visuros esse
credamus, quem spiritu sine intermissione videbimus. Nisi enim esset etiam interioris hominis
facies, non diceret idem apostolus: *Nos autem
revelata facie gloriam Domini speculantes in eandem
imaginem transformamur, de gloria in gloriam, tamquam
a Domini spiritu;* nec aliter intellegimus et quod in
psalmo canitur: *Accedite ad eum et inluminamini, et
facies vestrae non erubescent.* Fide quippe acceditur
ad Deum, quam cordis constat esse, non corporis.
Sed quia spiritale corpus nescimus quantos habebit
accessus—de re quippe inexperta loquimur, ubi
aliqua quae aliter intellegi nequeat divinarum
scripturarum non occurrit et succurrit auctoritas—
necesse est ut contingat in nobis quod legitur in libro
Sapientiae: *Cogitationes mortalium timidae et incertae
providentiae nostrae.*

Ratiocinatio quippe illa philosophorum, qua disputant ita mentis aspectu intellegibilia videri et
sensu corporis sensibilia, id est corporalia, ut nec
intellegibilia per corpus nec corporalia per se ipsam
mens valeat intueri, si posset nobis esse certissima,

---

[1] 1 Corinthians 13.12.
[2] 2 Corinthians 3.18.
[3] Psalms 34.5 (33.6 Vulgate).
[4] Wisdom 9.14.

" through my flesh." But if he had said that, Christ could be understood as " God," for he will be seen in the flesh through eyes of flesh. As it is, the words, " In my flesh I shall see God," can also be understood as if he had said, " I shall be in my flesh when I see God." And the words of the Apostle, " face to face," [1] do not compel us to believe that we shall see God through this bodily face and bodily eyes, for we shall see him in spirit without interruption. For if there were no " face " of the inner man, the same Apostle would not say: " But we with unveiled face beholding the glory of the Lord are transformed into the same image, from glory to glory, as by the Spirit of the Lord." [2] Nor do we otherwise understand again what is sung in the Psalm: " Draw near to him and be illuminated, and your faces shall not be covered with shame." [3] By faith, indeed, one draws near to God, and this admittedly is of the heart, not of the body. But because we do not know how close will be the approach of the spiritual body (for we are speaking of a thing beyond our experience, in regard to which no unambiguous Scripture authority comes to the rescue), the statement of the book of Wisdom must be true of us: " The thoughts of mortals are timorous and our foresights uncertain." [4]

To be sure, there is the reasoning of the philosophers by which they maintain that intelligible things are seen by the vision of the mind, and sensible things (that is, corporeal) by bodily senses, so that intelligible things cannot be seen through the body, nor can the mind of itself behold corporeal things. If we could be entirely sure of this, of course it would

profecto certum esset per oculos corporis etiam
spiritalis nullo modo posse videri Deum. Sed istam
ratiocinationem et vera ratio et prophetica inridet
auctoritas. Quis enim ita sit aversus a vero ut
dicere audeat Deum corporalia ista nescire? Numquid ergo corpus habet, per cuius oculos ea possit
addiscere? Deinde quod de propheta Helisaeo paulo
ante diximus, nonne satis indicat etiam spiritu, non
per corpus, corporalia posse cerni? Quando enim
servus ille munera accepit, utique corporaliter
gestum est; quod tamen propheta non per corpus,
sed per spiritum vidit. Sicut ergo constat corpora
videri spiritu, quid si tanta erit potentia spiritalis
corporis ut corpore videatur et spiritus? *Spiritus*
enim *est Deus*. Deinde vitam quidem suam, qua
nunc vivit in corpore et haec terrena membra
vegetat facitque viventia, interiore sensu quisque,
non per corporeos oculos novit; aliorum vero vitas,
cum sint invisibiles, per corpus videt. Nam unde
viventia discernimus a non viventibus corpora, nisi
corpora simul vitasque videamus, quas nisi per corpus
videre non possumus? Vitas autem sine corporibus
corporeis oculis non videmus.

Quam ob rem fieri potest valdeque credibile est sic
nos visuros mundana tunc corpora caeli novi et terrae
novae ut Deum ubique praesentem et universa etiam
corporalia gubernantem per corpora quae gestabimus
et quae conspiciemus, quaqua versum oculos
duxerimus, clarissima perspicuitate videamus, non

---

[1] John 4.24.

be certain that God could in no wise be seen through the eyes even of a spiritual body. But this doctrine is scorned by true reasoning and prophetic authority. For who is so far from the truth that he dares to say that God does not know these corporeal things? Has he therefore a body, through whose eyes he is able to acquire knowledge of them? Furthermore, does not what we said above about the prophet Elisha show well enough that corporeal things can be discerned by the spirit too, without the help of the body? For when that slave accepted the gifts it was certainly a corporeal transaction, but the prophet saw it not through the body, but through the spirit. So as it is certain that bodies are seen by the spirit, what if the power of the spiritual body is to be so great that spirit may also be seen by a body? For "God is Spirit."[1] Moreover, it is by an inner sense and not by corporeal eyes that a man knows his own life, by which he now lives in the body and causes these earthly limbs to grow and live, but the lives of other men, though invisible, he sees through the body. For how do we distinguish living bodies from dead, unless we see bodies and at the same time lives, which we cannot see except through the body? But with corporeal eyes we do not see lives without bodies.

Therefore it is possible, and very probable, that we shall see the corporeal bodies of the new heaven and the new earth in such a way that, wherever we turn our eyes, we shall, through our bodies that we shall be wearing and plainly seeing, enjoy with perfect clarity of vision the sight of God everywhere present and ruling all things, even material things.

sicut nunc invisibilia Dei per ea quae facta sunt
intellecta conspiciuntur per speculum in aenigmate
et [1] ex parte, ubi plus in nobis valet fides qua credimus
quam rerum corporalium species, quam per oculos
cernimus corporales. Sed sicut homines, inter quos
viventes motusque vitales exerentes vivimus, mox ut
aspicimus, non credimus vivere, sed videmus, cum
eorum vitam sine corporibus videre nequeamus,
quam tamen in eis per corpora remota omni ambi-
guitate conspicimus, ita quacumque spiritalia illa
lumina corporum nostrorum circumferemus, in-
corporeum Deum omnia regentem etiam per corpora
contuebimur. Aut ergo sic per illos oculos videbitur
Deus, ut aliquid habeant in tanta excellentia menti
simile, quo et incorporea natura cernatur, quod ullis
exemplis sive scripturarum testimoniis divinarum vel
difficile est vel inpossibile ostendere; aut, quod est ad
intellegendum facilius, ita Deus nobis erit notus
atque conspicuus, ut videatur spiritu a singulis nobis
in singulis nobis, videatur ab altero in altero, videatur
in se ipso, videatur in caelo novo et terra nova atque
in omni quae tunc fuerit creatura, videatur et per
corpora in omni corpore, quocumque fuerint spiritalis
corporis oculi acie perveniente directi. Patebunt
etiam cogitationes nostrae invicem nobis. Tunc
enim implebitur, quod apostolus, cum dixisset:
Nolite ante tempus iudicare quicquam, mox addidit:
Donec veniat Dominus, et inluminabit abscondita tene-

---

[1] *Most MSS. omit* et.

---

[1] Romans 1.10; 1 Corinthians 13.12.

It will not be as it is now, when the invisible things of God are seen and understood through the things which have been made, in a mirror dimly, and in part,[1] where the faith by which we believe counts for more than the appearance of corporeal things which we perceive through corporeal eyes. Now we live among living men who display the motions of life, and whenever we see them we do not believe, but rather see that they are alive. Though we cannot see the life within their bodies, still we see it in them by means of their bodies, all doubt being removed. In the same way, wherever we turn those spiritual eyes of our new bodies, we shall by means of bodies too behold the incorporeal God ruling all things. Either, therefore, God will be seen by means of those eyes because they in their excellence will have something similar to mind by which even an incorporeal nature is discerned—but this is difficult or impossible to illustrate by any example or testimony of the divine writings—or else, which is easier to understand, God will be so known by us and so present to our eyes that by means of the spirit he will be seen by each of us in each of us, seen by each in his neighbour and in himself, seen in the new heaven and the new earth and in every creature which will then exist, seen also by bodily means in every body wherever the eyes of the spiritual body are directed, and as far as their vision extends. Our thoughts also will lie open to one another. For then will be fulfilled what the Apostle said: " Judge nothing before the time," adding, " until the Lord come; and he will bring to light the hidden things of darkness and will make manifest

brarum et manifestabit cogitationes cordis, et tunc laus erit unicuique a Deo.

XXX

De aeterna felicitate civitatis Dei sabbatoque perpetuo.

QUANTA erit illa felicitas, ubi nullum erit malum, nullum latebit bonum, vacabitur Dei laudibus, qui erit omnia in omnibus! Nam quid aliud agatur, ubi neque ulla desidia cessabitur neque ulla indigentia laborabitur, nescio. Admoneor etiam sancto cantico, ubi lego vel audio: *Beati, qui habitant in domo tua, in saecula saeculorum laudabunt te.* Omnia membra et viscera incorruptibilis corporis, quae nunc videmus per usus necessitatis varios distributa, quoniam tunc non erit ipsa necessitas, sed plena certa, secura sempiterna felicitas, proficient laudibus Dei. Omnes quippe illi, de quibus iam sum locutus, qui nunc latent, harmoniae corporalis numeri non latebunt, intrinsecus et extrinsecus per corporis cuncta dispositi, et cum ceteris rebus quae ibi magnae atque mirabiles videbuntur rationales mentes in tanti artificis laudem rationabilis pulchritudinis delectatione succendent.

Qui motus illic talium corporum sint futuri, temere definire non audeo, quod excogitare non valeo; tamen et motus et status, sicut ipsa species, decens erit,

---

[1] 1 Corinthians 4.5.   [2] Psalms 84.4.
[3] Chapter 24, p. 325 above.

the thoughts of the heart, and then shall each man
have his praise from God."[1]

XXX

*Of the eternal happiness and perpetual sabbath of the
City of God.*

How great will be that happiness where there will
be no evil, where no good will be hidden, where there
will be time for the praises of God, who will be all in
all! For I know not what other occupation there
can be where no one will be inactive from idleness,
and no one will toil because of any lack. Of this I
am reminded also by the holy psalm where I read or
hear the words: " Blessed are they that dwell in thy
house, they shall praise thee for ever and ever."[2]
All the limbs and inner organs of the incorruptible
body, organs now assigned to various necessary uses,
will contribute to the praise of God, for then there will
be no necessity, but a happiness that is full, sure,
untroubled, eternal. All those numbers belonging
to corporeal harmony, of which I have already
spoken,[3] which now are hidden, will appear, arranged
through all parts of the body, within and without.
A delight in the rational beauty of these, and all
other things whose wondrous greatness will there be
seen, will inflame the hearts of all rational beings to
praise their great Creator.

The question what the movements there of such
bodies will be, is one that I am reluctant to answer
precisely, because I cannot get it clear in my mind.
However, both movement and posture, and the whole

quicumque erit, ubi quod non decebit non erit.
Certe ubi volet spiritus, ibi erit protinus corpus; nec
volet aliquid spiritus quod nec spiritum posset decere
nec corpus. Vera ibi gloria erit, ubi laudantis nec
errore quisquam nec adulatione laudabitur; verus
honor, qui nulli negabitur digno, nulli deferetur
indigno; sed nec ad eum ambiet ullus indignus, ubi
nullus permittetur esse nisi dignus; vera pax, ubi
nihil adversi nec a se ipso nec ab aliquo quisque
patietur. Praemium virtutis erit ipse qui virtutem
dedit eique se ipsum, quo melius et maius nihil
possit esse, promisit. Quid est enim aliud quod per
prophetam dixit: *Ero illorum Deus, et ipsi erunt mihi
plebs,* nisi: " Ego ero unde satientur, ego ero quaecumque ab hominibus honeste desiderantur, et vita
et salus et victus et copia et gloria et honor et pax
et omnia bona? " Sic enim et illud recte intellegitur
quod ait apostolus: *Ut sit Deus omnia in omnibus.*
Ipse finis erit desideriorum nostrorum qui sine fine
videbitur, sine fastidio amabitur, sine fatigatione
laudabitur. Hoc munus, hic affectus, hic actus
profecto erit omnibus, sicut ipsa vita aeterna, communis.

Ceterum qui futuri sint pro meritis praemiorum
etiam gradus honorum atque gloriarum, quis est
idoneus cogitare, quanto magis dicere? Quod tamen
futuri sint, non est ambigendum. Atque id etiam
beata illa civitas magnum in se bonum videbit, quod
nulli superiori ullus inferior invidebit, sicut nunc

---

[1] Leviticus 26.12; as quoted in 1 Corinthians 6.16.
[2] 1 Corinthians 15.28.

appearance, will be seemly, whatever it is, for nothing unseemly will be there. Surely wherever the spirit wishes to be, the body will at once be there, nor will the spirit wish anything which might be unseemly for spirit or body. True glory will be there, where no one will be praised by mistake or by flattery, and true honour will be denied to no one who is worthy, and conferred on no one who is unworthy. Neither will anyone who is unworthy aspire to it, for no one except the worthy will be allowed to dwell there. True peace will be there, for no one will suffer any hurt either from his own acts or from another's. The prize of virtue will be God himself, who gave the virtue and promised himself as its reward—and there can be no better or greater reward. For what else did he mean, when he says in the prophet's words: " I shall be their God and they shall be my people," [1] except: "I shall be that by which they are satisfied; I shall be whatever is properly desired by men—life and health and food and abundance and glory and honour and peace and all good things." That is the proper meaning also of the Apostle's words: " That God may be all in all." [2] He will be the end of our desires. He will be seen without end, will be loved without repletion and praised without weariness. This boon, this emotion, this activity will surely be shared by all, like eternal life itself.

But who is qualified to imagine, much less declare, what will be the degrees of honour and glory proportioned to the merits of each one ? However, there is no doubt that there will be such degrees. And that blessed city will see this great good in herself also, that no one who is lower will envy one who is higher,

non invident archangelis angeli ceteri; tamque nolet
esse unusquisque quod non accepit, quamvis sit
pacatissimo concordiae vinculo ei qui accepit ob-
strictus, quam nec in corpore vult oculus esse qui est
digitus, cum membrum utrumque contineat totius
corporis pacata compago. Sic itaque habebit donum
alius alio minus, ut hoc quoque donum habeat, ne velit
amplius.

Nec ideo liberum arbitrium non habebunt quia
peccata eos delectare non poterunt. Magis quippe
erit liberum a delectatione peccandi usque ad
delectationem non peccandi indeclinabilem libera-
tum. Nam primum liberum arbitrium, quod homini
datum est quando primo creatus est rectus, potuit
non peccare, sed potuit et peccare; hoc autem
novissimum eo potentius erit quo peccare non poterit;
verum hoc quoque Dei munere, non suae possibilitate
naturae. Aliud est enim esse Deum, aliud participem Dei. Deus natura peccare non potest;
particeps vero Dei ab illo accepit ut peccare non
possit. Servandi autem gradus erant divini muneris,
ut primum daretur liberum arbitrium quo non
peccare homo posset, novissimum quo peccare non
posset, atque illud ad comparandum meritum, hoc ad
recipiendum praemium pertineret. Sed quia peccavit ista natura cum peccare potuit, largiore gratia
liberatur ut ad eam perducatur libertatem in qua
peccare non possit. Sicut enim prima inmortalitas
fuit quam peccando Adam perdidit, posse non mori,
novissima erit non posse mori, ita primum liberum
arbitrium posse non peccare, novissimum non posse

even as now other angels do not envy archangels. And no one will wish for the place he has not received, though he be bound by the closest tie of friendship to one who has received it—no more than in our body the finger wishes to be an eye, since the peaceable structure of the whole body holds both members together. Therefore, if there is one who has a gift less than another's, he will have the further gift of not desiring more.

Nor will they be deprived of free-will because of the fact that sins cannot delight them. For the will will be free rather from the delight in sinning, freed even to the point of steadfast delight in not sinning. For the first free-will, which was given to man when he was created upright, was able not to sin, but was also able to sin. But this last free-will will be more powerful in that it will not be able to sin, and this also by the gift of God, not by the power of its own nature. It is one thing to be God, another to partake of God. God by nature cannot sin, while he who partakes of God receives from him the inability to sin. Moreover, there had to be steps in the divine gift—a first gift by which man should be able not to sin, and a last gift by which he should not be able to sin, the former that he might gain merit, the latter that he might receive the reward. But since that first nature sinned when it was able to sin, it is freed by a more generous grace, that it may be led to that liberty in which it cannot sin. For just as the first immortality which Adam lost by sinning was the ability not to die, and the last will be the inability to die, so the first free-will was the ability not to sin, the last the inability to sin. For

peccare. Sic enim erit inamissibilis voluntas pietatis et aequitatis, quo modo est felicitatis. Nam utique peccando nec pietatem nec felicitatem tenuimus, voluntatem vero felicitatis nec perdita felicitate perdidimus. Certe Deus ipse numquid, quoniam peccare non potest, ideo liberum arbitrium habere negandus est?

Erit ergo illius civitatis et una in omnibus et inseparabilis in singulis voluntas libera, ab omni malo liberata et impleta omni bono, fruens indeficienter aeternorum iucunditate gaudiorum, oblita culparum, oblita poenarum; nec ideo tamen suae liberationis oblita ut liberatori suo non sit ingrata. Quantum ergo adtinet ad scientiam rationalem, memor praeteritorum etiam malorum suorum; quantum autem ad experientis sensum, prorsus immemor. Nam et peritissimus medicus, sicut arte sciuntur, omnes fere corporis morbos novit; sicut autem corpore sentiuntur, plurimos nescit quos ipse non passus est. Ut ergo scientiae malorum duae sunt, una qua potentiam mentis non latent, altera qua experientis sensibus inhaerent—aliter quippe sciuntur vitia omnia per sapientiae doctrinam, aliter per insipientis pessimam vitam—ita et obliviones malorum duae sunt. Aliter ea namque obliviscitur eruditus et doctus, aliter expertus et passus; ille, si peritiam neglegat, iste, si miseria careat. Secundum hanc oblivionem, quam posteriore loco posui, non erunt memores sancti praeteritorum malorum;

the desire for godliness and righteousness will be as impossible to lose as the desire for happiness. For surely in sinning we retained neither godliness nor happiness, but though we lost happiness we did not lose the desire for happiness. Surely, though God himself is unable to sin, no one should for that reason say that he does not have free-will.

Thus the free-will of that city will be one will present in all, and inseparably fixed in each individual. It will be freed from every evil and filled with every good, enjoying incessantly the delight of eternal joys; it will forget past sins and punishments, but still will not for that reason forget its liberation and so be ungrateful to its liberator. As far as its rational knowledge is concerned, it also remembers its past evils, but as for actually feeling them, they are completely forgotten. A skilled physician knows almost all the diseases of the body as they are known in medical science, but he is ignorant of most as they are felt in the body, for he has not suffered them himself. So there are two kinds of knowledge of evils—one whereby they are not hidden from the grasp of the mind, the other whereby they stick in the feelings of a man who experiences them, for all vices are known in one way through instruction in wisdom, in another through the sinful life of one who is not wise. So also there are two kinds of forgetfulness of evils, for the well-educated, learned man forgets them in one way, and the man who has experienced and suffered them in another. The former forgets if he neglects his learning, the latter if he is free from distress. It is according to this second kind of forgetfulness that the saints will forget past evils, for they will be so

carebunt enim omnibus, ita ut penitus deleantur de sensibus eorum. Ea tamen potentia scientiae, quae magna in eis erit, non solum sua praeterita, sed etiam damnatorum eos sempiterna miseria non latebit. Alioquin si se fuisse miseros nescituri sunt, quo modo, sicut ait psalmus, *misericordias Domini in aeternum cantabunt*?

Quo cantico in gloriam gratiae Christi, cuius sanguine liberati sumus, nihil erit profecto illi iucundius civitati. Ibi perficietur: *Vacate et videte quoniam ego sum Deus*, quod erit vere maximum sabbatum non habens vesperam, quod commendavit Dominus in primis operibus mundi, ubi legitur: *Et requievit Deus die septimo ab omnibus operibus suis quae fecit, et benedixit Deus diem septimum et sanctificavit eum, quia in eo requievit ab omnibus operibus suis quae inchoavit Deus facere*. Dies enim septimus etiam nos ipsi erimus, quando eius fuerimus benedictione et sanctificatione pleni atque refecti. Ibi vacantes videbimus quoniam ipse est Deus; quod nobis nos ipsi esse voluimus, quando ab illo cecidimus, audientes a seductore: *Eritus sicut dii* et recedentes a vero Deo, quo faciente dii essemus eius participatione, non desertione. Quid enim sine illo fecimus, nisi quod in ira eius defecimus? A quo refecti et gratia maiore perfecti vacabimus in aeternum, videntes quia ipse est Deus, quo pleni erimus quando ipse erit omnia in omnibus. Nam et ipsa opera bona nostra, quando ipsius potius intelleguntur esse, non nostra, tunc nobis ad hoc sabbatum adipiscendum inpu-

---

[1] Psalms 89.1. [2] Psalms 46.10.
[3] Genesis 2.2. [4] Genesis 3.5.

unvexed by evils that evils will be completely erased from their senses. But by the faculty of knowledge, which will be strong in them, they will know not only their own past, but also the eternal misery of the damned. Otherwise, if they do not know that they were once wretched, how will they " sing the mercies of the Lord for ever," as the psalm says? [1]

Surely nothing will be more pleasant in that city than this song to the glory of the grace of Christ, by whose blood we have been freed. There will the words be fulfilled: " Be still and see that I am God." [2] That will truly be the greatest sabbath, a sabbath that has no evening. This sabbath God commended in the account of creation, where we read: " And God rested on the seventh day and hallowed it, because in it he rested from all his works which God began to make." [3] We ourselves shall be the seventh day, when we shall be filled and refreshed by his blessing and sanctification. There we shall be still and see that it is he who is God, though we wanted to be that ourselves when we fell away from him, giving ear to the tempter's words: " Ye shall be as gods." [4] Thus we departed from the true God, though by his action we might really have been gods, by partaking of him and not departing from him. For without him what is it that we were doing except to be our own undoing by his wrath? Restored by him and perfected by greater grace we shall rest for ever, and see always that he is God, and we shall be filled with him when he himself shall be all in all. For even our good works, at the moment when they are known to be his rather than ours, are at once imputed to us in order that we may gain this sabbath.

tantur; quia si nobis ea tribuerimus, servilia erunt,
cum de sabbato dicatur: *Omne opus servile non facietis;*
propter quod et per Hiezechielem prophetam dicitur:
Et sabbata mea dedi eis in signum inter me et inter eos,
ut scirent quia ego Dominus, qui sanctifico eos. Hoc
perfecte tunc sciemus, quando perfecte vacabimus,
et perfecte videbimus quia ipse est Deus.

Ipse etiam numerus aetatum, veluti dierum, si
secundum eos articulos temporis computetur qui
scripturis videntur expressi, iste sabbatismus evidentius apparebit, quoniam septimus invenitur; ut
prima aetas tamquam primus dies sit ab Adam usque
ad diluvium, secunda inde usque ad Abraham, non
aequalitate temporum, sed numero generationum;
denas quippe habere reperiuntur. Hinc iam, sicut
Matthaeus evangelista determinat, tres aetates usque
ad Christi subsequuntur adventum, quae singulae
denis et quaternis generationibus explicantur: ab
Abraham usque ad David una, altera inde usque ad
transmigrationem in Babyloniam, tertia inde usque
ad Christi carnalem nativitatem. Fiunt itaque
omnes quinque. Sexta nunc agitur nullo generationum numero metienda propter id quod dictum
est: *Non est vestrum scire tempora quae Pater posuit in*
sua potestate. Post hanc tamquam in die septimo
requiescet Deus, cum eundem diem septimum,
quod nos erimus, in se ipso Deo faciet requiescere.

---

[1] Deuteronomy 5.14.   [2] Ezekiel 20.12.

For if we ascribe them to ourselves they will be servile works, while it is said of the sabbath: " Ye shall not do any servile work." [1] Hence also it is said through Ezekiel the prophet: " And I gave them my sabbaths for a sign between me and them, that they might know that I am the Lord that sanctify them." [2] This we shall know perfectly at the moment when we shall be perfectly at rest, and shall see perfectly that he is God.

The very number of ages also, like the number of days in Creation, if reckoned according to the divisions of time which seem to be indicated in the Scriptures, throws more light on that sabbath rest, for it comes out as the seventh age. The first age, corresponding to the first day, is from Adam to the flood, the second, from then on till Abraham. These are equal, not in years, but in the number of generations, for each age is found to have ten. From this point, as the evangelist Matthew marks off the periods, three ages follow, reaching to the coming of Christ, each of which is completed in fourteen generations: one from Abraham to David, the second from then till the deportation to Babylon, the third from then until the birth of Christ in the flesh. Thus there are five ages in all. The sixth is now in progress, and is not to be measured by any fixed number of generations, for the Scripture says: " It is not for you to know the times which the Father has fixed by his own power." [3] After this age God will rest, as on the seventh day, when he will cause the seventh day, that is, us, to rest in God himself. To discuss

[3] Acts 1.7. On the six ages see the Introduction of Volume V, p. ix f.

De istis porro aetatibus singulis nunc diligenter
longum est disputare; haec tamen septima erit
sabbatum nostrum, cuius finis non erit vespera, sed
dominicus dies velut octavus aeternus, qui Christi
resurrectione sacratus est, aeternam non solum
spiritus, verum etiam corporis requiem praefigurans.
Ibi vacabimus et videbimus, videbimus et amabimus,
amabimus et laudabimus. Ecce quod erit in fine sine
fine. Nam quis alius noster est finis nisi pervenire
ad regnum cuius nullus est finis?

Videor mihi debitum ingentis huius operis
adiuvante Domino reddidisse. Quibus parum vel
quibus nimium est mihi ignoscant; quibus autem
satis est, non mihi, sed Deo mecum gratias con-
gratulantes agant. Amen. Amen.

each of these separate ages studiously at this time
is too long a task. But this seventh will be our
sabbath, and its end will not be an evening, but the
Lord's Day, an eighth eternal day, sanctified by the
resurrection of Christ, which prefigures the eternal
rest of both spirit and body. There we shall be still
and see, shall see and love, shall love and praise.
Behold what shall be in the end without end! For
what else is our end, except to reach the kingdom
which has no end?

In my judgement I have, with the help of the Lord,
discharged my debt of completing this huge work.
May those who think it too little or too much, forgive
me; and may those who think it just enough rejoice
and give thanks, not to me, but with me, to God.
Amen. Amen.

INDEXES

INDEX OF SCRIPTURE
CITATIONS
OLD TESTAMENT

389

INDEX OF SCRIPTURE CITATIONS

INDEX OF SCRIPTURE CITATIONS

INDEX OF SCRIPTURE CITATIONS

INDEX OF SCRIPTURE CITATIONS

INDEX OF SCRIPTURE CITATIONS

INDEX OF SCRIPTURE CITATIONS

INDEX OF SCRIPTURE CITATIONS

INDEX OF SCRIPTURE CITATIONS

397

INDEX OF SCRIPTURE CITATIONS

INDEX OF SCRIPTURE CITATIONS

INDEX OF SCRIPTURE CITATIONS

INDEX OF SCRIPTURE CITATIONS

INDEX OF SCRIPTURE CITATIONS

INDEX OF SCRIPTURE CITATIONS

INDEX OF SCRIPTURE CITATIONS

404

INDEX OF SCRIPTURE CITATIONS

INDEX OF GREEK AND ROMAN AUTHORS

INDEX OF AUTHORS

INDEX OF AUTHORS

INDEX OF AUTHORS

INDEX OF AUTHORS

INDEX OF AUTHORS

INDEX OF AUTHORS

INDEX OF AUTHORS

415

INDEX OF AUTHORS

INDEX OF SUBJECTS

417

INDEX OF SUBJECTS

INDEX OF SUBJECTS

420

INDEX OF SUBJECTS

423

INDEX OF PROPER NAMES

INDEX OF PROPER NAMES

INDEX OF PROPER NAMES

INDEX OF PROPER NAMES

INDEX OF PROPER NAMES

INDEX OF PROPER NAMES

INDEX OF PROPER NAMES

INDEX OF PROPER NAMES

437

INDEX OF PROPER NAMES

INDEX OF PROPER NAMES

439

INDEX OF PROPER NAMES

INDEX OF PROPER NAMES

INDEX OF PROPER NAMES

INDEX OF PROPER NAMES

443

INDEX OF PROPER NAMES

INDEX OF PROPER NAMES

445

INDEX OF PROPER NAMES

INDEX OF PROPER NAMES

447

INDEX OF PROPER NAMES

burning Troy only Minerva's statue was unharmed, I.287–289; she now shares the Capitol in Rome with Jupiter and Juno, II.39, where she and Juno have the services of a hairdresser, II.357; she also dwells in the upper part of the ether, II.39, 433; is the patron of crafts, II.43, 433; of mental endowments, II.45; and of Platonic ideas, II.481; II.75, 231, 375, 383, 387; II.177; V.389–397; 403–405.

Minos, son of Europa and Xanthus, King of the Cretans, V.403.

Minturnae, an ancient town on the Via Appia, I.235.

Mithridates, king of Pontus, whose war with the Romans lasted forty years, II.255; in one day massacred all the Romans in Asia, I.369; but was finally defeated, as Jupiter predicted, I.239.

Mizpah (Massephat), V.277.

Mizraim (Mesraim), son of Ham, V.19, 23, 69 and note.

Moses (Moyses), III.55; a long series of miracles was accomplished through Moses in order to rescue God's people, II.281–285, and the law was delivered with miraculous signs in nature, III.313; IV.11, 491, 575; "the frog" and "the locust" were among the ten plagues with which Moses smote the Egyptians, V.27–29, 197–201; Abraham and Moses given the title of prophets, V.211, 215; some have veil over their hearts when Moses is read today, V.277, 387, 399, 401, 481;

Greek theologians did not antedate our Moses, who gave a truthful account of God, though there was some wisdom in Egypt, in which Moses was instructed, VI.7–9, 15; 87, 429, 430, 433, 435; in working miracles, gods have been defeated by the martyrs, as the magicians of Pharaoh were defeated by Moses, VII.255.

Mother of the Gods, Great Mother, Cybele, brought from Pessinus to Rome in 204 BC, I.303; identified with the earth-goddess, II.41, 431, 435, 459–463, 481; in her rites the priests (Galli) follow example of Attis in mutilating themselves, II.329, 459–463, 469–471; her ship miraculously drawn up the Tiber, III.325.

Mucius Scaevola, failed to kill King Porsenna, II.73, 229.

Mucius, Q. Mucius Scaevola, consul 95, slain by the Marians in a temple, I.389, 395.

Murcia, goddess who makes a man lazy, II.61.

Musaeus, a mythical singer, closely related to Orpheus, V.413; VI.7.

Mutunus or Tutunus, same as Priapus among the Greeks, II.49.

Mycenae, after fall of Argive kingdom, people were transferred to Mycenae, V.415.

Naaman (Naeman), the leper, VII.359.

Naevius, early Roman comic poet, I.171, 183.

Nahor (Nachor), grandfather of Abraham, V.57, 73, 87, 157.

INDEX OF PROPER NAMES

449

INDEX OF PROPER NAMES

INDEX OF PROPER NAMES

that the soul is illuminated by a light from above, III.257; 293, 371, 385, 391, 393, 397, 401, 507; all philosophy is divided into three parts—physics, logic, and ethics, III.527. Plato plainly acknowledges, not that the world always existed, but that it had a beginning, although some believe that he held the opposite view, IV.55; he holds that all mortal animals, including man, were made not by the supreme God, but by lesser gods, IV.117-125; God held in his eternal intelligence the forms of the entire universe, including those of all animate beings, IV.127.

Platonists, III.27, 29, 31, 35, 39, 49, 63.

Plautus, best known writer of Roman comdey, I.171, 183; VII.49.

Plemmeus, king of Sicyon, V.385.

Plinius Secudus Maior, author of *Natural History*, IV.473.

Plotinus, and all well known Platonists of later times, prefer not to be called "Academics," III.57; 219, 257, 315, 351, 395.

Pluto, god of lower world, I.195; II.37, 45, 329.

poem *De Anima*, attributed to Augustine, IV.545 and note.

Poeni (Carthaginians), I.105, 349, 357; II.233, 441, 469; see Punic Wars.

Polemo, fourth in charge of Academy, VI.105.

Pollux, twin brother of Castor, II.101.

Polyphides, king of Sicyon, V.431.

Pomona, in charge of fruits, II.91, 129.

Pompey the Great, I.307; II.253, 267; VI.45.

Pomponius (perhaps L. Pomponius, author of Atellan plays), II.61.

Pontius, Lucius, messenger of Bellona, I.241.

Populonia, a goddess sometimes identified with Juno, II.359.

Porphyry, famous as Platonic philosopher, II.467, III.57; sets fourth, with some hesitation, the practice of theurgy, as a means of purifying the soul, III.287, 291, 293, 367; Porphyry's letter to Anebon, the Egyptian, asks for instruction about demons, III.299-305; he says that evil spirits must be appeased, III.347; that man cannot be purified by mystic rites, but by "principles," that is, God the Father, and the Son (who is Intellect or Mind), and Soul, midway between the two, III.351-353; Porphyry's treatise, *On the Return of the Soul*, III.389, 405 (cf. 271, 287, 345, 355); 393-399, 403-409, 415-417; IV.103, 125, 209; VI.215, 217, 223, 403, 405; VII.185, 271, 341; soul must shun every kind of body, VII.345; VII.349, 355.

Porsenna, Etruscan king, II.229.

Posidonius the Stoic, II.139, 142 and note, 143, 153.

Possidius brought relic of Stephen to Calama, VII.233.

Postumius, a diviner, I.237, 241.

Potina, goddess who serves drink, II.47, 127, 339.

INDEX OF PROPER NAMES

453

INDEX OF PROPER NAMES

454

INDEX OF PROPER NAMES

455

INDEX OF PROPER NAMES

INDEX OF PROPER NAMES

INDEX OF PROPER NAMES

459

INDEX OF PROPER NAMES

460

INDEX OF PROPER NAMES